BOUNDARIES IN MIND

American Academy of Religion
Studies in Religion
27

Editors
Thomas Altizer
James O. Duke

BOUNDARIES IN MIND

A Study of Immediate Awareness
Based on Psychotherapy

CHARLES E. SCOTT

THE CROSSROAD PUBLISHING COMPANY
&
SCHOLARS PRESS

The Crossroad Publishing Company
575 Lexington Avenue
New York, NY 10022

Scholars Press
101 Salem St., P. O. Box 2268
Chico, CA 95927

Grateful acknowledgment is made to
Vanderbilt University
for its assistance in the publication of this book.

Library of Congress Cataloging in Publication Data
Scott, Charles E.
　Boundaries in mind.
　(Studies in religion/American Academy of Religion ;
no. 27)
　Includes bibliographical references.
　1. Awareness. 2. Psychotherapy. I. Title. II. Series:
Studies in religion (American Academy of Religion) ; no. 27.
RC480.5.S37　　　　　150'.1　　　　　81-18366
ISBN 0-8245-0529-8 (Crossroad Publishing)
　　　0-89130-554-8 (Scholars Press)

Printed in the United States of America

For Donna, Mildred, Lester, Stuart, Rebecca, and Charles:
the best of boundaries.

ACKNOWLEDGMENTS

Edmund Keeley and Philip Sherrard, trans., *C. P. Cavafy: Collected Poems*, ed. George Savidis. Translation ©1975 by Edmund Keeley and Philip Sherrard. "Walls" reprinted by permission of Princeton University Press.

Wallace Stevens, "Martial Candeza," *The Collected Poems of Wallace Stevens*, ©1955, reprinted by permission of Alfred A. Knopf, Inc.

Charles E. Scott, "Psychotherapy: Being One and Being Many," *Review of Existential Psychology & Psychiatry*, Vol. XVI, ©1979, reprinted by permission of *Review of Existential Psychology & Psychiatry*.

Charles E. Scott, "Freedom with Darkness and Light: A Study of a Myth," *Studies in Non-Deterministic Psychology*, ©1980, reprinted by permission of Human Sciences Press.

Alphons Lingis, "Khajuraho," *Soundings*, Summer 1979, ©1979, reprinted by permission of *Soundings*.

Table of Contents

PREFACE

My purpose is to write about the awareness that occurs between organized fields of mental structures. On the one hand, there is communication among states of mind that are differently structured and organized. On the other, there are awarenesses that are characteristic of the borders between organized states. They are not like the awareness of personal identity or selfhood. I have called them boundaries in mind, and one of my tasks is to demarcate some of them and elaborate their meaning for our understanding of mentality. It is a peculiar subject since there will usually be a tension between the structure of the discourse, which is constructed in the identity of this culture for which boundary awareness is foreign, and the awareness under discussion. A demand is consequently placed on the reader. In order to give focus to border awareness one will need to decenter as much as possible the convictions, habits of mind, and certainties which form the largely unquestioned center of one's life.

The book's subtheme is found in the significance of immediate, boundary states of mind for an understanding of human well-being. I have drawn heavily from therapeutic communication because the issues at hand arise naturally in the processes of therapy. This coin of the experiential, therapeutic realm has not always been appropriated in the language and interpretations that tell us about psychotherapy. My goal, however, is not primarily to address theories. It is to re-think boundary immediacies with emphasis on their occurrences rather than on how they have been conceived. I have chosen this approach because these states of mind have been often forgotten or ignored. They need to be focused, recalled, given emphasis and place in our thinking if we are to understand ourselves in the full sweep of the awareness of which our intellects and personal identities form a part. They tend to dislodge the centralized dominance that has been given often to personal identity. They show that such dominance itself can be seriously distorting in relation to how we are with ourselves and each other. Their significance also lies in how they give depth, range and freedom in relation to all things. Their imagery often involves death and dislocation, and they consequently may be feared.

Since the topic of this book is immediate boundary awareness and not self-concept or personal self-consciousness, one might also wish to be aware of the limits that function in his/her personal and professional consciousness. Otherwise his/her own sense of self may intuitively resist the subject matter under discussion. When one has an open sense for the limits of who one is and for the limits of selfhood, the boundaries with other, vastly different awarenesses need not be threatening. The issue is more one of being open with the boundaries than one of "ego strength." Strength is important for this openness, but the strength that is often associated with "ego" is not necessarily that most desirable.

An important question is: how are "ego" or "self" to be conceived in a larger context of awareness? "Identity-strength" sometimes refers to an exceptionally well defended consciousness vis-à-vis boundary situations that has succeeded in making its own interests and energy or a developed sense of belonging into a closed, habitual pattern of self-reference. Tight confidence, unambiguous clarity of view, a serious sense of rightness—at best a feeling of narrow, if autonomous vitality and direction—are the hallmarks of this sensibility. But awareness without identity, death, indeterminateness, and states of that ilk are probably shadowy or are only "objective" to this manner of being. The boundaries are closed. Then awareness as identity may well find expression in the teachings of schools, a narrowness of mind, an overwhelming insistence on certainty. The non-identity of mind probably feels dangerous. The boundaries in mind, however, need not be a threat to identity. They may well threaten certain kinds of identity. But once they are allowed, they have the effect of freeing a person for boundary awareness, for experiences of radical otherness, and for all the contingencies in being who we are. Openness without fear of the contingency of identity and self is a basis for thinking and practice which is sought in the following pages.

Immediate states of mind are always intuitive, as distinct from conceptually objective, and they are often affective. One usually can approach such states by following feelings, staying uncritically alert with affect, or giving focus to emotions. These states find expression in indirections of all sorts: innuendo, irony, style, images, fantasies, depth feelings, desires, etc. A primary goal of this book is to use concepts in such a way that the intuitive and affective aspects of mind are intensified. Critique is a central function for theoretical investigation. But elaboration, variation, recollection, and play are the proper conceptual functions when one wishes to establish constructive, discursive relations with immediate states of mind. I shall frequently reflect and intensify certain immediate states of mind in order to specify them and then elaborate their meaning within specific contexts. Finding an immediate boundary state and speaking in its reference, then reflecting on it in a wider context, forms the rhythm of the chapters.

The chapters will set forth a theme, such as how interpreting occurs in Chapter One, often by finding the images or metaphors that express or indicate how the subject matter happens. The meaning of the focused awareness in relation to other situations is then developed as theoretical questions are raised: such as, how is fantasy to be conceived? What does fantasy mean for our understanding of mind, our concepts of personal unity, our understanding of distortion? Chapters Two and Four elaborate the ideas of Chapters One and Three respectively with emphasis on psychotherapeutic processes. Chapter Five brings to bear the forming ideas of the previous chapters by showing how immediate awareness may be considered. Elaborations in that chapter are primarily by means of therapeutic interchanges instead of myths. That chapter concludes the book's development of the claims that mind is the occurrence of immediate awarenesses and that boundary awarenesses provide a key to understanding immediate awareness.

I am particularly indebted to friends whose insights, criticisms, oppositions and support have been provocative and helpful. Edward Casey, John Compton, Mary Watkins, James Hillman, William Richardson, Medard Boss, Edward Farley, Hans-Georg Gadamer, Lee Rowen, Gerald Epstein, Gary Deason, Albert Hofstadter, and those in the Vanderbilt Seminar for Semiotics Studies are among the many influences, doubtlessly much changed by my chemistry, that have been woven into the text. I have been aided greatly by the Society for Values and Higher Education, the National Endowment for the Humanities, and the Vanderbilt Research Council. I am especially indebted to Donna Jeanne Scott for her unswerving support. Several people with whom I have worked therapeutically generously have allowed me to use excerpts from our sessions. I am aware of occasional conversations, often seemingly incidental snatches of writing, and other exceptional moments in which an idea formed or a shift of mind happened: an unexpected book, a series of remarkable days in southern France, hospitality and beauty in Greece, insights in a student's paper, conversations at Notre Dame University and on Falls Branch Road, Tennessee, the character of this woman or that man. These and a few experiences that dislocated my habits and expectations have played essential roles in giving form to this book in which the contingency of form is born in mind. Sheila Mitchell, Patty Smith, and Vera Langerova have each shared stoically and with my appreciation the task of making sense of my script.

I say to you; one must have chaos in oneself in order to give birth to a dancing star.

Nietzsche, *Thus Spoke Zarathustra*

Under the tyranny of the eye, that glutton for frontiers, this is the prime alienation of the cinema; always inherent in the theater, yet obscured there because of different performances and productions of the same text. But the final cut allows no choice, no more than one angle; no creative response, no walking around, no time for one's own thought. In the very act of the shooting, it destroys the past of the mind of each spectator.

Images are inherently fascistic because they overstamp the truth, however dim and blurred, of the real past experience; as if, faced with ruins, we must turn architects, not archeologists. The word is the most imprecise of signs. Only a science-obsessed age could fail to comprehend that this is its great virtue, not its defect. What I was trying to tell Jenny in Hollywood was that I could murder my past if I tried to evoke it on camera; and it is precisely because I can't really evoke it in words, can only hope to awaken some analogous experience in other memories and sensitivities, that it must be written.

John Fowles, *Daniel Martin*

A statement to Ezra Pound by a Russian reader of his poetry: "I see, you wish to give people new eyes, not to make them see some new particular thing."

Gaudier-Brezeska

INTRODUCTION

A reliable indicator of the presence of Eros is a person's experience of his/her solitude. In silence, or in the absence of company, a person may find him/herself not repeating what he/she has heard or been told. One may find, rather, his/her *own* dreams or words or notions; memories and hopes; relations; interests and desires for interest; readiness to move or attentions to the present. However Eros is manifest, a person in his/her deepest solitude feels related and alive, whether in pain or satisfaction. In this awareness of life, a person also has a sense of his/her own presence, a quiet preparedness to be, knowing him/herself to be alive in being alert with living things, with Eros' reflection, however it is found. Such a state of mind is hardly a personal accomplishment. It goes too deeply, is too far beyond the reach of what a person can do voluntarily. It pervades one's life. And its absence goes far beyond failure. The absence of Eros is apathy *in* one's interests and vacancy in what fills one's mind.

Creating and dying carry us beyond our identities to regions of mind where we experience ourselves as strange. In both, Eros is implicated. The emergence of a hope or fantasy, for example, may leave us with an indelible sense that we are a part of a region that is vast and creative, that we are creatures even in what comes to us as most our own. We may also experience something like bottomlessness or chaotic vacuity when neither hope nor fantasy will come, no matter how hard we work at it.

Immediate awareness, the subject of this book, is a state of mind that we live, but do not make, and one in which the relations of Eros are always at work, building up or tearing down. We do not experience immediate awareness as produced by something. It is not a representation. It is accessible to accounts, as we shall see, to the extent that it is self-aware or is apparent in bearing other states of mind. It is our alertness as we live, and as such it is particularly at issue in sickness or health, when the whole of our lives is fundamentally affected. I have consequently given particular importance to the engagements centered on sickness and well being. In those engagements—in "therapy"—the primary focus is on the immediate state, not on accounts about it, and the participants' relations are directed by fundamental ways of suffering and being well, i.e., by ways in which relatedness is going on in one's life. It is focused on the "erotic". Those ways are themselves immediate experiences, which, as experiences, carry ultimate import for us. They may be fecund or barren, unruly or tightly ordered. But however our immediate state of awareness may be, it is bedrock for our daily lives. As we interpret immediate awareness we are interpreting how we are fundamentally in relations, how we are basically alert.

Immediate awareness has been said to be essentially different from concious processes and not susceptible to description. It might always precede observation and thus be past when it is seen or spoken of. It might be totally nonconceptual and fundamentally changed when it is grasped conceptually. Or it might be a completely different region than "consciousness," such as the Unconscious, to which we have access only by inference and speculation. These observations about the unavailability of immediate awareness, however, are based on misleading interpretations about consciousness.

Some of the assumptions of such interpretations, which I shall call into questions, are:

(a) That "consciouness" is the sole locus of self-awareness. This interpretation pays attention only to the development of self-consciousness in a person's identity and usually understands it as an ability to report about itself and to give historical narratives about itself: "I have these characteristics; I act in these ways; I am. . . ." I shall call attention to the enormously diverse ways in which awareness happens and show that awarenesses can become self-aware without the involvement of personal identity or what is called "consciousness." The hallmark of self-awareness is the capacity to address and respond with other awarenesses.

(b) That "consciousness" is always observational and synthesizing in nature. When human awareness is interpreted as necessarily judgmental and conceptual in nature, we expect it to be essentially distanced, even cut off from every other kind of occurrence. I shall deal primarily with awarenesses that are not activities of observing and judging. Their fundamental kinship with observation and judgment is the event of awareness as such: in awareess there is no necessary abyss between conceptualizing and being nonconceptually aware. The issue is one of learning how to think, attend, and speak with and of immediate states of mind.

(c) That "consciousness" is essentially personal, and consequently separated from everything that is not personal. I shall show that personal identity happens in the immediacy of non-personal and indifferent awareness, that absolutizing the personal for its own region is not necessary.

(d) That meanings originate in "consciousness." The anthropomorphizing of meaning leads us to overlook the ways in which things and people come to be as they are through processes and events of which people are a part, but often neither the controlling nor defining part. I shall develop the observation that meanings originate and develop in events, which are not the activity of a subject or of "subjectivity."

(e) That "consciousness" is a desiring state and that it is separated from all non-desiring states of being. By interpreting awareness as event, rather than as subjective activity, I shall be able to show that desiring states and non-desiring ones are immediate and aware with each other.

(f) That "consciousness" is not intrinsically worldly and that consequently it is essentially different from occurrences in the world. I shall show that awareness is intrinsically worldly and that all aware events happen in the same as well as in different ways.

When these interpretations of "consciousness" and mind are found to be unnecessary, the expectation that immediate states of mind will be distant or unapproachable will diminish. We shall rethink how immediate awareness happens, with emphasis on the immediate diversity of awareness. Immediate awareness is not primarily subjective. It is the happenings of existing things and their regions, and by interpreting them we are interpreting how we are immediately in the immediacy of what is. This claim forms a central focus for the first chapter.

I shall make frequent use of myths in the conviction that they are narratives that reflect varieties of immediate awarenesses which are best spoken of indirectly in order to preserve their truth of occurrence, as distinct from accuracy of claims and assertions about them. The power of myths is found in their expressing immediacies, in their power of Eros. They tend to make explanation a side issue, and that is probably one of the reasons why "mythical" and "not true" tend to be associated in modern speech. Myths do not create accuracies of statement. They recollect happenings, re-enact meanings, remember in the manner of story, poem, music, custom, or language. The occurrence is done, or perhaps re-done, not as a claim about something, but as the occurrence itself in the telling or singing or whatever. One need know nothing about the myth to be a part of it. Seeing *what* is mythically going on, reflecting the event in knowledge about it, as in Oedipus' knowledge of his incest, can intensify one's involvement. But this perception need not essentially change the event, since knowledge about it is founded in it, is also a part of it, and perpetuates it. Myths are present in our methods of coming to know things through basic images and tacit understanding, in the destinies of methods that are unknown, even to sophisticated practitioners, in the relations that provide basic directions of knowing and doing.

Given these characteristics, myths are different in a polar way from the self-understanding of much of our modern knowledge, to the extent that we think of knowledge as self-founding or self-perpetuating. Our reasons and approaches always tell stories other than the reasons and approaches themselves, stories that are far more extensive than the range of our explanations. Explanations, even when they forget their own powers of creation and destruction, are parts of larger destinies which escape the confines of the explanations that they spawn.

We need not choose, however, between the goal of accuracy in knowledge about things and the enactment of occurrences in their immediacy through myths. We need to see the inevitability of myths if we are not to lose our thinking in a morass of clear argumentation, evidence, and method. Knowledge about things is an inadquate basis for thinking because that type of knowledge cannot countenance appropriately an entire dimension of realities that I shall refer to with such words as *event, occurrence, happening, immediacy, awareness, mind, truth,* and *communication.* We have the capacity for giving accounts that are self-aware in the accounting, not merely in the mode of an outside observer. Cultivation of this self-awareness in the event does not lead to methods as much as it leads to a discipline of attention and reflection, about which I shall say more below.

In psychotherapy, both knowledge about events and intrinsic development of self-awareness in events may be legitimate goals. Aside from some poets and artists, contemporary psychotherapists are probably more alert than most of us to the development of immediate self-awareness. I have resisted the powerful, modern philosophical temptation to give a structural description of this immediate self-awareness and its development, thereby losing the subject and its milieu in the accounting and denying the bespoken in the manner of speaking. Rather, as I interpret immediate awareness I attempt to speak out of certain kinds of psychotherapeutic occurrences, to reflect them, to find language appropriate to them. They provide an experiential entrée into the immediacies of awareness. I have often wanted to classify these occurrences, to give myself a handle to keep grip on them. I have composed pages, now discarded, on methods for conceiving them. I have worked on interpretive schemes that would provide a basis for judging developments of awareness in hierarchical terms. I am not prepared to say that such investigations might not "advance" our understanding in some ways. But I can report that the subject of this book would not tolerate such treatment. The subject simply disappeared and another subject, another genre of being, took its place. Reflection, indirection, metaphor, insight, contemplation, these kinds of approaches are appropriate if one wishes to understand the immediacies of things. Accuracy is less an issue than perceptiveness. Recounting is less a problem than bespeaking. Explanation is not the first problem. Seeing and hearing are.

As a philosopher I found frequently in the literature related to psychotherapy remarkable sensitivities to immediate awareness, closer in spirit, if not in language, to Fichte and Schelling in their old age than to modern social science or mathematics. I suspect that dealing face to face with madness, dislocations in awareness, and the occurrences of well-being drives one to these sensitivities that we might otherwise miss when we only think about things without the intimate and disciplined vis-à-vis. Yet a certain craziness persists, often remarked in relation to Freud, viz. the clash between the experiences of therapy and the scientific language he used to deal with the psyche. We are prone to think of human awareness in the language of systems, forgetting the chaos, the element of Eros, that is always present.[1] We think of events like maps, surely one of our most abstract devices, and miss the unmapable, the utterly concrete that will not abstract. We quantify our health and lose the liveliest things of all, the happening of creative, fantastical energy. Our madness is found in what we leave out of our ideals and analyses.

The kinds of events and insights that go on in therapy—not necessarily in the school languages about these events—provide an an entrée to what we tend to forget and leave out in our public self-understandings. The awarenesses that spawn therapy, as well as anti-therapeutic destruction, give us occasion to rethink some aspects of our awareness, aspects which tend to be left out of our disciplines as well as out of popular speech. And further, the languages of those awarenesses—night dreams, waking dreams, fantasies of all sorts, deceits, myths, weirdness, shades of indefiniteness, bright and shining gods, awful depths, terrors at home, and familiarity in foreign lands—these are languages that we must learn to speak if we are to escape the destructive madness of a cultural prison made up of abstract accuracies about the surfaces or forms of things.

I am a contemporary academician, and I am inclined to think of methods as *the* means of providing order. A sound method allows us to secure knowledge with self-aware justification. It allows responsible control in therapy, for example, particularly when the therapist is out of his/her depth or simply does not yet understand what is going on. Methods preserve traditional wisdom and practice. They teach us in responsible and addressable ways. I am inclined to think of responsible education as methodologically structured and as capped by sophisticated expertise regarding methods of evaluating and using still other methods. I am inclined to look for the methods which justify claims and which save us from personal arbitrariness.

I am also persuaded, however, that methods as such can obscure major regions of reality. Our predisposition to define truth by reference to methods is one of the problems that we need to address. It may also be a pathology from which we need to be cured. Methodologically structured and justified intelligence appears to block us from an entire region of occurrence: the occurrence of things that is contingent, non-predictable, neither accurate nor inaccurate, not a subject or an object, not epistemological. We tend to ignore happenings in their freedom from our methods of observing them. In the

[1] By "chaos" I have in mind a region of awareness other than our ordered and systematic realms of "consciousness." The contrasts that I shall develop are between occurrence and isolated thing, awareness and conceptual knowledge, truth and fact, strangeness and controlled familiarity. This awareness is not to be understood from the perspective of control, but from words and notions that are generated by its presence. Learning to think with and from this region of awareness constitutes the discipline which I shall discuss below.

language of this essay, we tend to ignore their truth, their presence that gives us a non-methodological basis for observing them.

We are now accustomed to thinking of different methods as issuing in different, but legitimate, knowledge. In our climate, we are generally not inclined to think of monolethic methods. We are latitudinarian in a wonderful way that allows phenomenological methodologies to exist with methods in theoretical physics and behaviorial psychology. We seek compatabilities, not exclusions, and we are presently inclined to learn about each other's methods for finding out things and doing things—not unlike ancient storytellers who used to visit each other's provinces, learn each other's languages, and listen to new stories which would later be incorporated into their own traditions. We even develop our schools of learning around methods of exploration, discovery, and uses of knowledge, not around canons of metaphysical principles or the authority of a particularly successful investigator. The investigator's lab or department can always be disbanded or attended by someone who suspends his/her methodological training in order to learn this other person's approach. But we never doubt that any investigator is expendable. More frequently we look to an on-going team based in methods of investigation to provide the context for discovery.

In psychotherapy, in spite of a tendency to collect professional identity around particular methods (viz. Gestaltist, Jungian, Freudian, etc.), most of us are probably pursuaded that other therapeutic methods that we judge to be misleading or wrong can be nonetheless therapeutic in practice. Therapy in some sense appears to go on in spite of the therapeutic method. People may find an increased sense of themselves, of their own limits and possibilities. They may find themselves more able to do what they intend to do and to intend without fateful repetitions of early, now destructive patterns. Those discoveries may occur through the help of Jungian, Existential, Freudian, or Primal Scream approaches. Awareness that tends to heal (as well as that that tends to be destructive psychologically) happens with many different methods and appears not to depend totally on a method for its occurrence. Hence our emphasis falls on therapeutic events rather than on the school literature.

The free, open bestowing, taking, destroying, nurturing occurrence of things that will not be harnessed by methods seems to shadow us particularly in this time. We have done well with our methods. Unheard of discoveries, remarkable prosperity, ways of healing diseases, approximations, at least, to humanitarian organizations, a sense of power and dignity through order: those are enormous things that are founded in methods. But, although "we may want to shun (the pit) and attain honor in the world, . . . it draws us still."[2] Our "sympathy with the abyss"[3] is puzzling in light of our successes in organizing things for what appears to be our great benefit.

[2] Thomas Mann, *Death in Venice* (N.Y.: Vintage, 1960), p.72.
[3] *Ibid.*, p.13.

Probably our expectation that there are essences, whether "in" the mind or "out" in nature, is one of the assumptions that is most in need of reconsideration. The notion can be suspended that the words "there is" should indicate something inviolate like a "fact" that is carefully observed or a "structure" that provides continuity and has a special, abiding character. Not because these notions are wrong or unhelpful. They are neither. But because they are limited. Search for facts or essences involves, I suspect inevitably, a dominant interest in exact certainty—rigorous, hard-nosed methods again, and that leaves out most things that simply are not subject to the certainty of fact or essence. The trickster has often functioned to open people to the non-essence. "Coyote" in some American Indian lore created much that is real, free of the laws of cause and effect and logical connection. Those familiar with Coyote were as familiar with the non-rational contingencies of animal behavior and natural occurrences as Husserl was familiar with certain structures of consciousness. Hermes, who plays a special part in this essay, embodies the immediacies of mind that are the opposite of essences: the given, bestowed particular that is real without general justification, as well as the happening of disclosure.

Barry Lopez points out that some Eskimos have more sensibility in relation to wolves than our best trained Western naturalists because the Eskimos "have tended to develop the same kind of efficiency in the Arctic" as wolves, so that a special kinship exists between them.[4] This kinship means a special perceptiveness for meaning and detail in wolves on the part of Eskimos that is simply not usually available to "Westerners" and that is not produced by our sciences of observation. "Scientific" observation, Lopez shows, has difficulty grasping the kind of "detail" that is not generalized or viewed within a tendency toward generalization. The Eskimo does not expect the wolf to be fully understood or to be grasped by categories. To the contrary, conjecture informed by personal knowledge of an individual wolf's actions, or those of a specific pack that is dominated this year by certain wolves known to this Eskimo in these ways are their opening to the reality of wolves. What is anecdotal for biologists is the stuff of understanding for the Eskimo, who is attuned to the roving details of particular things and individuals and who has found no reason to generalize or to seek knowledge with essential certainty. Instead of thinking about wolves as interesting strangers, he lives with them in the continuity and kinship of ways of living and sameness of environment. He knows the wolf with an open-ended set of expectations developed out of hundreds of years of community experience. "The lack of separation from (nature's) elements" distinguishes the Eskimo from the naturalist, who comes from a community of separation from nature, even if the naturalist lives in a cabin, walks in snowshoes, and speaks the native tongue.

[4] Barry Lopez, *Of Wolves and Men* (N.Y.: Scribners, 1978).

The Eskimo, says Lopez, speaks of and looks for exceptions to rules in order to understand the particular, natural situation that confronts him. He speaks of likelihoods, of specific wolves, of what he has learned about this one or that one. The line is a fine one. Our task is to learn to be so taken by events and occurrences that our culturally natural inclination to classify and generalize and essentialize passes away into another kind of seeing, closer to an awareness that often characterizes therapeutic relations among people. My persuasion is that these inclinations toward classification and generalization, which have been marvelously productive, have distanced us from the occurrence, from the non-factual, non-structured dimension of things, from "nature" in a certain sense. As thinkers our task is to follow the trickster, to see deception, exception, violation, perversion, and distortion. This is nothing new for many therapists who deal with the vagaries of mind and have learned, at least in therapy, not to look so much for instances of general things, as to follow the movements of awareness, which are far closer to the lore of Coyote than to a structured logic.

Our goal is to re-think awareness and mind in order to engender inclinations and language for concretenesses and disclosure, although those very inclinations and language may seem often very abstract in our generalized knowledge, when we make structures of facts and essences seem like individual things and the very element of what is apparent.

Intuitive perception is better able than other forms of reasoning to see (or hear) whole events in their hues, qualities, and simultaneous interrelations. It is often noted in its generative function, as people find new directions and relations "suddenly" or unexpectedly. It is also noted as a function within systematic structures in such forms as mathematical or logical insights. But taken on its own terms, intuitive perception poses a problem for modern intelligence. Intuition does not happen as a procedural process, as a methodologically developed structure of concepts, or as step by step understanding or as a personally arbitrary activity. It is seeing into or in something as it happens. As I shall show, intuition need not be a subjective event. An entire environment happens in intuition: style of life, the history of the awareness in action, quality of attention, predispositions and moods, commitments and disaffections, the arrangement of things around one, the natural setting, and so forth. It is a world event. It sometimes happens like the flooding of light, sometimes as a sharp and focused fix on something, sometimes as quiet realization over a period of time, always as awareness *in* the placement and juxtaposition of things. It usually depends on a person's and on a culture's quality of mind; how loving and hating go on, for example, is a prime factor for intuiting, as is the quality of intensity and concentration in an event. Intuition also usually involves drawing near to things. It is not an abstracting gaze, but is touching awareness, alert proximity, intimacy of a sort, like a son's knowing his father in a close relationship, like a person's knowing a region in which he/she has lived long and intensely, or like the emergence of familiarity with a person without explicit expectation.

By the standards of accuracy, intuition is highly fallible. It not only may be mistaken *about* something, while yet knowing that something well, it is more inclined to intimate and to guess about specifics, to suppose, to muse, than to expect exactness or certain accuracy. Although intuition is not the way by which one usually would want to establish the quantity or measurement of things, it is the way by which some of our most significant kinds of familiarity happen. As one intuits one is deeply in touch with the whole situation of awareness. One can hardly say that intuitions are his/her own. One participates in them, finds growing proximity through contemplation or attention, gets taken up into events and settings, finds him/herself expanded, somehow grown in the intuitive event. The dangerous side of intuition is the possibility for possession by the things that one encounters. Its positive side is the degree of kinship and familiarity that happen in it, a quality that one might long for if he/she is dominated by discursive, systematic, bureaucratic, or pragmatic types of consciousness. Those latter kinds of consciousness tend to distance one from things for the sake of abstract clarity, imposed order, and efficient use—goods that are essential for our well-being, but goods that cannot replace closeness with and within the world.

Some type of kinship, far excessive of individual preference and intention, appears to be fundamental in intuition. Lopez's astute observation is that the profound similarity between a tribe of Eskimos and wolves is the kinship that shapes the Eskimos' remarkable perceptiveness relative to wolves. These people and the wolves hunt in similar ways, appear to approach death in similar ways, cope with the same kind of environmental problems, and have similar social structures. They have a fundamental and apparently common strata of awareness that provides a kinship in perceiving and knowing. Analogously, a person of one community has a fund of awarenesses for most of which he/she cannot give an account, but which is a thorough part of his/her way of being with things and in which a person from a very different place or time does not naturally share. The "I don't know why. I just know" response is often an accurate report about intuitive relations with things and about insights that can be penetrating and on target.

These shared situations, these kinships are lived and aware and do not belong to any person in particular. They make up traditions, languages, customs, and basic world-relations. As lived out they are ways of being alert that make up both individual minds and the mind of shared experience and knowledge. We shall focus particularly on world-relations as awarenesses in the first chapter. Presently we note that familiarity joins people in common awareness. Later I shall develop the observation that our awareness in common may be specifically cultural—this people at this time—or funda- mental for human being over a considerable sweep of time—an awareness common for us in how we occur, regardless of our culture. In both cases, our focus will be on common familiarity that is a non-reducible awareness and that serves as the basis for thought about it. Our goal is an increase of alertness as intuitions are reflected in conceptual attention, an attention of which the intuition may become an active part regarding itself.

This essay is descriptive, although it is not limited to categorial schemes or attempts to find essences to describe. I am also disinclined to the "here's one, there's one, and here's another" kind of description that merely enumerates things or groups. My goal is a growth of explicit consciousness by highlighting how some things occur as aware. The word *describe* has the original Latin meaning of "to write" and can mean simply to state something in writing. It also means "to give account of something" or "to give a mental image." "To describe" used to mean "to represent by drawing, by a statue or by a picture," although we do not now find the word used that way. If I follow a pattern, such as a dotted line or a conception, I may be said to describe it.

Describe obviously means much more than to talk or write accurately about something. Giving a descriptive account of something may be analogous to following a pattern or outline, viz. your words may engender perception of something that was there, but not apparent to us. A description may be a literal re-presentation of something, or it may be a narration. "To narrate," "to express," and "to depict" are synonyms of "to describe," just as "to explain," "to characterize," and "to delineate" are.

When we take *describe* in its kinship of meaning with *expound*, we see that telling a story or a dream can be a description that sets something forth or presents it. How one frees something from obscurity is his/her interpretation of it. But the crucial point is that as something is exposed to view, is made manifest by words, description is going on. Describing is a way of giving place and apparentness to something (i.e., it is a way of ex-posing). Our task is to come to perceive things that are present in and through their presence. Our means are images and words. Our method is a type of writing. Our goal is description in all its forms with the purpose of respecting the full eventfulness of what is to be described. I shall categorize and express, narrate and outline, represent and present: whatever helps to attune our awareness to how something is going on in its own happening. At best the movement and meaning of the words will articulate the movement and meaning of the event so that an immediacy of insight can take place which frees both the reader and writer for other words, thoughts, and insights.

Philosophical thinking at its best brings one to what is thought about. It disciplines and directs our intellectual capacities around something. If we begin with what is itself not directly familiar with the reality in question, with other theories, for example, without regard for the reality of their own enactment, we as philosophers shall begin and end without much closeness with the part of the world that we are attempting to think. If we begin with intuitive occurrences and take our reflective cues from them, on the other hand, we may intensify our familiarity with the world as we think. The key issue is learning to discipline our thinking in our regard for what is thought: the subject should arbitrate the language and approach. In that, phenomenology is right: the thing to be thought is to be the master of our thinking. That is a remarkably difficult principle for us who are accustomed to finding forms by which to orient things for knowledge. The phenomeno-logical principle means that we have to learn how to forget the notion that method, use, and interest are primary for our touch with things. Our task is to find the touch that makes possible our further actions regarding things, i.e., our interest is to re-inherit our immediate awareness in the world.

What happens to the perpetual observer/hearer, even if he/she has learned not to interfere and has found how to avoid voyeurism while being aware? Even if he/she has found how to love by seeing and hearing? With-out him/her, no book would be written, certainly. But just as there are mo-ments in madness when the dimensions of observing and hearing, and indeed most dimensions of perception, fall into terrible forgetfulness and perhaps die, there are also moments of profound well-being when observing of all kinds cease and there is non-observant immediacy in which events bear of themselves all that is remembered and that lives. It is a poor life when such immediacies are not honored and appropriated in what one expects of his/her observing. If observing, hearing, smelling, feeling, tasting, thinking—in a word, and at best, interpreting in the light of Hermes— return one to such immediacies and their appropriation, if they allow the awareness that all interpretations are to cease, then we shall have found some degree of self-awareness in our observant dimensions and shall less likely go mad in our passion to know with unobstructed clarity.

The issue is consequently one of discipline, not method. In my twentieth century academic robes I also think of method when I think of discipline. But the connection is not necessary. Allowing something that is quite present to be as it is is probably one of the most difficult undertakings for us. That is even more difficult than paying heed to fantasy, because our poets and novelists have not given up the awareness of fantasy. But most of us doubt that a non-imagined thing, there before us, being as it is, utterly, is to be "known" in any way other than through some subjective structure, be that structure poetic or scientific. The discipline of not interfering and yet being very alert and knowing is hard enough so that we are inclined to find a method for the discipline. Phenomenologists especially have been caught in this trap, after hearing with sympathy Husserl's call "to the things them-selves." He found things usually as structures of a subject, and this accept-ance of the primacy of the knowing or experiencing subject carries with it a particular and sometimes obsessive concern for a rigorous method, as distinct to a rigorous discipline for letting things be as they are in their occurrence.

This kind of discipline assumes that things are already apparent when a person, or a consciousness, turns to them. I shall develop some of the issues related to this assumption in each of the chapters. The discipline we are now addressing involves a trust of the disclosiveness of things, patience in allowing a clearing of apparentness to occur in the midst of fogs of interference, and willingness not to expect much, not to anticipate rapidly, not to inject direction or directives. It involves cultivating a way of experiencing and seeing things out of which such ideas as dualism, subjectivity, intentionality, the primacy of perception, and so forth do not arise. A quieting discipline, not schoolish or even inclined to cultivation for its own repetition. Until the words "being free" make immediate, experiential sense with an accompanying feeling of allowing things to be, one has not taken many steps in the discipline of being alert in his/her immediate awareness.

The discipline, the way of seeing that I have in mind, also may involve an effort to see and hear with words what one sees/hears without verbal articulation. It involves cultivating a state of mind which issues in ways of seeing/saying through which the openness of the world is apparent in both what is said/seen and how the seeing/saying occurs.

This essay is not intended to be a study of this discipline, a piece of meta-discipline, but it does assume that cultivation of a way of seeing is a primary philosophical goal and that giving up, at least for a while, our usual concerns for method is an important first step in coming to see things themselves.

"Sympathy is a condition and mode of perception," says Corbin.[5] Our deepest sympathies are our positive sensibility, our basis for attraction, our bonds with things. They constitute the erotic. Languages and customs also have indigenous sympathies. Proculus is right in saying that all realities are webbed by sympathies (as well as by antipathies). Immediate draw is part of Eros' being. Usually those sympathies are invisible, and we are drawn to things without knowing it, by attractions and repulsions that are not apparent to us. The discipline that I have in mind is one in which our thinking is not only alert to the sympathies and antipathies of our being, but is responsive to them and in them through our approach, style, and language of reflection.

[5] Henri Corbin, *The Creative Imagination In the Sufism of Ibn' Arabi* (Princeton, N. J.: Princeton University Press, 1969), p. 107.

This dignity lies in keeping watch over the unconcealment—and with it, from the first, the unconcealment—of all coming to presence on this earth. It is precisely in enframing, which threatens to sweep man away into ordering as the supposed single way of revealing, and so thrust man into the danger of surrender of his free essence—it is precisely in this extreme danger that the innermost indestructible belonging of man in this granting may come to light.

Heidegger

But what if we gave free rein to ill will? What if thought freed itself from common sense and decided to function only in its extreme singularity? What if it adopted the disreputable bias of the paradox, instead of complacently accepting its citizenship in the doxa? What if it conceived of difference differentially, instead of searching out the common elements underlying difference? Then difference would disappear as a general feature that leads to the generality of the concept, and it would become—a different thought, the thought of difference—a pure event.

Michel Foucault

I

INTERPRETING

1. Hermes

Although discussions need not have patron saints or divine guidance, Hermes shall here serve both functions. I shall be dealing with the coming of meaning and the distortion of meaning. I shall attend to the "Hermes dimension" of mind and world, which is primary when we want to understand the psychological, the soulish, the unconscious and the conscious. The myths of Hermes tell us a remarkable amount about how awareness goes on, and that telling is also an activity of consciousness that is seeded deeply in our language and tradition. *Insight* is the word that seems most appropriate as one comes to Hermes in the mind. His stories tell us much about seeing that is neither voluntary nor agency-centered. Some of his admirers followed magic in his name. But that is unnecessary, unless "magic" encompasses all that is psychic, but not routinized under some decade's or century's intellectual canons. He names the divinity of movement in and out of the unexpected, and, as we shall see, he may guide us to parts of our own being which are excluded by the normalcy of our ordinary days.

We shall want to read him metaphorically. He can bring many different messages, but the trail we are following points to the happening of mind and shall lead us toward our own experiences of coming to see, viz. to what we call interpreting.

(a) The origin of Hermes[1]

Kerènyi comments that Hermes "is most likely the same dark depth of being from which we all originate."[2] His father is Zeus, Lord of the Sky and source of divine order. His mother is Maia, a nymph about whom little is known other than that she was majestic, beautiful, shy, and able to satisfy Zeus. She preferred her cave to Olympus and may have had some relation to the Titans of older times. Hera was asleep the night Zeus and Maia lay together, and Hermes' origin in infidelity, at night, with the greatest of the gods and a nymph who was not quite a goddess will come to bear shortly. Kerènyi's observation, however, is not a cynical statement about our parents'

---

[1] Unless otherwise noted, these observations are based on *The Homeric Hymns*, trans. Andrew Lang (London, 1899).

[2] Karl Kerènyi, *Hermes: Guide of Souls* (Zurich: Spring Publications, 1976).

morality, but is his guess that our souls, our consciousnesses, our human worlds have their continuous beginning, at least partially, in common with Hermes' origin: a cavish femininity, shy and darkly wonderful, sensuous, able to dwell alone and outside of clear orders of relation, and a powerfully fecund, demanding, raucous, terrible god of order who reigned over earth's vault. Sky and earth, height and depth, sound and silence, Zeus and Maia copulating in a vast and rich cave before Eos rose blushing in the eastern sky or Caephalus blew his cold dawn's wind and Hera rose to see to hearth and home.

Out of this union comes, at dawn, in "ten moons," "a child of many a wile and cunning counsel." Kerènyi shows that Hermes combines indications of the hard cruelness and bloodthirstiness of the Titans with the compassion and gentleness of the Olympians: although there are overtones of a murderous and consuming night power, he is governed, by the time of the Homeric hymn, by devious, divine charm, if not by gentlemanly grace. The combination of tendencies is our interest. Hardly is he born before he darts to the cave's threshold, kills a turtle, invents with its shell the lyre, and sings beautifully in roguish chants of how Maia and Zeus conceived him, of the riches of Maia's place and of the splendid gods of Olympus. He procedes to steal Apollo's cattle, apparently because he wanted fresh meat, but sacrifices two of them to the Olympian Gods and eats nothing. Playing, almost dancing, he steals, worships, deceives, charms, and sings his first hours of life, and then his angry half brother, Apollo, full god, long born, arrives to reckon his injury with Hermes. The youngster first appears as a mere child in the cradle, one who could do no deed at all. When Apollo is unpersuaded, he gentles his half-brother with "twinking eyes," wit, and lies. Apollo laughs, but is prepared nonetheless to punish the thief. As Apollo, God of Cleanliness and Purity, picks up Hermes, the cave-conceived divinity who is to become the messenger (Angelos) of the gods, "let forth an Omen, an evil belly-tenant, with tidings of worse, and a speedy sneeze thereafter. Apollo heard, and dropped renowned Hermes on the ground."

There follows an encounter with Zeus, who bursts out in laughter over Hermes' misleading account of himself and his deeds. A deal between Hermes and Apollo is struck, in the light of father Zeus' wisdom, and Apollo receives the lyre while Hermes receives guardianship of cattle and a cattle whip. Apollo remains privy to the mind of Zeus, but Hermes is soon to become the ambassador to man from the gods.

So was the first day.

Hermes, who is born in the coming of light after a dark conception, brings light and life wherever he is. He is virtually without order. His worship of and sacrifice to the gods, of whom he is already one when the hymn was written, is out of delight in them, not out of obligation. He is an event of light, like the play of light on the infinitely reflecting Mediterranian waves seen on a cloudless day. But his enlightenment has no set of principles to be ingested and followed. His half-brother, Apollo, knows the abstractions of the universe in their purity, but he is not the angel to human beings. Hermes scoffs at honor, seeks no position based on prestige, farts and "threatens worse" in Apollo's hands, lies, cheats, and is roguish with what he also delights in. But he created the lyre; *he* gave music to Apollo, a creation that meant the gouging and tearing death of a peacefully grazing turtle. Without seeing blood on the first lyre, and also pieces of skin, and without catching a whiff of the first lyre on its second and third days, one misses something in the origin of music. It did not take place in the mind of Zeus or in the austerity of Apollo. This god is the guide of human beings. Darkness and light, gods and half-divinities, delight and spilt blood, wit and an overtone of vague malice, liveliness through deception and trickery, creation in deviation, divinity without dignity, progeny without respect: an origin we humans all share. In what way could we possibly find Hermes as a guide, as an occurrence of our own souls?

(b) Hermes the Guide

The name *Hermes* probably is related to the herm, a four cornered stone (or, at times, perhaps a pile of stones) that was a way-marker on a road or path or an indication of a border. This combined experience of marking a way and marking a border points to Hermes. A road goes two ways, a particularly perplexing reality if we reach a road without a map or a clear sense of direction and do not know which way leads toward home. And a border may mark familiarity and strangeness—my region and theirs; each side is strange to some degree from the other side. And a border marks same and different. We on this side are the same in the sense that . . . , while those on the other side do not share these things with us and are different.

Hermes is related to the experience of ways, but he is not related to a person's search for *the* way or *a* way. He marks out ways. He is related to the experiences of foreignness, strangeness, and familiarity, but not to the specific perspectives inside the regions. He marks and even defines differences, but he does not take sides. His is not a side over against something else. He is presenter, giver of sameness and difference, herald of the gods, proclaimer and announcer, swift as light, but unaligned. He appears to love realities, to take delight in the presence of things, but he is not inclined to quarrel or to take anything, least of all himself, with heavy seriousness. Whatever he takes, he seems to take it lightly. He makes ways and differences manifest without being identified with what he presents.

Hermes is consequently never fixed into a sustained individuality. From the perspective of steady character he is always perplexing and mysterious. He consorts with all mortals and immortals, says the *Hymn*, but his presence does not confirm anything or anyone as right or wrong. I, in a hurry, take the wrong turn and end at a place opposite where I intended to go: Hermes is no less present there than if I had arrived where I intended. Hermes as guide does not mean that he guards what I want or sends me on the way, which by *my* best light I should travel. He may announce love when I seek pure concentration. He may herald Hades and the forgetfulness of death as I seek more life. He may bring the message of Apollo as I seek more earthiness and ordinary relationships. Hermes the presenter is not guided by a person's interests or by an order internal to himself that he seeks to imprint on reality. In what sense is he a guide?

W. F. Otto reports that in earlier years, when a remarkable silence occurred in the midst of lively friendliness, Hermes was said to have entered the room.[3] One did not know, at first at least, what the silence, that interrupted the easy flow, meant. And his presence was also recognized with a sudden burst of darkness in times of clarity or by enigma when the situation had been straightforward. As the ever present border between the familiar and the strange becomes apparent, Hermes is recognized. He is also found when the well-traveled way appears as a place on which I can be lost *because* it goes somewhere, and I do not know if I should be on it. He is a guide in the sense that he marks and makes apparent the other, the strange, the dark, the unfamiliar, the mystery-in-this-context.

In my home town there is a line along an alley that marks the border between two Indian nations. In earlier times tribal members of the Creeks and Seminoles forfeited their rights upon crossing that line. Each was a no-man when the border was crossed. That seemed strange and puzzling to me as a boy, when I walked down the alley and criss-crossed from side to side. There was a sameness to the sides that made the border seem artificial. Yet men had died for crossing. I could imagine sitting on one side and looking across to the other. Maybe, I fantasized, I had never been across the line, but I had heard stories, and the border seemed then to define safety and belonging. But, in my imagination, I see the sameness of the sage grass on both sides, the sameness of the air that the hawk flies through, passing with impunity over the line on the ground. That other, foreign side, arbitrarily created, is somehow the same. The strangeness over there and the familiarity over here mean sameness in some way. Say that I cross over to the strange land and run over the same ground and through the same grass toward the grove of pecan trees for some of the same shade, and I laugh suddenly as I run in the realization of sameness and arbitrariness and non-necessity and kinship, and as I approach the pecan grove a shot drops me in stride, and I am left, no man, to die without right of recovery or burial. Hermes, now the devious one, given my own interests, was just as present as guide as if I had remained seated on my side and suddenly seen, in a spiritual leap, that the sides do not mean that we are un-brothers, that the sameness of the hawk's element is like the sameness among us who are otherwise separated. Hermes, now not devious, would have been manifest in this manifestness of same with mystery and familiarity. And as he marks borders

---

[3] Walter F. Otto, *The Homeric Gods*, trans. Moses Hadas (N.Y.: Pantheon, 1954).

he manifests their non-necessity in their reality, just as when he marks he sews ambiguity into any certainty that is founded in the notion that one way in its familiarity is the *way*.

Hermes as guide and Hermes as trickster do not contradict each other. They reflect each other in the light of Hermes' difference from individual motivation, interest, and will.

But he is said to be the friendliest of the gods. Not only did he create music and the lyre, but also fire. He harbors no heavy grudges. He does not have to be pleased by sacrifices or obedience. He extracts no particular price, he gives no commands, is untainted by moral seriousness. He is a wonderful companion, at least for gods, and he shows compassion for dead souls. He means, I believe, that nothing is finally defined by human will and that not even human existence is defined by the interests of the person. In that is his friendliness to us most clear. Hermes is the guiding event. He is enlightenment with all its elusiveness. He manifests the limits of all personal or folk compasses. He reveals the borders of all identity, the other realities that face and cast their shadows on each certainty, the dark mystery that shadows our best clarity. As guide he shows ways and borders by always being with opposites, differences, and othernesses. He is to be thought only by paradox, irony, and ambiguity, and he reveals to us in that something of our own, perpetual origin.

(c) Being with Hermes

Being with Hermes on ways and borders is an experience of being alert in a setting that far exceeds the consciousness characteristic of our personal character and identity. His myth imagines us accompanying a kind of shooting star to a region of awareness where ordered security is not a primary principle of life, where accuracy is not a measure of truth, where creation and event take enormous priority over confirmation, status, lineage, citizenship, and propriety, and where the presentation of whatever announces itself is a source of attention, no matter the practical consequences. Being with Hermes is being open to the borderline of words, ideas, situations, and circumstances. Being with him involves that remarkable capacity of being in something and also being aware of a beyond-this-something with which we have a kinship that seems strange right now.

Hermes is a thief. One struggles to gain independence from a parent, say, and does, and in the possession of new independence finds that he/she has lost something too, other than dependence. Perhaps he/she has lost an old security or a certain youthful charm or a kind of optimism. Hermes. And if one laughs, as well as grieves, and feels a little tricked and stays with the sense of loss or the unexpected emptiness, one is with Hermes. One has found a border of his/her particular identity. In the loss, the thievery, one experiences an intrusion in one's own plans from an unknown region, as though trading were going on with participants other than I. Or, a couple experiences days of intense attraction and involvement, only to find not only a dissipation of the intensity, but a certain emptiness quite other than physical tiredness or spentness. In the absence that comes so surprisingly on the heels of the experience of full presence, one may catch the footprints of our divine friend, if he has not wiped them out. We also have occasion to experience that the whole of things, the sameness that pervades differences, is sometimes to be found more in loss and absence than in intensities that demand so much of our attention, as though these involvements were themselves the whole world. The inexhaustibleness of being borders our strange exhaustion in this case.

Walter Otto says that Hermes "is the spirit of constellation which recurs in the most diverse conditions and which embraces loss as well as gain, mischief as well as kindliness."[4] "Constellations" can occur in many different ways. Things may be brought together and related through powerful or heroic authority, through sovereignty, as when people and things are arranged according to one or a few persons' will. Or they may be brought together for the sake of production, acquisition, or conquest. But Hermes is absorbed by or identified with no heroes or wilful directions. He manifests decency by being lewd, the heroic by being concerned with little things and by finding the crass and cowardly worthwhile. He can also border weakness by his great strength and ugliness by his beauty, his songs, or his movement.[5] He forever marks the limits of all things, including most particularly those enormous religious and moral realities in the seriousness of which we can all lose our sense of finiteness and play, as well as our capacity to catch the meaning of our lives in the flash of white in early morning or twilight on the wing of a flying bird.

Hermes as presenter constellates always with the border in view. Apollo tried, but failed, to tie Hermes down on the first day of his life. Hermes' freedom from all bonds is his remarkable power. He as myth gives personality and vividness to events of presentation, and not just of one thing or even of a large group of things, but to the event, the coming forth of all things— of ticks and fleas and flies and maggots, as well as of Zeus, my own self, and the British Parliament.

Being with him is like a wise man's being open to his dream of an idiot woman, a cruel person's being open to a fantasy of compassion, a deeply committed person's being open to a sense of profound doubt and depression, a mother and housewife's openness to her androgynous symbols, a clergy person's happiness over a dream of rape. Hermes brings things together in the appearance of a mysteriously, perhaps infinitely larger whole. Being with him is found as weakness in strength and as the perverseness and madness of whatever is established as complete and sufficient, even for just a

---

[4] Ibid., p.122.
[5] Rafael Lopez-Pedraza, *Hermes and His Children* (Zurich: Spring Publications, 1977), is the best account that I know of Hermes' relation to deviation, perversion, and opposites.

moment. His heralding all things divine and his attention to all things means the infinite reach of being and the arbitrariness of every standing place. Being that knowledge, he smiles most of the time.

My own emphasis will fall on how the experience of Hermes provides entrée for the experience of interpreting, i.e., of a person's coming to see something through a process of developing awareness. In the course of the discussion I shall attempt to persuade you that *World* is to be conceived as an event of awareness that is not primarily personal, but is subject to self-awareness. How a person relates with the world and how the world is an event are the Hermetic relations that we shall pursue. Our next step is to consider hermeneutics.

2. Interpreting

Am I being perverse to approach interpreting by means of the God who fathered Priapus and Pan and who has a heritage not only of fecundity, but also of perversion and deviousness?[6] Perhaps. But perverse in what context? The unencompassableness of Hermes would not have impressed Homer, I think, as being different from the context in which mortals understand things. Nor would his unpredictability have seemed opposed to many of the realities that we understand. Interest in his meaning has also increased among those in our century who deal in depth with human awareness and who find contradiction, androgeny, misshapenness, as well as creativity and delight in living to be only a few of the constant characteristics of the human soul. Hermes' perverseness is largely his not fitting into the fitting of a given time and situation, and his divinity is partially found in his limitless heralding or manifesting opposites as well as other divinities which differ from what we hold to be sacred and holy. He seems to give, without judgment, place and word to whatever is. In that sense he calls into question all interpretations that give priority to judgment or to any kind of absolutes. His perverseness in our time is most likely to be found in the ways he shows methods of scholarly and scientific certainty to be transcendable by regions bordering, but otherwise untouched by our desire for certainty and accuracy. We shall see, in that light, what Hermes might show us about our own understanding and our experiences of interpreting.

Our experiences of interpreting are reflected in the meanings of the word. "To interpret" primarily means "to explain" in the sense of telling the meaning of something. I might interpret an institution to you by saying or showing that it means that exchange of money is very important in this country or that another institution means that education is a public responsibility. Or you might tell a story to your six-year-old, who had been playfully misleading you by acting as though she were drowning in the swimming

---

[6] Ibid.

pool, about the shepherd boy who called "wolf! wolf!" You would be interpreting her action to her in a larger context of danger, concern, and reliableness. We interpret in such situations by bringing out their forgotten or unnoticed present meaning of something. In that sense, to interpret is to bring something to light. "Elucidate" says the dictionary. "Lucidas," the root of "elucidate," means full of light. We experience a kind of illumination when an interpretation is successful, and ideally we speak from clarity of meaning as we interpret. It is not like the experience of shining a flashlight on a dark object but is the experience of coming to light, like when dawn comes and we begin to see. Although "explain" originally meant to flatten out or to make level, a meaning we retain when an explanation simplifies and removes shadows and roughness, "interpreting" is closer, in its first meaning, to the process of making something apparent with all its obscurities and unevenness. The emphasis falls on developing an awareness of meaning, however complex or strange in our setting that meaning might be.

Another meaning in "interpreting" is "to construe in light of individual belief, judgment or interest." "Construe" has the sense of to construct or to pile up or to set in order. It is what we do with what is scattered or strewn about. We are interpreting as we provide order. When I tell the meaning of something I am giving order. Or when I arrange things, such as flowers, ideas, people, or spaces. Interpreting in the sense of construing has the sense of a configuration of awareness that reflects individual judgment and interest, but that configuration is not necessarily under the aegis of that individual's interest and judgment. The configuration is there, in the apartment complex, in the temple, in this language or those customs. How things are together is an interpretation, and we are deeply imprinted by interpretations as we live in and through orders of words, orders of customs, or orders of material things. The orders are postures of awareness—interpretations— which are embodied in how things are together. Interpretations are by no means limited to the consciousness of individuals.

A third kind of interpretive experience is apprehending and representing by means of art. That kind of apprehension goes on *in* an activity of presenting. It is not the same thing as thinking about what a work of art means. If you act a part in a play, for example, the persona may begin to take over. Not only do you interpret the part, but the part itself in the context of the whole work lends apprehension to the persona in the situation of the drama. You the actor and I the observer both find ourselves taken into an order of presentation that is at once an interpretation and an apprehension.

This word, *interpret*, founded in the Roman way of being with things, always carries the overtone of simultaneous order and awareness. The classical Romans knew that the orders of their language and empire, their civilization, were apprehensions. To be under the Roman civil authority and to speak the Roman language were to be in an awareness, an interpretation, that was the meaning of *Roman*. Rome was presented in how the individual was who he/she was. One was always in an interpretation as one interpreted his/her world to him/herself.

The Greek word, however, is *hermeneuein* and it indicates a significantly different experience. The word may or may not be directly descended from Hermes, but the experience of Hermes, as reflected in his myths, will shed light on how our understanding goes on in the Greek aspect of our heritage.

The Greek emphasis falls more heavily on the givenness of things. The first direction in the word is toward the bestowal (ref. heralding) of meanings and things rather than toward their order. The gods, for the Greeks, give personality to kinds of order: Ares, the order of belligerence, boldness, battle, competition, high spiritedness; Hephaestus, the order of inventing, solitary making and forging hard substances, heat, etc. Divine powers, rather than citizens and other individuals, are the source of order. My present interest, however, is not specifically theological. I am noting that in our Greek heritage the experiences of givenness and non-human origin are more dominant than in our Roman heritage. The Latin *interpres* could also refer to an interpreter or negotiator, but the idea of messenger, which is given in the *hermetic* side of *hermeneuein*, does not come across strongly in the Latin. Hermeneutic may also be taken to assume orders and the task of coming to see the orders, but Roman organization is not implied. Rather, transcendence of human originality is implied.

The ungraspable, elusive quality of meaning should not be overlooked. If we are sidetracked by literalizing mythical personages and actions, we lose the power of myths to speak of the non-literal dimensions of our world. That non-literal dimension includes the occurrence of meaning and significance, an occurrence that Hermes helps to focus. We experience meanings in how things are together or come together, in the way things are present. We are encompassed by meaning in the sense that we always are in a world filled with orders and presences. Not only is our particular awareness structured by relations, orders, and relations of orders, so are our dreams, our physical environment, our language in which we come to awareness, and all to which we can specifically refer. Each meaning or relation of meanings (i.e., each thing or relation of things) merges with other meanings, carries with it meant opposites (i.e., not this, such as not male, not neuter, but feminine, etc.), shadow off into backgrounds, penumbral areas. We shall look in detail at these aspects of the presence of meaning. Now, however, we need only the initial notion that coming to understand and understanding— involving what as children of Rome we call interpretation and as Greek progeny we name hermeneutics—are ways of coming into the presence of things with our own presence. Both are kinds of reflection, a countenancing that will not allow us to think of interpreting as only our particular activity. As we come to see and understand, we are in occurrences close to the way Hermes is said to be.

3. The Situation of Interpreting

As we come to understand things, as interpreting goes on, we are in a vast situation, a good metaphor for which is the reflective play of light. A slightly disturbed sea on a bright day, or a prairie of grass, appears as neither a single bright light nor as a web of discrete lights. They are plays of light in which discreteness is forever blending into other discretenesses, in which there are vaguely shadowed reflections upon reflections upon reflections, dazzling an individual beholder by their apparently infinite movement. They present the strange situation of luminosity: full of light and yet empty of substance. The play of light casts its tone for visibility, and in looking at it one sees by it and yet sees nothing in particular. The Greeks were astute in their perception that coming to understand, no matter how much limiting order is present, involves an infinity, a kind of wholeness, an unreachable light, an excessiveness of the orders that can be spoken of most appropriately by indirection and through mythical persona.

Hermes, whose birth is closely associated with the coming of light, and who means shadow, border strangeness, and guidance always in the presence of opposites and differences, allows us to see that orders in relation to orders do not circumscribe the situation of interpreting. The borders, the shadows, and the appearance of infinity, with its effect of distorting the pretensions to totality characteristic of any of the parts: all these clouding and unsettling factors are part of the appearance of the light of the world, i.e., of meanings in their interrelation.

The Anglo-Saxon word *mind* gives us an indication of this situation. Historically its first region of meaning is the experience of remembering, an experience that involves heeding, being reminded, recollecting. In remembering we live out continuities in which what has gone by is linked now with the upcoming. *Mind*, in this context, means the occurrence of continuity in which something of the rootage, perhaps of the origin of the present is given experientially as recall. Such connections might happen through retelling or exposition, or reversion to something that is now left out or forgotten. Minding or reminding in this sense means reestablishing, recalling, or commemorating linkages and kinship, and hence resonance, celebration, and symbolization are important overtones of *mind*, as well as overtones of holding together and staying in touch. Mind as recollection occurs as the past kinships and rootages of the present situation come to bear as awareness. As that happens we individuals may also gain lucidity, our understanding develops, and part of the vast depth of any given moment may vaguely emerge in our particular grasp of things. A richly remembered present presages at least intimations of possible whole.

Another area of meaning for the word *mind* involves disposition. Mind is not made up primarily of *what* is thought, but is thinking, judging, intuiting. Disposition, in the sense of the bent of thought or the inclination of a conscious situation is the mind's state. *Disposition*, in this context, means inclination, a kind of desire, although desire as the drift or direction of a state of awareness, not of a single agent within that larger state (that is, not the action of an "ego" in, say, a Freudian or Jungian sense of the word). The mind is a place or region of entertainment, in which specific goals are like fish within a powerful drift of the sea. It is a state of feeling awareness that pervades, but is not isolated as any one thing or set of things. The mind is, says the OED, a kind of vision. In light of the recollecting aspect of mind, we can say that mind is awareness, with a disposition of flowing presenting passedness, that comes to bear in how perceptions, thoughts, horizons of the future, the gatherings of things, and so forth happen now.

The mind, in other words, is filled with borders, with disjunctions, opposites, with a vast array of "what-has-gone-on." As disposition it is felt and inclined conjunctions of reversions, encounters, and, as predispositions, it happens as anticipations. Mind is the occurrence of awareness that has within it multiple directions. At the same time, it is our immediate awareness, an immediate sense of its own occurrence. I know of nothing else in the universe like mind, this self-aware event that encompasses conscious and nonconscious relations and that is lived by a particular person as a surpassing enormity of directions, depths, mysteries, meanings, and other powers and experiences with which he/she can be only vaguely in touch.

As we consider the Hermes-quality of mind, we shall look to one more word that carries with it helpful experiential insight: *bear*. Its very old and now obsolete meaning is *wave* or *billow*, still vaguely present in the sense of "to bring forth." It means also "to carry," but usually with the continuing overtone of bringing forth, as in "to support," as "muscles bear the hand"; "to take a companion along," as "he bears with him a son"; "to bear witness," "to give" as "she bore her hand to him"; "to entertain or to harbor or cherish;" "to share in," as to bear a part; "to endure," as "to bear many things." It may also mean to extend or stretch, as the line bears east, and to sail or go in a certain direction. And it may mean to yield and to give birth.

Mind bears. Even as we may bear in mind. In one sense, mind is bearing, as disposition and past-determined setting. It is bearer as yielding and bringing forth. It is carrier as harbor of relations and events, as constant accompaniment, as continuity, and, playing on the intersecting meanings, we can say that our identities are born in mind.

As a self-aware event, mind means an occurrence of beholding, an attending regard, that occurs with whatever is going on. It is bearer of past in its present moment, it is a vis-à-vis in the midst of conscious happenings. Like Hermes, it seems to be everywhere at once, it seems to have been conceived in darkness, being, as it is, self-contained, but its coming heralds light. It happens like the multiple reflections of light, without substance, without explanation, compatible with all that appears. It is the region for enlightenment, that with which we in our limitedness must come to terms if we are to "find ourselves." And yet it gives no exactness in its guidance, no preference for character. Mind is illuminating passage, the illumination of presence, self-awareness with identity, the basis of our understanding, judgment, and specifying desires.

4. Mind as Distortion

Hermes, closely related to thieves and deformed people—in a word, closely related to deviation from normal expectations—is perpetually the guide in a landscape that exceeds the familiar. The unfamiliar may become apparent as a vaguely familiar valley found to have a different horizon over that hill and different arrangements of trees and rocks, even though the stream looks like the familiar one and this spot where we are standing looks like a place we remember. Or our familiar family may become strangely dislocated in the developing silence between our parents or in the sickness that has caused deviation from our habitual ways. Is this the same family in which I felt known and secure? Or in a time of intense concentration my room, so known to me, may change: a sense of timelessness might shimmer over the desk and from the walls, the bed may stand out with utter individuality, a dislocation in the habitual continuity. I may feel strange and alien as the unfamiliar comes breaking through the everyday significances of this place. Neither space nor realities of any kind are finally owned or totally possessed by the habits and expectations in which we are familiar with them. Dreams are well known for their power to dislocate the familiar and to blend the known with the mysterious. Hermes is closely related to such experiences in which deviation occurs as the in-breaking of the unencountered or of the unheard of in "the normal."

Our encounters with "our" minds are often marked more by unfamiliarity than by familiarity. The familiar usually encompasses an arrangement of things and people in our environment, by a "normal" interpretation. We may be most familiar with ourselves as how we are usually viewed: we are in touch with ourselves through the roles we play and through the identities given to us by people around us. I may know myself as one who seeks to please or as one who is inclined to rebel, as one who wants unqualified acceptance or as one who depends on criticism. I may know my character through my obedience or refusal of certain inherited norms. In such cases, I am reflected to myself by my social environment, and depth encounter with mind or with the disposition and recollections that happen as I think, act, and feel are alien to me. My dreams, in this instance, will feel strange and probably irrelevant. The very milieu and region of dream and fantasy will seem unreal. The experiences of numenosity, symbolic powers, radical otherness, and difference within "my" awareness: such things will hardly appear likely or rational. Certainly not normal. They would appear to be tantamount to losing my mind.

In counseling situations I have frequently heard a person say that what used to appear normal seems crazy now. One young woman, in a few intense weeks, experienced the full range of her life in light of her death. Relations that were rote became charged with possibilities for intense awareness. She felt the cold insight that her life was hers and valuable and worthwhile and that she was wasting it, not living very much. She was shocked at the banality of most of her conversations and contacts, at the loss of life that happened as insensitivity, trivial ambition, thoughtless rising in the morning, tasteless consumption of food, habitual walking, unreflective talk that meant very little beyond social function, and a pervasive absence of gratitude, outrage, love, or profundity. She had crossed a border to awareness of death, an awareness around every corner in "our" minds, and her familiar terrain became altered and cast in a very different light. She said that she had been out of her mind to live as she had. One could also say that the security of the banal had been stolen from her as she crossed a frontier, a frequent form of Hermes' trickery.

Mind, the self-aware region of so much that transcends our particular postures and points of view, dislocates those regions of familiarity that domi-nate us or define us. Mind may appear as dreaming when waking seems absolute, as dying when life seems total and complete, as pragmatic affairs of everyday life when we are ethereal in most of our relations, as the sheer fact of difference when we are most comfortable with what we know, as chaos and absurdity when we are locked in our orders, as unbroken silence when we are filled with "our" sounds, as total other to all pretenses to suffi-ciencies, and so forth. Mind dislocates by its transcendence of all particulars and any totality of particulars. It seems like an illusion when we are set or fixed in one way of being who we are.

5. Mind as Event of Illusion and Fantasy

Worthwhile events enhance human life. *Enhance* in this context means to increase or to elevate or to encourage human life. Not necessarily more things or more goodness of character or even more days. More life: more intensity of perception, deeper and higher awareness, greater capacity for pain, commitment, affection, distance, closeness, love, hatred, deceit, adven-ture, greater openness to all that is alive, greater distaste for the deadening. Whatever is therapeutic aids human living, and we turn to mind as fantasy and illusion in the context of recalling that being alive is in some sense a question of quality of involvement with living beings. This quality is intrin-sically "fantasy."

The notion that mind happens as fantasy or image (or as notion) is ap-propriated in many quarters.[7] In this discussion I shall use the word *fantasy*,

[7] Henry Corbin, *Creative Imagination in the Sufism of Ibn' Arabi*; Mary M. Watkins, *Wak-ing Dreams* (N.Y.: Harper, 1977); Gerald N. Epstein, "The Relation of Healing to Imagination," *Studies in Non-Deterministic Psychology*, ed. Gerald N. Epstein (N.Y.: Human Sciences Press,

since its Greek root (*phantasia*) meant making visible and was founded in *phantic*, a possessed person. *Phainein* meant to show, to appear. In scholastic psychology "fantasy" meant a mental apprehension as well as the faculty of apprehension. The word rightfully means "coming to visibility" or "appearing" and carries with it an overtone of the in-breaking of the unexpected or of the unknown into a region of knowing. Although *fanatic* now has a completely negative sense, a *phantic* in much earlier times was one through whom people discovered what was blocked to them in their ordinary and usual knowledge. *Phantasia* meant the appearing of the hidden, and in our context we can say that it meant coming to an explicit awareness of mind. The phantic minded the hidden and forgotten.

I shall not use *image* frequently, even though it is much more frequently used and fits better into our ordinary conception of what is knowable. It usually has the overtone of *copy*, and we hardly think of it as a verb. Without thinking about it, *image* probably means to us a re-presentation: an image of the dance last night; I carry your image in my mind. Or we may think of an unrealistic concoction: that is only an image of economic reality, as distinct to the real thing. Or imitation: a close copy is "the spitting image"; "in the image of the president" might mean in the likeness or semblance of another reality, for example, the president. At worst an image is a mere copy or a public illusion that hides a private reality, such as when image-makers create the impression of what a group of consumers or voters want. That means that "imitating reality," as distinct to being real, is probably lurking in the background when we say *imagination*. Or if not imitating, producing something that is not really real, but is like something else that is real.

The topic of this section is the presentation of mind. In the next section we shall deal with the non-subjectivity of mind. Our goal is to see how mind happens as event, as the coming forth of happenings or realities. We shall strain our words in order to free ourselves from an inclination to understand things primarily through substantives and literalisms rather than through happenings and verbs. These strains and awkwardnesses will help us to see the life of mind as the occurrence of the utterly real. As we deal with mind and fantasy we are dealing with the life of mind, with the coming and staying of things, with creation (as well as death). We are also moving toward a notion of "world" as a region of reflection that is not the work or product of a knowing subject. If we come so far, we shall see that interpreting means allowing things to be as they occur, that being true is event, is coming forth or happening. Then we shall be prepared to think about being well and ill, hopefully free of a subjectivistic notion of ourselves, a notion that may not "mind" human being as well as we could wish.

1980); Gerald N. Epstein, *Waking Dream Therapy* (N.Y.: Human Sciences Press, 1980); James Hillman, *Re-Visioning Psychology* (N.Y.: Harper, 1975); James Hillman, "Further Notes on Images," *Spring* (1978).

I assume that how things are present and referrable is a major question for our modern interpretations of things. I am assuming that we must deviate from much of our ordinary language usage and from many of the assumptions that gird our theories about ourselves, because we tend to think in terms of subjects knowing objects. That has bred an enormous predisposition for literal accuracy. The emphasis falls on *literal*. We naturally assume that knowing is re-presenting things because we are self-enclosed, neurological structures. We are perceptive beings in the sense that we are able to get what is outside of us into us in the form of patterns, that is perceptions, ideas, brain structures, etc. These patterns are copies of what they are not. There is controversy over whether we know only the patterns or the non-patterned things through the patterns. Or perhaps the way the patterns come together and behave is reality. Or perhaps reality stands forever outside of the patterns, only to be approximated by human states of mind. In any case, we tend to want the real to be something that is exactly as it is—literal, not fictional or imaginal or fantastic. We tend to want to be free of our gazes and regards, to be in touch with how things *really* are. *Really* then means out there, by itself, just as it is without regard for my regard of it. So we seek to be exact. If we can get a predictive bead on where something is headed or developing we suspect that we are knowing *it* in *its* situation. And we measure. Our goal is an honest exactness, unshaded by deception, speculation, imagination, or even history. Things are present to us as objects of interest and use and so forth. Behind this cluster of assumptions, preferences, and predispositions lies a considerable suspicion of fantasy and imagination, unless *imagination* means technical or theoretical ingeniousness.

Fantasy consequently retains its sense of deviation. It deviates from the dominant expectations and goals of our time; from quantitative exactness, literal reality, hard-nosed approaches and methods, linear, step by defined step ways of discovering. It also retains now a slight overtone of being possessed, except that presently it is a "mere" possession. Nothing divine or important about it, simply a non-substantial foolishness, one's being possessed by some irreal notion or other. The very thought that fantasy might itself compose the life of mind and world, that everything hard-nosed, careful, responsible, honest, accessible, and right is founded in fantasy is itself mere fantasy, although perhaps repulsive for its pretensions. Being fantastical is itself a deviation from our day to day norms. Consequently dreaming and fantasizing strike us intuitively as playing with nonrealities. The idea that illusion, mistake, insight, appearance, and truth are to be closely associated seems particularly foreign. We have to break away from the everyday ways of our ordinary and educated lives in order to appreciate fantasy.

Waking dream therapy sets us in the direction of appreciating the creative and destructive ways that fantasies appear.[8] The first issue often is being free and open for a fantasy.[9] Corbin has developed thoroughly the observation that the realm of fantasy is *sui generis*, that it is neither abstract nor "matter," but is a region of transformation in which things gain a life—I would say meaning—that changes their valence and gives them a power for creating and engendering further life and meaning.[10] *Soul* is the name Hillman gives this region.[11] Watkins usually says *imaginal* as she thinks of this region. *Imaginal realm* is Epstein's preferred term.[12] All four people are naming a "place" where a depth of the person's life happens and one in which one's particular personality and identity are subsumed in a considerably larger whole. This larger whole, which distorts the ordinary experience that I am "just" who I am, may give one pause at its threshold. "I" have limited control there. I find myself with all manner of influences, forces, persona, histories, and destinies. "I" am not ballasted by ordinary cause and effect or the reliability of familiar standards of measurement. "I" am in a "crazy" world of transformations, shadows, strangers, and non-orientation. Well might I pause.

Watkins refers to the waking dream as "the conscious experiencing of the imaginal."[13] "When we observe what we are doing," she says, "who we have become, and where we are aimed, it is often as if our lives were dreamed by another, and we are some two-bit or noble actor or actress executing a part."[14] That kind of experience breaks down our sense of being simple, continuous identities. We realize that our existence is composed of much more than our identities with a physical body. There are many faces "influencing our thoughts, emotions, movements, and actions. One can no longer say that it is a god or a spirit and yet one has those ancient feelings of possession and movement by a force that does not answer to logic or common space and time."[15] Speaking of the imagination as masculine, Watkins says:

[8] Epstein and Watkins have helpful bibliographies on this topic. I have had some experience in this form of therapy. I speak both out of that experience and out of the work of Epstein and Watkins.

[9] I shall continue to use the word *fantasy*, although the literature on this topic almost universally uses *image*. Most of the authors whom I have read, however, do not have a copy of something in mind, but have in mind an event that is present as autonomous, sometimes as a feeling or thought or recollection, but one that is not produced by the action of the "who" with whom one identifies him/herself. An image, in this context, happens, like a dream, as a region of awareness in which one may find oneself as a participant.

[10] Corbin, *Creative Imagination in the Sufism of Ibn' Arabi*.

[11] Hillman, *Re-visioning Psychology*.

[12] Watkins, *Waking Dreams*; Epstein, *Waking Dream Therapy*.

[13] Watkins, *Waking Dreams*, p. vii.

[14] Ibid., p.7.

[15] Ibid.

But suddenly we may see that it is not the visible he has been talking about. In his gestures, he has sought to make the invisible visible. He is talking about something we do not know and thereby cannot judge according to our usual·standards. He does not use our language because he does not speak of the things our language was created for. He has, like Proteus, donned the costumes of countless images, assumed the voices of many gods, to live out the drama of experience. He has used the material from our houses, our lives, as props for his art. . . . We must grow accustomed to the twilight of his space, his images and metaphors, by dwelling there. In this way we can begin to travel within toward that which he points to.[16]

One begins by discovering a "new" region in which relations are remarkably different from those he/she has grown to expect. Frequently, in a relaxed state, one may enter this region and participate in what happens, like an intense daydream that takes one up into its way of happening. One young man followed his wife into a harem and discovered much about her of which he was not conscious. A woman followed an old lady, after initial fear and distrust, into an area of terror and darkness which previously she could not approach. A woman found her mother in a fantasy and had a painful and long overdue conversation with her. In these instances, the confronted people spoke back in their own voices and with their own ways. One frequently comes upon figures, situations, feelings, and other parts of the fantasy that are totally new and strange to them: a man who is to be known for the first time, a voice in a cave, a bear speaking, great light, new sensations. And these and the countless other ways fantasies happen are in a region of awareness that one may block, but that one can neither possess nor use.

As Watkins says, "The image is a vehicle in that we can move in it, but its space has no terminus . . . only unending depth."[17]

Another frequent aspect of the experience of fantasy is that when one does let go and allow the fantasy its full sway, uninterrupted by checks or refusals, what happens in the fantasy, like in a dream, conveys and communicates itself on its own terms. The remarkable, communicative autonomy of the fantasy, in this non-waking, non-sleeping milieu, allows one to experience his/her ordinary waking life in a depth that one does not encompass, but that reveals no end to itself. For some people, the key word is height, rather than depth. But in either case, a different element faces the element of waking. It feels utterly different, this element, in comparison to the milieu of being awake. But it is an element of awareness. Everything in the fantasy that one finds or hears or sees or smells or tastes, though utterly strange, is relational and communicative in the sense that one can be excited, afraid, interested, non-plussed, or whatever. Appearances are going on: there the black, fast swimming seal goes past; the angry, pounding sea sweeps in; the grey-eyed serene lady glides toward us; the wild, caged stag

[16] Ibid., p. 12.
[17] Ibid., p. 13.

leaps through the gate, pounding away from the wire meshed fence. Like anything that communicates, these fantasies can mean quite different things in different ways of hearing or seeing. They are kinds of lives, not mere pictures, but events that no nouns manage to capture. When I recall the fantasy in which the old, hunch-backed man looked at the pheasant and laughed, I may, depending on who and where I am, experience rejuvination in extreme fatigue, or I may experience the wildness of a beautiful bird over against a tired old human. Or I may feel like a dumb, beautiful bird, stupidly domesticated and laughed at by a wise old man who sees beyond the beauty of my feathers. And so forth.

The point is that in fantasy what happens "sticks to itself."[18] The fantasy is a whole, an inherence in which the parts form an appearance that will not boil down to one thing, any more than you or I can be boiled down to some simple nugget or essence. Each part of the fantasy reflects the other parts. One can see the aspects from any one of the aspects, by imaginatively varying his/her posture. I can, for example, see the fence from the wild eyes of the stag. Or I can be a fence, containing wildness. Or I can be the distant forest, mutely present, neither waiting nor anticipating, but hiding and placing wildness. All of these "postures" are ways of being in the fantasy. The fantasy, as an aware occurrence, without a single, positing subject, allows such multiplicity in its polyvalence of meaning, in the wholeness of its event.

Hillman illustrates this reversability as he elaborates this part of fantasy,[19] which Patricia Berry developed in *Spring*, 1974.[20] Speaking now of a dream of a blue arrow:

> Not only does your arrow—and I am addressing the dreamer—take you into the blue, come from the blue, brings the blues, is true blue, and so on. But also, in reverse, your blueness comes in arrow shape, straight as an arrow, arrowing sharply. You have an arrowy blueness, and the nature of blue in you, according to this dream, is pointed, swift, shafting, feathered, straight, airborne, flying aimed. . . .

This quality of mutual reflection in the fantasy is part of its depth: mind happens here as a circumscribed, reflective infinity of reference, as an event which, qua event, never seems exhausted. It may cast its light on my waking world, but the difference from the waking world as I ordinarily live it is the fantasy's plasticity, its reflexive flexibility that seems foreign in the usual. In the next section I shall show some of the ways in which world and "fantasy" are the same. The issue is not whether the figures of fantasy are the same as these rocks and trees and people in this park. They aren't. The issue has to do with the way appearances happen, and I am calling to mind that how fantasies happen reflect how the non-fantastical happens. Fantasies

[18] Hillman, "Further Notes. . . ."
[19] Ibid.
[20] Pp. 63-69.

put us in touch with something we have forgotten about our world. The radical, immediate move from the charging lion to the still, deep, deep blue pool may be the basis for seeing not only the difference between one aspect of my aggressiveness and a region of depth of feeling. It may also shed light on ravenous experiences and serenity, on a struggle and a related disturbance. And so forth. In the fantasy's radical juxtaposition of place, time, mood, speed, and sound, a juxtaposition that seems to violate common, waking experience, I come to touch realities that I had overlooked or to which I have been blind: the move from my lionine aggression to my depth of serenity is without mediation, like day and night without twilight or dawn; or, the lionine and depth of nonconscious awareness are close and immediate in me. The fantasy's meaning depends on what it sheds light on, what it finds relation with. But whatever it means, its meaning is found in a sameness of fantasy-relation and relation in the waking world. Fantasy's difference from my common sense, highly educated and trained expectations, my normal assumptions of universal efficient causation, of my life without lions or deep deep pools, and so forth, that difference is where the sameness of the fantasy event and some part of my waking life is to be found.

The reversibility of postures in fantasies and the mutual reflections of aspects in an event of fantasy may well be an entrée into how we are in the "non-fantastical" world, in spite of our beliefs to the contrary. When we approach mind through its dimensions of fantasy and illusion we find a region that tends to be excluded by our present intelligence and our common ways of life, but a dimension that happens in ways that have remarkable revelatory power through its sameness with situations in the waking world.

6. Mind as World-Event

Why is sustained contact with our night dreams and waking dreams therapeutic? That they are able to be therapeutic indicates some kind of likeness, or bridge. We have seen that the likeness or bridge may be found in the difference between fantasy and the type of experiences that largely make up our conscious, waking life. Fantasy and non-fantasy, however, are both events of awareness. The literalness and exactness of this board being cut to fit that space are in a region of relations: this space in relation to these spaces, and this place where the space is in relation to the porch that is attached to the house, and that in relation to the larger intentions of the builder and the community and so forth. Non-fantasy is a happening of mind. This mathematical formula and that computer bear and recollect traditions far richer than any history could report. They both have indigenous predispositions—toward calculation, precision, formal relations and formal causes, intellectual awareness, etc.—that make up a kind of tide or drift and set horizons of possibility. This formula and that computer help to form an environment of meaning and significance that yield a future way to be with them and in their presence. They are events of mind as recollecting bearers that form significant environments and horizons of possibility. As we find things in the world, they mean, they form contexts and identities. In future millennia, a discovery of one of our cars would reveal an enormous amount of information about our lives now, because the car means something as an individual thing that intrinsically reflects a huge context of relations. In that sense, discovery of a car by people in a far distant society that has forgotten our time is analogous to our discovery of cuniform or our encounter with a very strange dream. Discoveries can be made because the car, the written characters, or the dreams are real. They bear meanings; they are made up of intricate relations of meaning and significance, quite indigenous, thay may be ciphered if the conditions are right. They are events of mind in the sense that they bear meanings that constitute identity, relation, partness, and so forth.

Being of this strange region that we call mind, fantasy and non-fantasy are able to mean something in relation to each other. One does not appear to be reducible to the other, nor is one a copy or an imitation of the other. But communication is possible among fantasies and non-fantasies in the forms of shedding light, elaborating, giving added dimension, concretizing or illustrating, attracting and repelling, contradicting, and differentiating. Fantasy and non-fantasy form borders vis-á-vis each other. The laws and customs and occurrences in each of those regions are very different. Happenings in one are not identical with happenings in the other. But crossing the border appears not only to be possible, but in many lives to be frequent. The qualities of mind—recollecting, bearing, giving horizon, and so forth—seem to remain the same, and these qualities are some of the characteristics of presentation and being, whether the being and presentation are fantastical or non-fantastical.

We shall look further at the notion of world-event in order to see more clearly that mind is event whether of fantasy or of non-fantasy, and that its eventful quality gives us an opening to understand mental relations more in terms of Hermes the guide and border-marker than in terms of relations primary for any one region of mind, such as intellectual connections or flights of fantasy. We should then be in a good position to ask further about what happens as we interpret.

How does fantasy occur, whether in waking dream or during sleep? I am thinking now of how the fantasy is present. It is direct, full, and absolute for the moment. To be savored and attended. Often it is evanescent, perhaps hardly recallable, or recallable only under certain conditions, not always subject to my will, as when a dream comes to mind during meditation, or perhaps one recalls in a dream a previous night's dream that had surfaced during the day. The fantasy-event is always passing, always transfused with a fragile quality. Yet, it is also plenteous and often vivid and filling as it happens. All that goes on in fantasy seems to go on in this milieu, this region that happens as absolute yet passing, recallable but immanently loseable, full yet without plenitude, vivid but easily faded. This region names how fantasy comes out or is present, and in this sense names the event-dimension of whatever goes on as fantasy.

Event means to come out or to happen or to come to pass. What may we say about non-fantasy world-events? Take as an example my daughter's glance across the table as I mention with a hint of irony and in a context of good humor that women's liberation has brought on more work and responsibility for women. This young and independent teenager, who wants her way as a way of being free and who resents the restraints of responsibility, has caught a point to be enjoyed, resisted, ignored, but hardly to be argued. A slight smile and a flash of half-serious outrage before she lifts her glass of milk and looks straight ahead as if she were sizing up silently a battle that will last for some time. It is direct and full, this event, absolute for a moment, to be savored and attended. Without paying it special attention, it might pass quickly from my recall, forever lost. Or it might come back to me much later, through a dream or as I drive absentmindedly down a turnpike. It was such a passing moment, fragile, yet remarkablly plenteous. Its event shared much with events of fantasy.

There are many kinds of things that are much longer than the moment with my daughter: a lengthy friendship, a long involvement in a community, a sense of identity, the duration of a stone or tree or mountain, a culture's life. But as a happening, as coming forth and being present, as event, all these things carry with them an utter presence and a forever passing that give them, as event, a translucence and a density, a fullness and an ultimate non-necessity that we may find at every turn. Events seem to be complete in their being always beyond a possessive grasping of any kind. To allow an event, qua event, is to be open for a depth and height of awareness that does not stop, because it is always evaporating beyond the compass of any given experience or set of things. Events are not to be stored up, except in other events as recollection, reflection, recall, i.e., as minded. And those preserving events are themselves utterly passing, utterly eventful. We are dealing with an indefinite infinity of happening: coming forth and passing away at once.

We shall look at four aspects of events of things in the world in order to develop further the similarity of the events of fantasy and non-fantasy.
(a) Invisibility

The more involved I am in specific tasks and their materials, the more I am inclined to see and hear what is substantially there. I am vaguely irritated when I am involved in a careful institutional process between, say, two offices attempting to assess the uses of a limited supply of money, to hear of visionary experiences or I-Thou relationships. Such things seem distracting and irrelevant to the issues at hand. The more my character is molded by absorbing tasks with things and their relations, the more my perceptions and consciousness are cast in the sensible and intellectual stuff of things. I am fixed by attention to what matters for solving problems, completing jobs, realizing goals, assessing purposes. My world is lived by reference to the visible, i.e., to what is perceivable within practical contexts. Networks of relations, such as is in a cybernetics framework, make sense to me. Even the uncertainty of tomorrow fits in. But I am strongly inclined to overlook or thoroughly ignore the non-substantial gappiness and the invisible non-substantial dimensions of where and how I am.

Michel Foucault has not been inclined to overlook the invisible, and we shall look for a moment at some of his observations.

There is something utterly visible about a corpse. It lacks an inaccessible interior. We can find out about it, with some technical knowledge, by prying it open and analyzing its contents. We are hard pressed to think of a dead body as suffused with invisibility. But to take the corpse as a mere surface is to miss much of its reality. Foucault penetrates the surface, as we shall see, by finding how a corpse reflects its place and time and the history that is part of its event.[21]

The invisibility of an opposite is reflected in an identity: the meaning of sanity, for example, is reflected in madness, as Foucault showed in *Madness and Civilization*.[22] How madness is recognized shows a structure or grid of perception and order that is quite invisible to the perceiver as he/she perceives, although the invisible in this case is the very order of knowing in which the person's recognition takes place. As I see that person as mad, I immediately reflect a recognition of the opposite of madness, as well as the order that allows and to a certain extent generates the recognition. "A silent configuration" of discourse is what Foucault calls it, in which the light of recognition is anterior to every gaze.[23] This depth order of perceiving and knowing and reflection of opposites can be unearthed. It is susceptible to being known historically as a power and structure for knowing and perceiving. Its invisibility, its not being the visible thing in any gaze or regard, is present as a describable, encompassing transcendence with any group of things or observations. The possibilities for kinds of knowledge are reflected in what is known, but are never sufficiently held or instantiated by what is known.

The invisibility of the orders in which things have their place, their meaning, their time and so forth, is well illustrated in the remarkable 18th-century painting by Velasquez called *Les Meninas*.[24] It is a painting of the artist himself, who is intent on the subjects of his painting. They, the subjects,

---

[21] See particularly Michel Foucault, *The Birth of the Clinic* (N.Y.: Vintage, 1975).
[22] Michel Foucault, *Madness and Civilization* (N.Y.: Vintage, 1973).
[23] Foucault, *The Birth of the Clinic*.
[24] See the Preface to *On the Order of Things* (N.Y.: Vintage, 1973).

are reflected vaguely in a mirror behind him. He stands with a huge canvas before him, well dressed, while a young princess and her attendants pay close attention, not to the painting, but to the subjects being painted. And in the background a nobleman has stopped at the open door to look into the castle room and observe what is going on. Everyone in the painting is there because of the subjects of the painting, and they, the king and queen, are shown only in the mirror's vague reflection. They are the hardly visible sources for the painting's order. They are the nearly invisible subjects of the painting, whose power and influence Velasquez could capture best by painting, not their likenesses, but how they give presence and order to the highest people in the land (and to the next queen as well as to the finest artist alive). Velasquez reflects through his painting the meaning of ordering power and influence, a kind of power virtually unnoticed until the president dies, the style of life changes quickly, or we are unable to speak our own language or to follow our own customs.

Are we to think of a corpse in a way similar to a great painting? The corpse as we know it is a reflection of detached pathological analysis. Not the corpse of the child, just killed, held by the mother of the once-breathing son. But the dead body which functions as a source of medical knowledge. At one time medicine regarded the body as an instance of rational order, not subject to mere perception, but knowable by means of the rational laws of nature. Rational knowledge and logical inference were the means proper to understanding a disease. Hence the physician observed and classified symptoms in order to reach the essence of the illness. And he assumed that the body was essentially a rational structure, a logically ordered organon, to be treated as a whole of rationally collected parts. The body, as matter, hides the rational essence, but like nature manifested indirectly the nature of its creator. The body showed discretely to the careful, well thinking observer what its essence was like.

But this rational gaze, ordered by the intuition of a system of balancing opposites in an organon of pure essences, transformed slowly into the modern way of glancing to find a case, an instance, the data, the causal relation. The corpus of medical knowledge thinks of itself as based on the immediately seen, not on invisible rational essences. One waits with a silenced imagination, free of fantasy, unperturbed by visions, to see what happens for empirical observation. Out of this silence arises signs rather than symbols, cases and patients, a corpus of related facts to reveal the nature of this or that disease. In this quiet and invisible order of knowing the modern corpse emerged, through anatomy, as a thing that had no essence to hide. It is a penetrable surface that allows a total description.

Detached pathological analysis, the open field of observation, which needs order to be tolerable, and an expectation of making all things visible, are conditions for the "corpse" and are reflected in the corpse as we know it. Anatomy, not personal encounter with body, as central for medicine is another. An emphasis on orders of classification is yet another. And discovery of dissection. But behind these immense discoveries and notions lies the rationalists' idea of essence: a timeless, spaceless, non-body thing that, without a history, defines life and relegates history to mere appearance. From that idea of essence Foucault traces a direct line to "the absolute eye that cadaverizes life and re-discovers in the corpse the frail nerve of life." He shows that the modern research hospital has at its center the anatomized corpse because of an invisible order of knowledge that has never known its own history or its own historicity other than as an object of its own gaze, a gaze that instantiates the ahistorical intention. In his words, "the [modern] Gaze that envelops, caresses, details, atomizes the most individual flesh and enumerates its secret bits, is that fixed, attentive, rather dilated gaze which, from the height of death, has already condemned life."[25] The "death bearing perception" is one in which the discourse quality of reality, its fundamental historicity, its transmissional development, are left out, with the consequence that the unspeaking dead thing, lying as though it were not history in its very presence, becomes a cornerstone for a huge edifice of knowledge.

Foucault shows how an invisible order that leaves out its own life, that is, its own historical development, is expressed in ways of giving unconscious primacy to death in the visibility of both life and disease. His work is remarkable for us on two counts. He shows us something about how invisibility happens in the world around us, and he develops his point by attending to a way of knowing that is unaware of how its own time and limits occur. By taking the corpse, a most thoroughly objective thing, as his focus, he has given us an uncompromised example of the invisibility that is part of things that happen in the world.

The invisibility of things is found in how they are together, in their relations, in their coming forth as what they are. *Relations*, we see, are not lines among things which essentially are non-relational. *Relations* are in the happening of things as they are. Change relations and things intrinsically change. Change things and connections, and communications, meanings, and identities change. *Invisibility* names how things happen, and their happening, we find, is how they are. Their *how* and their *who* are inseparable. Everything, in its occurrence, is "more" than can ever meet a perception, and this more, far from being mere material density, is its coming forth as it is. Invisibility is in a thing's being "in the light" and available for perception and recognition.

(b) Luminosity

Consider two series of paintings, Monet's *Waterlilies* and Cezanne's *Mt. Saint Victorie's*. Each presents the artist's perceptions of the same subject or kind of subject over several years. They are paintings of things, objects, non-human, and quite utterly different from us. They present, however, with

[25] Ibid.

unusual sensitivity the occurrence of those objects. Cezanne, sitting on a cottage terrace outside Aix-en-Province, found the large stone mountain at times so dense that only the light around it and off of it and from it was translucent. The space to the mountain was clear, and light poured from over it, the opposite of a fog tumbling over and down a mountain side. But it itself is like a dark shell, blocking all passage and all illumination. In other of his drawings, Cezanne found it so luminescent that only its outline, where it met the sky and the earth, had an absence of light. He could not see through it, as he could through a veil, but it itself gave visibility, cast light rather than shadow and defined itself against the sky as the merest outline. Cezanne found it to claim a kinship with the light around it.

I once read an account of a noted biologist who returned the algae and amoeba to their original environment after he had taken his observations because, he said, they had little in common with his laboratory, and they "belonged" where he had found them. This simple alertness, like Cezanne's insight into light's presence in density, notes familiarity and kinship in usually overlooked ways. Monet's waterlilies articulate this kinship of light and matter with unsurpassable eloquence. Stand back from the huge canvasses and you see pastel lilies, in a leafy, light, watery element. They fill your vision, subtly claim the world for a moment, until they appear to undulate as though a breeze has passed. I have looked for the flying dragonfly and heard the fall of silence as they refused the surrounding noise of the museum. But if you approach them closely, there is no outlined form to be seen. There is rather a play of light, color and shadow. That is all. And as you back away that play without outline shapes into waterlilies again with their leaves and water. Monet found water, its reflections, and the flowers to happen more like shades of light then hard stuff. He had an uncanny ability to see things happen with endless difference. The more he saw, I believe, the more he experienced the thing's own happening, the less he could touch with his hands the material reality before him. He painted the reality as it happened, and our incapacity to touch physically what the painting presents is not a small part of the art before us.

Where Monet painted there was water in which a person could drown. The lilies budded, blossomed, faded, and sank to the mud below. And his painting is on canvas covered with paint made from various elements and paid for by francs. Yet these blunt aspects, quite real, are suffused with a luminous porosity, with occurrence, which Monet particularly celebrates and minds. In addition to a thing's fixity in its place and identity, it happens as multiple reflection, as an occurrence of reflection upon reflection that defies exact outline or precise limits. In this reflexivity one finds luminosity, light play that carries all manner of shades, meanings, innuendos, possibilities, shadows, unknowns, and a continuing sense of mystery that will not dissolve into whatever perspective in which we find ourselves cast. This luminosity appears to be pervasive of the worldly happening of things and to cast doubt

on the notions that density occurs apart from shaded evanescence and mere
light.

(c) Dislocation

We are familiar with the dislocation that occurs with dreams and other
fantasies, and we have noted that mind is apparent in dislocation as borders
are crossed into areas of awareness totally unfamiliar to our identity. Dislocation also occurs as I experience my entire region of familiarity in its
non-necessity, finiteness, and deathliness. Not only will I cease to be. The
very context of life, everything, is suffused with the capacity not to be. As
this dimension of the world becomes apparent, I discover that familiarity
does not totally define the "place" of my being. A complete absence of life
in any sense that I can recognize appears to be immanent, and the familiar
seems to be located in a dimension of uncanniness. *Deathliness*, suffering,
and evil open us to an other-realm. They are means of perception through
which we become conscious of the limits of the ken of human life, and we
become conscious of the presence of a of non-human region that is alien to
our lives. In "our" region we find a commonality of need and suffering as
well as of possibility and enjoyment.[26] We find a rightness in compassion
that surpasses belief or judgment: compassion brings us together and facili-
tates a recognition of ourselves in our common humanity, a recognition that
is not bounded by systems of belief and custom. In our own region we can
recognize courage, even when the cause that is defended or created by the
courage is repulsive to us. We can find meaning in our being human in
concentration camps and wars as well as in business and idleness. We are in
a region that allows depth of recognition and worthwhileness in living.

But this human region of kinship is transient and bears no sign of being
necessary. Not only may the courageous person become corrupt leader, or
brothers and sisters destroy each other. Love and courage might well fail in
individual instances in a region where love and courage might in time
triumph. But the region for human discourse and relation offers no basis for
believing that it will endure infinitely. We know that the earth itself can be
snuffed out with heat or cold or by the slightest alteration in a balance of
forces within our solar system. We know as well that we are quite capable of
destroying ourselves and that the cultural reality of individuality, upon
which courage and compassion, as we know them, depend, is a recent
development for our species. Such knowledge prepares us for a different
order notion: that the circumference of our realm is a border at which
appears foreignness-for-humans, a kind of silence which offers no support or
resonance for what we find best and most beautiful. Sometimes this border is
most apparent in the experience of radical cruelty, dissolution, and death.
We experience *that* such anti-life reality can happen, and in the happening

---

[26] For an elaboration of this notion, see particularly Camus's *The Myth of Sissyphus* and *The Plague*.

we know a foreignness to ourselves and the elements on which our lives depend. This border may also appear as we experience the silence of space as distinct to the resonance of the space-of-our-lives. The simple experience of immensity can also open us to a region alien to our being.

Camus called this disjunction between the human and the alien to human, absurdity. He meant by that word that human life generates fundamental ideals and basic purposes for human life which are bordered by a non-resonating, non-nurturing dimension that appears to us through calamity and disaster. It announces something like Fate, which means only the inexplicableness of the failure of life. It is the silent backdrop for human hope which persists in spite of the pervasiveness of dying, suffering and radical perversity. The human heart may be corrupt, but that corruptness is endlessly transcended by a silence beyond our ken in which our orders appear to unravel and the best of our creations begin to dissolve into nothing that we know.

Such experiences of the alien dislocate the commonality of our world in the sense that our world as a whole appears to be founded in no location. Location itself seems to be finite and bordered. We are oriented in our world, but the region of orientation itself lacks orientation, and this lack seems to shine through things as they come to be and cease and provide no justification for their being in space and time.

(d) Indifference

By virtue of our interests and the postures or our consciousness, we inevitably differentiate. When we lose our passion and interest, however, our connections with things weaken, and in our fatigue or depression we experience the world as flat and dull. Those same things by which we are so unmoved were alive and interesting to us at another time when we had energy and passion. That is a common enough experience. But when we are deeply attuned in our experiences to the things with which we relate, we discover that even when we are involved and interested, far from bored, there is still a backdrop, a dimension of no interest and no care in the presence of things. That perception can happen as a key of depression that accompanies our interests, in which case our "being down" functions as a way of being aware of the things' difference from our interest and involvement with them. They will not finally slack our thirst for a world of infinite interest and passionate life. Or as we come out of involvements tired or fed up or vaguely unsatisfied, we may experience a growing emergence of the background sense that meaning and fullness of interest do not totally define the presence of things. We discover that our passion and interest do not make meaninglessness and insufficiency go away. Even in the moments of rapt attraction and total involvement, things are with us in their difference from our passion as never to be absorbed or identified with our attraction and intensity. Our connections with things do not eradicate a dimension of indifference in which things only border all our kinships. Their indifference is part of their non-location in the regions where we are who we are at home with our kind.

Wallace Stevens had a remarkable grasp of what I am calling indifference. He saw that it is a part of the world, that it is aligned with life, although it is not at all aligned with personality and identity or exclusively with any real thing or set of things. Consider, for example, the following stanzas from "Martial Cadenza":

I. Only this evening I saw again low in the sky
    The evening star, at the beginning of winter, the star
    That in spring will crown every western horizon,
    Again . . . as if it came back, as if life came back,
    Not in a later son, a different daughter, another place,
    But as if evening found us young, still young,
    Still walking in a present of our own

II. What had this star to do with the world it lit,
    With the blank skies over England, over France
    And above the German camps? It looked apart
    Yet it is this that shall maintain—Itself
    Is time, apart from any past, apart
    From any future, the ever-living and being,
    The ever-breathing and moving, the constant fire.

IV. The present close, the present realized,
    Not the symbol but that for which the symbol stands,
    The vivid thing in the air that never changes,
    Though the air changes. Only this evening I saw it again,
    At the beginning of winter, and I walked and talked
    Again, and lived and was again, and breathed again,
    And moved again and flashed again, time flashed again.[27]

"Not the symbol, but that for which the symbol stands," in this case the rising, evening star of winter, ever there for a time, real and utter, if passing. And strangely beyond the differentiations and personalities that we share or give to it.

The coldness of the star, and its distance, or, in another poem, the coldness and distance of the northern lights, give Stevens a medium for pointing out the non-human, non-breathing, non-earthly dimension, perhaps non-living dimension of the world. This dimension is strangely enlivening for us. Its very indifference to us and with us is a condition of our warmth and creation.

In "The Auroras of Autumn" Stevens makes his subject the auroral lights, with their enormous, wave-like flashes of illumination that strike up into the fall's northern sky, dominant, ephemeral, cold, virtually lost at sight. They are airless. They heighten light in the midst of a dark sky without a sound or an effort. They simply come as reflections as though they were

[27] Wallace Stevens, *Collected Poems.*

aspirations. They remind Stevens of the flash of images and things. They relieve the darkness, not like a passion relieves boredom and not like a friend relieves loneliness, but like a whole event of illumination that comes in the midst of a whole darkness. We are, says Stevens, parts of the cast light. In its "frigid brilliance" we find our partial ways, make out our lives, and in an undefined way depend on the whole illumination for our partial sight.

This cold and indifferent light is reflected to Stevens in the fading whiteness of a closed beach cabin and in the flowers, also fading at the end of summer by the cabin's wall. That light is reflected in the reminders of life that has gone, in the blank visibility of a white that is losing its vividness. The "ice and fire and solitude" of the northern lights reflect the aging and loss and passage of Stevens' life in their kinship with an empty cottage that recalls summers at the ocean in its solitary and pale moment. The indifference of creation is also reflected, in this poem, in the dissolution of the young mother who had made "that gentler that can gentle be." Her once soft and touching hands have become a motion, but no longer a touch. Mother dies in the boreal night of illumination. As the light passes from mother's eyes, says Stevens, the windows of the house find their own light. Light remains through a painful and grieving psychological growth, seemingly indifferent to pain and anxiety.

And father too. Once strong and commanding, he passes away, no longer a measure of yes and no, no longer a giver of limit and provider of place. He is transformed into a speed of insight not to be measured by human scale. That father of identity changes to "The deep ear that discerns/At evening, things that attend it until it hears/The supernatural prelude of is own. . . ." The father dies and is transformed in this kingly and profound light, in this "motion of ever-brightening origin."

In these transforming passings away, Stevens says, there comes a chaos of light, like a primitive festival, like a play without words or plot, illumination without meaning. This light is without substance, not like water, but like the transformation of clouds. "A season changes colors to no end. Except the lavishing of stuff in change. . . ." Of this indifference with our differences, he says, "The scholar of one candle sees/An Arctic effulgence flaring on the frame/Of everything he is. And he feels afraid."

"Its nature is its end/That it should be, and yet not be, a thing/. . . ." "But it exists/It exists, it is visible, it is, it is." Not from us, not of us, but with us, and visible, this pervasive quality of indifference in which things happen.

Invisibility, Illumination, Dislocation, and Indifference name four (among many) aspects of the way things come forth in the world. We are paying attention to how things happen, and we find in their happening a communality with the happening of fantasy, although we find no hint that a subject, whether a person or a subjectivity like ours, contributes the commonality. The occurrence of things and fantasies involves us and not us at once, a commonality that means that as we come to terms with the happening of things we become more open to the happening of fantasy, and the reverse holds as well. The issue is how we are with the event of existence, regardless which existence. And the commonality of events is the linkage of fantasy and non-fantasy which enables one to encounter the reality of his/her world by means of dreams, specific counseling, or whatever. I have been calling the commonality of event *mind*, since the word lends itself to this meaning and sense it carries the connotation of awareness. After developing a suspicion, I shall turn directly to the issue of how awareness occurs as mind (not primarily as conscious, personal subject).

7. A Suspicion

I suspect that one of the issues for human well-being has to do with how one comes to terms with the event of being, regardless what kind of beings are around. We experience, of course, terrible illness when we have been repeatedly abused as children, when we have lived with very little affection, or with unspeakable deception, or when some terror has convinced us that if we do *x* or *y*, such as seek our goals relentlessly or trust openly and completely, we shall die or suffer terrible pain. These destructive kinds of events are so apparent that as therapists we have difficulty looking through them and beyond the person's life history. That sounds like forgetting the individual. As I shall indicate later, however, the situations that foster healing appear to be those in which how things happen is allowed. There are surely at least a hundred and perhaps a thousand ways to allow the happening of things. Few of us could give an account of our accustomed ways of freeing and allowing, except in the most inadequate terms. When I am with you, however, and I am free for uncaring indifference, dangerous borders, invisible influences, shaking dislocations, trickery, and theft in the depth of my awareness, as well as unspeakable and awesome enormity and brightness and darkness, then I am coming into my own, regardless of the specific issues that we talk about. As I come into my own, as I am able to live with how things and fantasies are happening, I become freer and freer for the pain, enjoyment, frustrations, anxieties, gains, success, etc. of my daily world. As Stevens puts it in "The Auroras of Autumn," we are an unhappy people in a happy world in the sense that happiness, at the world's engendering height and depth, is the coming and persisting of light, of creation and life, of awareness, regardless how turbulent the surface be. No one believes, I suppose, that therapy is to eliminate turbulence or trouble. The issue is to realize together the situation of our existence, so that we are in touch, however non-verbally, with the events of light and creation which are quite other than who we chance to be. I doubt that human well-being can occur except in a profound and open acceptance of a cacophonous, senseless passage of good and bad things in an occurrence that is simultaneously as serene and careless as the coming of a cloudless dawn.

8. World-Event and Interpreting

Event (or *happening* or *occurrence*; I have used these words inter-changeably) has been the center of our attention as we have looked into how we are in common. We have seen that how fantasies and things in our environments happen have many factors in common. We shall look now at meaning as a common factor in order to see that how things, fantasies and non-fantasies, happen is always an interpretive occurrence. We may then see that interpreting is not necessarily something that we do as a personal-ized or individual activity. Interpreting is intrinsic to events. But with a Hermes-quality. Events happen as interpretations in which things fade into each other, contradictions emerge from samenesses, and enemies become friends. Mind, we have seen, appears to name this region of occurrence. Perhaps the notion that non-voluntary fantasies are aware, even though I do not "do" them, is easier to see than the notion that world-events are intrinsically aware. We may even have difficulty at first thinking that there is depth awareness that is not a personal activity. To say that world-events are intrinsically aware, non-personal, and interpretive may also seem coun-ter-intuitive to us at first.

On the other hand we are familiar with finding that we have been in a peer group or cultural stream and that we have been taken up by it or deeply formed by it. We expect that to go on all the time. We are formed by how our families are structured. We are also formed by family structure itself, as distinct from a society that has no families as we think of them. We are formed in relations, even though we resist the relations that we are in. And by our milieu and ten thousand other things. We experience trauma when we are wrenched from the familiar—a kind of deep wounding goes on because we are formed in and by the familiar. We live it, and *our* lives are at stake when the familiar is totally threatened.

In what sense may we say that awareness constitutes these orders that are not private or subjective? We have noticed that fantasy frequently breaks into our ordinary awareness and may even create a crisis if it, the fantasy, radically contradicts our self-understanding. The fantasy-awareness not only minds what we have forgotten, it also heightens our awareness of the non-linear, non-intellectual, and abnormal eventfulness of mind. It, as event, allows us to see that normalcy can be in ways in which we, through our narrowness and over-literalization, tend to lose touch with mind. As we get into a fantasy, our consciousness intrinsically changes, we see in and through the fantasy. Perhaps we look at the way we move dully from task to task to task and see, in the fantasy of flying to that far galaxy, seen as only a twinkling light here, that we are half-dead and half-crazy in our undisturbed rut. The fantasy is also an awareness that we can live if we cross its border.

The set of customs in a rural area is also an awareness. If I have been tied down to an awareness of the world in and through institutional practices, and I get into a rural form of life, the meaning of an individual person will probably be altered as I live out the immanence of the animal and the vegitative and the distance of the authority of bureaucratic structure. The world happens as relations among things that are themselves structures of awareness as one lives through them. The anonymity of a large aspect of our awareness is the collective awareness that we share as we live through the social and cultural commonwealth.

Probably our being upright and bi-pedal and enjoying our particular brain structure, etc., also constitute a species awareness. It is certainly not an individual perspective, but a way of being aware in common with all my kind. But presently we need only note that the world happens as an event of relatednesses, seemingly unfathomable in its reach and complexity, that is lived out as certain inclinations, intuitions, pre-reflective understandings, and ways of being in the world. That is, the world happens as interpretive structures, as ways in which things are transmitted. There are so many of them, these configurations that make things out in so many related or conflicting ways. And consequently we speak so differently out of our different kinships and histories and minds. Like fantasy, world is lived out and lived through, often when we do not know what we are doing, or why.

And like fantasy, world is a happening that is indiscriminate regarding the contents of what goes on. Event. Coming forth. Illumination. Happening. The event of world as simple luminosity and presentation is the place of location that tends at once to dislocate all pretensions to totality or exclusive validity or primary reality. World is no less of mind than fantasy is. And no less articulated by the quicksilver of Hermes' passage. In world-events the presence of each thing and things in their totality passes invisibly in the indifference of being, the light of reality that illumines and refuses all our categories, all our grasps, all our desires, all our efforts, and remains as our commonality with elves, whales, generals, and beggars.

When we fix our sight firmly on interpretation as event, as a non-subjective occurrence of mind and world, and when we recall that we are dealing with orders that merge into the non-order of emergence and being present, we are able to see that our own activity of interpreting reflects orders of things, both in fantasy and non-fantasy, as well as the very occurrence of whatever is present. Interpreting can be a self-aware event that shares immediately in the eventfulness and ordering quality of fantasy and non-fantasy alike. Self-aware interpreting may evolve a style of awareness in which the non-permanence of things in their relations is immediately reflected. It may be founded on the coming forth of things; it may be Hermes-minded and see immediately, in its own event, that incompleteness, mystery, strangeness, as well as kinship and ordinariness, are involved in the very way interpreting goes on if it is true to its own basis. In that insight, the sameness of mind and world are evident, without even a slight inclination in the interpreter to subjectify or objectify either.

9. Truth and Therapy

The sickness and absence that mean life and death for us are the fabric of the world. We seem to lose significantly part of the ways things are with us if we over-accentuate either the bounty or poverty of events. If I fix, for example, on the continuity and predictability of events, I shall, in my fixity, be blocked and probably deeply fearful of the dimension of things that is subject neither to linear perceptions nor predictions. The radical differences in the presence of things will threaten my investment in continuity and prediction, and I shall try to live as though the world were essentially different from how it happens. I would be a little mad, no matter how adapted I might be to the behavioral norms around me. Indeed, my madness might be founded in norms that originated in this fear of disjunction, non-rationality, and brokenness. Or I might try to live as though there were no invisibility in reality, or no indifference, or whatever. In any case the plenitude of being that allows for full satisfactions and intellectual reliability is always accompanied by a kind of poverty, a lack of fullness, a certain gappiness in things. This emptiness may be recognized as indeterminacy that accompanies determination, finiteness and deathliness, insubstantiality, or contingency. Things happen with an absence of final justification and without ultimate guarantees of their reality or their future. This pervasive not-having-to-be means, as we shall see, that uncertainty and doubtfulness may reflect a direct apprehension of how things happen.

If insubstantiality, shot through with absence of reality and deathliness, is intrinsic in the happening of things, fantastic or not, how are we to understand truth, the self-disclosure of things?

We begin with Kariel on Christo:[28]

"At Valley Ford in California's Sonoma County people remember Christo's fence. They recall the parties, crowds, and traffic jams, the record number of hamburgers sold, the network T.V. publicity—all the theatrical events that had centered on the fluttering, shimmering expanse of white nylon anchored on cables and steel posts along a twenty-four mile stretch through Marion and Sonoma counties for two weeks in September, 1976. To install what he called his Running Fence, Christo . . . had the help of contractors, engineering consultants, and over 300 college students. Beyond these collaborators—and beyond the local merchants—there had been attorneys to appeal the denial of a land-use permit; and beyond them, some sixty financial sponsors, art dealers, and collectors of Christo's sketches and collages; and beyond them, Jeanne-Claude, his wife who publicized the venture and raised the two million dollars needed to sustain it. Fifty-nine ranchers were persuaded (and paid) to give permission to let some 2,200 sheets of nylon, each 68 feet wide, snake across their property toward the

[28] Henry A. Kariel, "Shifting with Art," *Soundings* (Spring 1979).

coast. What is more, Christo had overcome the resistance of all but one of the public agencies charged with safeguarding the environment. He cajoled and conned his way toward success, coping with individual skepticism, local politics, bureaucratic routines, and an economy geared to appreciate nothing but palpable pay-offs. . . ."

"Today, the fence is gone. Only preliminary drawings, legal briefs, the record of some 16 public hearings, travel vouchers, contracts, receipts of money spent, an elaborate environmental impact report, a documentary film of the fence's construction, and Sonoma County Landmark No. 24 (a solitary fence pole) remain as testimony to Christo's guile and energy. Nothing but these artifacts intimate what had actually spanned the countryside, what despite its sheer sweep and range had been devoid of message and point, generating only by-products, achieving only side-effects, ultimately amounting to nothing weighty enough to be measured or rational. Christo's ephemeral object had merely given shape to his impulses, dramatized a landscape, and engaged a quiescent populace."

Kariel says that Christo's fence was "a structure of perception directing us to discriminate not among completed cuts but among alternative ways for transforming the fields into which reality has been authoritatively divided and frozen."

"Gathering and reflecting" are two words that come to mind as I think of Christo's fence. This aesthetic event, "devoid of message," created a considerable occasion in these two California counties. I can imagine an elderly couple talking, puzzled, wondering what he was up to. High school students talked about it, their bored teachers even became animated over it in conversations with each other in their lounge. A lawyer laughs and shakes his head when asked what the hell his client is up to. An art critic talks with an engineer about the relation of the fence to the countryside. Students go to work setting line, hard work for God knows why, but find it fun and vaguely important. A rancher and his wife stand on the porch and look at the fluttering nylon. She says, "You know, John, it's crazy but I like it. I'm glad you let him come over us." A government environmental bureaucrat alternates between anger and attraction as this pushy Bulgarian immigrant politics to override the bureau's negative ruling regarding the fence's extending into the sea.

The fence gathered interest and relation, occasioned conversation over something without a clear objective other than to take place. It happened as an opening for a vaguely different way of perceiving, gave pause to ways of life made rigid by certified expectation and tight controls on what is acceptable to be. It engendered expectancy and anticipation, not over what it would accomplish, but expectancy and anticipation in relation to whatever was going on: an opening out into the openness of the world without the need of a prescription, at least for a brief moment. For some, maybe for a few brief days. For a few, maybe for two months. Maybe a year or more for one or two people filled with grace. But in any case, it reflected an open, purposeless liveliness and simple playfulness with all the foolishness and nonsense that we live with anyway.

Imagine an old couple close to the fence's crossing. They are seventy-five, bored without clear reason for boredom. They have what they need. They have been married fifty-one years, have four children and eleven grandchildren. He worked for the state of California for fifty-four years and was the head of a division when he retired ten years ago. They went around the world when he retired, a "wonderful" trip, even if they had known very little about most places they saw. They got a lot of slides. But after several home slide shows, trips to children's homes and even a summer making their way to Washington, D.C., and back in a small camper, they had less and less to say to each other, even less than before he retired, and each noticed the other's "aging and slipping a lot."

She read out of the paper to him that an artist named Christo was trying to put up a fence of nylon, costing an estimated one and a half million dollars, etc. He thought it sounded like a damn fool thing. "More crazy people in California than any state in the union." More articles and TV coverage. Why would anyone want to do a thing like that? And she vaguely remembered their trip around the world with a vague recollection of the feelings she had as she planned it. Around the world just in order to do it! She had never left her home town until she was 18. And flying. It wasn't so much like going somewhere as it was like simply being off the ground and going fast. She had felt younger than when she was 45. She had wanted to live and to do other things that interested and excited her. And he saw a fourth TV report, he had a flash of his office in Sacramento, the desk, the flag, the pictures on the wall, the smell of the stuffed couch and chairs and the one view out the window that had been his only source of non-artificial light for sometimes ten hours a day; the way the feds got harder and harder to deal with. And the middle-aged men under him who wanted his position; his disappointment when his retirement seemed like a relief to people around him with whom he had been associated for years, no matter the engraved silver plate and the speech by the Commissioner for Transportation. When he retired he felt like he had not enjoyed his work and that he had mattered little in a very big state government. He got up and made himself a whisky sour. The next morning he read the newspaper article twice about a man in Sacramento saying that the fence would not be allowed to cross the public beach. He put down the paper and said, "I'd like to see this thing." His wife set down her coffee cup and raised her eyebrows. But she wanted to see it too.

It, the fence, gathered feelings, associations, people, agencies, money, energy, all manner of foolishnesses and very intelligent observations as well because as a "fence" it did not mark or limit anything, Except, perhaps, the limited, i.e., it cast some kind of limit on the limits of people around it and reflected a borderless, limitless non-necessity that did not have to have practicality or sensibleness or efficiency to be. It allowed a fleeting perception of how I live in fixed ways that tend to freeze rather than to free my life. It even directed "us to move around that sliver of death we invariably feel at the center of success, consummation, climax, victory."[29] In that kind of detachment from purposes and completions, it reflected, as it snaked its 24 miles, fluttering uselessly over property that was defined almost totally in market values and in the face of people struggling hard to make a living and find something, almost anything worth living for—it reflected a play and a laugh, almost like light in semi-darkness, that was as free as most of us would like to be. Not freedom of choice in this case, but energy to choose. Not freedom from commitment, but openness for what is alive and real around us. "Narrowness and exclusiveness are lethal," Kariel says. The opposite of killing narrowness is openness for what does not prevent us from hoping, fantasizing, believing, and wanting to be.

The freedom found as one experiences what will suffice for a moment and in its moment will not guide us in our practical endeavors. But to be open for impractical, endless, and momentary sufficiency is one key experience for understanding a state of mind that may regenerate routines and engender meaning rather than fall prey to a flat, non-symbolic life that loses the energy to anticipate, strain, envision, quit what has lost regenerative power, or risk transforming a dying usual. The word *ever* probably comes from this experience. It does not mean something that does not die. It names "at all times" and should not be thought of as a line that does not stop, but as a region not defined with the lines and things that cross it or shadow it. "For ever" can mean in a moment that seems limitless. It names a kind of freedom in which we are limited, but a freedom that we may reflect in how we seek to be, in how we cross borders and allow border-crossings that so deeply relativize who we are and what we are.

This region of peculiar freedom allows, but it does not propose anything. It is "ever" in the sense that what is gathered and reflected is not of final consequence. It gathers and reflects by allowing whatever is coming out to be. It happens as freedom from the limits and borders that define things. Our kinship with this freedom is in our finding ourselves through fantasizing, our discovering new energy by refusing the absoluteness of securities and finding regeneration and even creativeness through playful, purposeless presence with people and things. Very hard when the earth and even the sky seem to belong to people, agencies, and governments.

I have a fantasy about the truth. There was a time when meaning happened without benefit of writing, and recollection was solely through brain activity. As writing developed with Hermes smiling, first through lists of merchandise stored or delivered, and then through codes, orders, and letters,

[29] Ibid.

the brain developed entirely new capacities, stimulated by reading, writing, and the symbolic character of letters and numbers. A new kind of knowing came to be and the physiology of the brain changed as this knowledge through letters engendered a different kind of awareness. Slowly the power of the spoken word moved in the direction of music, drama, poetry, recitation, and story, while that exactness made possible by the stability of writing had more and more to do with the notion of "knowing." People came to know through texts rather than through encounters with sound and expressions. The certainty of myth, the divinity of poets, and the angelic, messenger-character of the storyteller quietly passed away as the new awareness changed the human brain, and the changing brain changed human awareness.

I then fantasize a group of scientists and other learned people who have developed a computer that is able to hold enough information patterns to provide a sufficient, explanatory account of a large number of things by causal analysis. It is only a matter of time until similar accounts will be given of anything subject to careful research and, in principle, we will have a complete knowledge of the reality of things and the ability to predict with a high degree of accuracy what most things (and kinds of things) and persons (and kinds of persons) will do in different circumstances, which are also reasonably predictable. Then Hermes smiles. A strange development has begun in industrial countries around the world. People are learning to communicate through a new kind of music. Out of this development have come communities of people who, by highly sophisticated sounds, have been able to heal physical and psychological maladies, develop remarkable growth in plants and establish previously unknown human relationships and bonds free of all sense of authority or control. As this new discovery is more and more widely practiced, the brain slowly, through multiple generations, develops new capacities for hearing and translating sounds and other capacities for picking up ever higher frequencies. Structured speech as we know it passes more and more to the side, and motivation for controlled experimentations, explanation, and prediction wanes with mathematics in our present sense of the discipline. Science, the social sciences, and metaphysics are less and less needed. The entire field of knowledge and interest in which the notions of "complete explanatory are account" and "predictability" had their lives slowly becomes vaguely recalled and not much appreciated sounds. (In this fantasy, one also hears the stars and empty space.)

Freedom for being without purpose, for possibility, and for change of fields within which our best knowledge resides seems to have an important relation to truth, particularly if we do not equate "truth" with "accuracy within a field of reference." One alternative to truth as accuracy or correctness is the Greek understanding of *aletheia*. That word means unhiddenness or absence of darkness and through Heidegger, particularly, and other contemporary philosophers has come to mean disclosure or coming forth.

Something is its own truth as it comes to be present or is available as something. Truth is not taken as a property of judgments in this case. When I say something that corresponds with some state of affairs, such as "that child is sick" or "it's fourteen miles to town," I have been accurate. But we are looking for the truth of things, not correctness about them, and consequently we are not looking for a conceptual relation when we look for or speak of the truth of human being or the truth of technology. Our word *truth* has the Anglo-Saxon history of meaning faithful and constant. It may be taken to have the overtone of abiding presence or reliable presence, a meaning which approximates the Greek sense of unhiddenness. How something is apparent and abiding is its truth.

I have suggested that a goal-less, gathering, and reflecting event that crosses borders freely and insists only on its own being, like Christo's fence, resonates deeply with our being and appropriately may have the effect of occasioning our sense of being free from constrictions that make false claim to absoluteness for our lives. I have also fantasized that our most certain knowledge is within fields of reference that are dependent on brain processes and histories that are subject to transformation. If we accept these notions, then the free eventfulness of things and the contingency of the regions of our certainties need to be appropriated in our particular interpretations of ourselves and our world, as well as in the styles in which we make claims and assess things. The truth of things, how they occur and are apparent, will most likely involve the dimension of eventfulness and our interpretations will appropriately involve a sense for the contingency of how knowledge occurs.

(a) The dimension of eventfulness

We have already reflected on the world as a non-substantial event. We are noting now that how things are apparent involves a purposeless occurrence of being, "mere being" Wallace Stevens calls it, which is something like a call to that dimension of us which is not the same as who we are in particular. *Freedom*, in the sense of being open in this openness of the world, a non-prescriptive place, totally the opposite of a compulsive mentality and quite different from a subject who intends something, names a way of occurring that is different from a state of volition. It names the occurrence of human being, our being able to be other than who we are, our being able to change fundamentally, our being able to transcend our past, our being able to be, and so forth. It carries the overtones of engendering endurance, not of ego production necessarily, but a predisposition to be and to be freely open with whatever occurs in our world, no matter how much we may also hate or fear some particular things. This freedom is part of the truth of human being, part of its occurrence and its presence, and it is in common with the eventfulness of the world.

(b) Interpreting contingently

The contingency of the regions of our certainties means that fantasy and non-fantasy have in common a non-necessity, a perishableness, a certain initial indebtedness to humility. If the very style of interpreting reflects this pervasive contingency, its use of language and notions, as well as the fantasies that it tends to engender, will mean that the context of assertion is due to pass away, that good humor at the heart of our seriousness as well as play with essences are utterly appropriate. It would appear that the sheer enormity of our structures for controlling our environments and for producing certain knowledge, as well as the criteria for soundness used by committees that judge what is fitting for public or governmental support, hide profoundly their contingency. Even though that observation be more personal than universalizable and even if such pretense to stability be inevitable, at least how we understand ourselves and our certainties can reflect how our understanding occurs. Our interpretations can reflect their own occurrence, by which one comes to expect when he/she is inside the interpretation, for example. A bank building in Toronto has an enormous, ten story glass wall that reflects light onto fountains and trees, and inside that building one expects what goes on to open out into a green, flowing world of light. A nice illusion. Inside some religions one comes to expect deathlessness. Inside medical materialism one expects the development of control over disease, analogous to our control of some diseases, and a radical improvement over natural selection by control of physical processes of generation and inheritance. The acceptable style for communicating knowledge in both science and social science reflects a sense that facts and structures of knowledge are utterly non-fantastic, literal, unsoulish, nonpoetic things to be reported with a dryness that is only imperfectly approximated by thirteenth-century scholastic debates, a style that means ad nauseum that one need not attend the gappy nothingness that shines through and around every fact and our knowing as part of the contingent event in which all things happen.

An interpretation is an occurrence which is relatively open and closed to its own event. One way openness to its own event can happen is playfulness with how the interpretation borders and closes things out: humor and play at the border. Our reputations, identities, and social and personal lives depend on borders and exclusions as we become and maintain who we are as individuals and as members of societies and traditions. Being playful at the borders is close to not taking one's life with final seriousness. It is quite different from holding on quietly and deeply to what is most important. It is like catching a wild, beautiful bird inside your house, carrying it to the window and letting it go with the hope that it will return. In the dream in which that event occurred, the dreamer reported that the bird flew away quickly after being frightened to have been inside the room, where it had flown about wildly, hitting the walls before it was caught and held. It turned in mid-flight, however, when it realized it had been freed, and flew back to the man, still at the window. They looked at each other as the bird fluttered in mid-air. It seemed surprised to know that the man had freed it. The man in the dream felt deep joy. Later the dreamer reported that he had let go of something that needed not to be captured and that it had returned of its own accord.

This kind of experience of letting go what is "captured" in an interpretation is almost impossible when systematic completeness or closure is a tendency in one's manner of thought. It is particularly difficult, if not simply impossible, when a group of people want to establish a school by means of a set of doctrines which unite them and distinguish them collectively. An abstract structure of ideas, if it does not have a built-in principle for self-suspicion which repeatedly sends the person outside the structure for "knowledge and truth," will in fact pretend a sufficiency and adequacy that tend to close borders and to make crossing them or intrusion from the other side traumatic. Methods for establishing certainty usually tend to promise adequacy within its borders, even when those methods practice experimentation and seek out their own inadequacies. I know of an eminent philosopher of science who made the doubting of hypotheses and openness to change central for his philosophical method and who wept in anger and disappointment when another philosopher, who had been a follower, read a paper deviating from some of the older man's fundamental principles. The older philosopher, wise and much honored, cut off his younger colleague and refused even to answer his letters. I have also known therapists, psychiatrists, and psychologists to be certain enough of their methods of work and thought that they could condemn other well developed methods as simple foolishness. And sometimes the fool danced, while Hermes played, and the established ones looked silly in their heavy robes and tall hats, carrying heavy Certainty on their backs.

We interpret freely as we find things and people to be in certain ways, to name how they are, and to attend to the people and things in whatever ways seem appropriate. In reference to a dream: that dark door at the end of the descending marble stairs is too dangerous to open. One may allow that, reflecting it, not only in therapy, but on the street, while reading the paper, while bathing. I may find my life too rushed and crowded. I allow that, see how it occurs, perhaps change my way of life, perhaps radically. One may find his/her discipline strange and foreign. One may find a way to predict the collision of two kinds of molecules. And so forth. Interpreting in all cases is finding how things are going on, with whatever method or assumptions we use, but it does not necessarily mean putting high stakes on the interpretation, even when we are motivated enough to spend great energy and take considerable risks. If the results and the process are not worth the energy to us, no need to disguise the loss. Interpreting as it is lived out is itself the reality to be focused. If being in this or that way of interpreting deeply bores us or consumes our energy without much return or causes us to forget our being, then the task is to look around, cross a border, let in something else, perhaps a foreigner. A final issue for all interpreting is life in mind, not accuracy within a field of reference, and no interpretation is true that weakens passion for being, regardless its accuracy, tightness of method, and capacity to hold things in what appears to be deathless certainty.

I have made most of the observations in this discussion out of experiences in therapy. Not all of these experiences have been in one to one situations or in groups designed explicitly for psychotherapy. Some have come in the course of friendships, others have happened as a group of people have been drawn together by some shared intensity, some moments of experience in which I or others found transformations happening. Still other experiences have happened in the form of musicians, poets, and, most often, in the form of philosophers who in their communications have gone far beyond the reach of my conceptual grasp and transformed ways in which the world happens for me, thereby giving me a modified basis for what and how I feel and think. Through such experiences, I have found directions for interpreting therapy and for interpreting interpreting as therapy. Therapy is transformation through which a person is open to previously closed dimensions of the world. I have tried to show that world happens as mind, that mind is not primarily a subjective happening, and that fantasy is one access to the commonality of all things. Finally I have said that the truth of things and people is their free and open self-disclosure, the happening of however they are in the world. Interpreting is how we are with things. It is our particular way of minding things. The therapeutic issue is not whether, but how we interpret, and the most serious issue for interpreting is not intellectualization— always a flaw when it means hiding behind thoughts—but openness to the boundless indeterminacy that crosses our borders and shines through our specificaties. I suspect that the free open-ness of our being, so utterly deathly and so utterly alive, so crossed by boundaries on which we depend for our lives, and so wholly not the same as any one bounded area or all the areas totaled up—that free openness scares us like a small child's fear of walking in the dark night in which it senses total strangeness in its most familiar room. That free openness leaves us unguaranteed, unconfirmed, unneeded, and unnecessary in our being. It leaves us free to be. A meaning of therapy is to allow this strange wholeness that we are, whenever and however we can, usually in small doses and short moments, with the hope that one should become free for how mind, world, and being happen and thus free not to live with deathly constraint, with armed borders, and with most of one's psychological budget going for ingenious, but costly methods of defense against the not-I and consequently against our own being.

The contemporary emphasis on the therapeutic techniques probably reflects an understandable fear of the openness of our being as well as a desire to be helpful and genuinely therapeutic. We use cybernetic models of communication, the language of roles, biological models for the organon of our souls, the cause/effect structures of science, and on and on in our hard and honest search for clarity, understanding, and effectiveness. But what is the truth that we are after? My guess is that it has more to do with the myth of Hermes and the profound, pre-cognitive experiences that spawned his myth, than with techniques of approach. When we think and relate out of openness with the openness of the world, the place of techniques changes: we search for ways to overcome whatever prevents us from being attuned with the free openness, the truth of our being. The issue for therapy is this free openness and the interpretations that issue from it.

Isn't it certain that everything longs for what it lacks, and that nothing longs for what it doesn't lack?

Plato, Symposium

He now has gone a little ahead of me. This is of little significance. For us believing physicists, the separation of the past, present, and future has only the meaning of illusion.

Einstein, regarding a recently deceased friend

. . . so the adepts of hieratic science take as their starting point the things of appearance and the sympathies. They manifest among themselves and with the invisible powers. Observing that all things form a whole. . . .

Proculus

II

BEING ONE AND BEING MANY

We turn now to discuss the relation of part/whole in a specifically therapeutic context. If mind is a whole event of diverse, perhaps infinite, and always frequently distant, disjunctive, shifting parts, how are we to think of therapeutic goals for human beings?

We shall consider the part/whole distinction as one that reflects a pervasive and experienced dimension of human awareness: in being who I am in particular I am in my awareness beyond my particularity in common with all. I shall interpret this situation by focusing on how we occur in common. That *how* is a particular event that reflects non-particular commonality. The coming forth of beings, how things are available with us, is the place to look for a thematic understanding of how we are in common, i.e., form or matter or subjectivity are not the places to look in order to understand how we are in common. Hence, the experience fundamental for the part/whole distinction, not its various theoretical formulations, is our linkage with our philosophical predecessors who have written on the part/whole "distinction."

1. Theory and Therapy

The relation of theory and therapeutic practice is seldom clear. When a philosopher speaks about therapy, the therapist is inclined, intuitively in the present cultural climate, to hear abstraction and intellectual exercise. And philosophers are inclined to discount as unsophisticated those ideas developed by non-philosophical therapists. Experiences, however, may link theory and practice. We practice out of basic experiences, and we think out of basic experiences. When, for example, the categories fundamental for our thinking have to do for the most part with explanation, with causes and results, we speak out of a desire for intellectual order and out of projects related primarily to conceptual structuring. Those desires and interests mean that thinking in an explanatory manner is separated from therapeutic practice in which people attend to meanings and events in terms of fundamental affections and affective relations. At least that appears to be the situation presently in that the meanings of affection and the meanings of explanation are usually ordered in highly different ways. But if the thinker and the therapist find common experiences to think out of and use discipline in attending to these common experiences, an accord of theory and practice can occur. In that accord, thinking enriches and guides practice and practice guides and enriches thinking. Our interpretative aim should be to find and attend to common events and to relate and speak out of those specific instances of commonness.

When we attend to our commonality and see that commonality in relation to therapeutic events, therapeutic practice and thought regarding therapy will reflect each other in an area of growing awareness that is made up at once of theory and practice. That awareness is our aim, and it is not attainable as a thought or as an object of thought. Rather, this kind of awareness comes as one listens to the events and experiences out of which this discussion arises and which are reflected in the discussion. As concepts reflect and speak of events common for us, our awareness develops. Then we may say that interpretation, in the sense of growth of understanding and development of common meanings, is going on.

2. Plato, Parmenides, and Heraclitus

There is a relation between unity and order that has been experienced as not efficiently caused. Order is found not to be done by any particular direction of will. The Greek experience of destiny is an instance. Directions are ordained by the fabric of possibilities, nature, and particular human beings. Like their inexorable moving of a suspended wheel, like the seasonal course of the heavens, situations move toward fulfillment of directions, toward intrinsic completion, without regard for specific human interests or personal fulfillment. Destiny is a self-completing unfolding of situation or setting that is not defined by its many participants. This notion of destiny has spoken out of people's awareness that the whole of the situation of which they are a part is not deeply informed by the strength and character of individual passion. That whole may be thought of as the Cosmos all around a located human being, or it may be thought of as the non-personal dimension of human being. In either case, the person is deeply and sometimes terribly aware of an infinitely transcending region which is regardless of the individual's fulfillments and suffering. My emphasis presently is to fall on how this non-personal and non-volitional region has been found and how it is significant for understanding our own well-being.

I want to note, without developing further, how Plato, Parmenides, and Heraclitus spoke of the immanent presence of a region which transcends individuals, is in some sense comprehensible by them, and which is present as a direction of non-personal unfolding in personal experience.

Plato speaks of the intimate and intrinsic link of unchanging beings to changing beings by saying that the unchanging "becomes in" the changing being or is "to be in," "to lie in" the changing being. The non-personal is definitive of what is personal, for example, as the non-personal "comes to be" in the individual's circumstances. A particular finite being is "in common with" its defining, but transcending reality. They are "in communion with each other," and the finite being "imitates" or "is like" its present and transcending destiny as it lives out and toward what is given to be.

The defining reality of a given thing is not the specific, existing thing, but is its order, its particular unity. This unity is found to be different from the vicissitudes of the existing thing, but definitive of what the thing, in spite of itself, can be and become. It is an instance of destiny. And for Plato, unity means goodness. The unfolding of a being's destiny, its definitive reality, is a reflection of the unity and wholeness that enjoys sway over everything. I understand that to mean that Plato discovered that the present non-personal directions of his being, when thoroughly included in the individuality of his own way of seeing, inspired a fulfilling completeness that was good in its occurrence.

This experiential correlation between well-being and non-personal unity is also reflected in Heraclitus' and Parmenides' fragments. Heraclitus combines a method of reflection that "distinguishes each thing according to its own way of being" with an encompassing insight that "what is common to all," how we are in common, can guide us. Guides us in what sense? "Nature loves to hide," he says, and is not usually available for direct knowledge. Things, however, find their "repose in changing," and "conflict" and "strife" provide direct access to the repose in common of all things. Such claims are paradoxical only if we view all things solely from the perspective of individuality. How we are in common guides us in how change occurs. The measure of kindling and dying down, waxing and waning, victory and defeat and so forth is defined by none of its instances. Again we find the insight that order is an event of relation between individuals and non-individual aegis, a relation susceptible to sight, but not to explanation. The meaning of this aegis is found by Heraclitus in that soul that lives out its "inner law" to fulfillment as a "dry beam of light." Seeing for Herclitus, as it is for Plato and Parmenides, is an occurrence in which one gives way to the seen and does not interfere with how it is. Only then can human awareness undergo an ordering in which it finds its partiality to reflect thoroughly that unity or wholeness which defines awareness without being that awareness.

"Gaze steadfastly," said Parmenides, "at things which, though far away, are yet present to your mind. For you cannot cut off being from being; it does not scatter itself unto a universe and then reunify." He found being to be one, common and utterly the same in all of its instances. This sameness is utterly compelling when seen, only and simply as it is; it is that without which differences could not occur; it is present always and always not an instance of anything. The intensity of Parmenides' experience of the meaning of the sameness of being should not be overlooked: the scattered is always in common and reposed in its being; the scattered is not to be denied, but the common repose is to be intimately known.

Plato, Heraclitus, and Parmenides each know that order is found in a present non-object which need not will to be and which in its presence makes possible an accord among the many that need not overcome differences, strife, and relative agreements in order to be at one and deeply at peace.

3. Difference and Diversity

We experience difference and diversity in terms of puzzlement, privacy, opposition, resistance, indentity, and self-differentiation. The child discovers that he/she is not the same as his/her mother. The adolescent discovers that he/she is not the same as his/her father. The adult discovers that he/she is not the same as life itself or being itself, i.e., he/she discovers that he/she is to die. We all discover that we are different from the world of which we are intimate parts, and I believe that puzzlement accompanies these discoveries. One may not think about the discovery. He/she may not ever know that the discovery is going on. He/she may simply see his/her mother or father or him/herself differently. He/she may feel pause or doubtful or set apart. He/she may laugh or fall quiet in his/her puzzlement, but an experience of question occurs as such transitions occur. The words *odd* or *remarkable* or *strange* would probably be appropriate for such experiences. I suspect that most of us at one time or another wish, out of our puzzlement, that we were more at one with things such that doubt and question were not so pervasively appropriate.

In the puzzle of being different, we are immediately aware of ourselves in our silence, in what we do not say, in how no one absolutely knows us, in our capacity to say yes and no. We occur as private in our differences. As private we are opposed. We can experience the "no" of others, their privacy, their differences, their refusal of us or of our intentions. And we have a sense of who we are in our difference and privacy. We are name and identity to ourselves in our being different with others.

But the most problematic experience presently appears to be self-differentiation rather than differentiation with others. We tend to think of ourselves exclusively in terms of our specific identities with others, which means not only that a backdrop of loneliness is particularly characteristic of our present manner of being together, but also that we expect to be just exactly who we are. I take this literalism of identity to be expressed in resistance to one's dreaming awareness, in remarkable conceptual stress on the ideas of personality and character when one wishes to understand human reality, in the identification of consciousness and conceptual mentality, and so forth. When we occur to ourselves as significantly different from the way we usually are, we may be surprised, shocked or traumatized. If I am this one identity, private and different from everyone else, how can I possibly also be different from myself? How can I be mother and father to myself? How can I be my own shadow? How can I desire what I abhor? And so forth.

I shall indicate later that this kind of literalism is lived as a refusal of one's sameness, of one's own being. Presently I want to stress that difference from everything else but oneself and difference from oneself are aspects of how we are in common. Consequently, doubt, question, puzzlement, and a thorough absence of sameness are given aspects of our world and of ourselves in our particular being.

4. Indifference

Difference, as distinct from indifference, occurs by virtue of immediate interest and concern. As I feel desire, things distinguish themselves, and as desires change, foci and penumbra change. I am a region that is alert in desires and interests. I am aware of myself in relations marked by intricate and familiar networks of interests, commitments, concerns, i.e., networks of desires. Desires are living, aware directions which have the power of singling out and ignoring and which give energy in some relations while letting other relations fall out of importance.

As a person I am a self-aware region of desires. That region is subject to changes in the hierarchy of interests, to shifts in relations, satisfactions, failures, and so forth. But I am immediately aware of myself in desiring, in being interested, in seeking, avoiding, finding, struggling, etc. Differentiating in concrete relations is at the core of personality and character.

As I differentiate in desiring, I find all manner of things that are not what I am after. Intense desires are particularly powerful ways to distinguish things. Hatreds and loves, as we know so well, set things apart and bring things together, discover sames and not-sames, and give fundamental identities to things in their desiring contexts.

Not desiring at all might well seem like death to us, at least the death of our identifiable selves, our individuality, our character. Our being particular, that is, our specific way of being just who we are, occurs in distinguishing things. Our identity is intimately involved in the manyness of beings. In our desiring we find the world highly diverse, potentially fulfilling and threatening, filled with beings that come and go and change always.

Indifference has a puzzling quality about it. By *indifference* I do not have in mind ignoring something or someone. Ignoring is an attitude. I have in mind an absence of attitude. This absence of attitude is seen in the notions of one and whole. The whole context of all our many situations is not attitudinal or personal. What Heraclitus, Parmenides, and Plato knew, viz. that indifference is always an accompaniment of differentiation, that indifference is never resolvable into differentiation, that the one is not the many—that knowledge was partially recovered some years ago when nature ceased being viewed through the metaphor of mother and, after some initial, heated disappointment, was allowed to be impersonal, indifferent, and yet beautiful. I say partially recovered because we have yet to appropriate fully in our contemporary setting the fact that indifference is the horizon of all differentiation. The nursing mother, for example, who provided so much meaning for people's experience of nature, is not only personally and uniquely related with her child. She is also mother. It is child. Feeding is occurring. The very quality of eternity which we might experience in the nursing situation is beyond all the individual caring and specific nurturing that is going on. The metaphor of mother nature can mean that mother is pervaded by indifference even as she particularizes and gives individual nurturance.

This absence of attitudes, as we saw in Chapter One, is a dimension of human awareness. It is constitutive of the world as we live it. A pervading sameness, a non-differentiated, non-individual unthing-like quality may be found with all instances of things. It is a non-caring, non-desiring, non-differentiating dimension that we are sensitive to when we know, for example, that we die without regard for our interests, that we change regardless of how we change, that meaning occurs in spite of what meanings there are, that being is regardless of our desires, that personality and character occur no matter what their content.

Indifference names one aspect of how reality is. It is important for our interests because it also names one way in which what has been called the one, the same, or the whole appears. Therapeutically indifference is important because it not only names a dimension of our own existence which can be terrifying, but it also names the wholeness of our being which can be refused or blocked only with enormous expense to our being well.

If we absolutize the personal for psychotherapy either in our language or method, we shall leave out of account the very being of our existence, that is, the event or the coming forth of things, in such a way that plurality and individualism will be limits for our understanding of health. Desire, in that case, would appear to be the foundation of human existence, and all experiences would be lost in which desire steps back of impersonal insight, uncaring contemplation, aimless intuition, and desire-free communion. Our refusal of indifference means insensitivity regarding not only nature in its difference from us, but also the very quality of seeing the undesired or the totally unexpected, as frequently happens in insight. Such refusal means that our appreciation for the non-personal, such as I-Thou occurrences, would be seriously damaged. It would also mean that we would tend to identify knowledge of objects with awareness as such. Indifference names the non-objective, non-particular, non-desiring dimension of our awareness, the immediacy of awareness, in which no person is found and on which personal well-being is founded.

5. An Instance of Part/Whole: Awareness of Meaning
   and Awareness of Meanings

By looking at our sense of meaning in relation to our senses of meanings we shall take one example of the simultaneity of particular and whole, and

that will give us at least some orientation toward understanding and meaning of our being at once one and many. My aim is to direct us toward an
interpretation of human being in which we can see that oneness is a
fundamental event, not an accomplishment, and that as that event is lived in
denial it is accompanied by psychological illness.

I want to focus on how meanings reflect the sheer event of meaning,
how a meaning is a phenomenon of an event of which the particular meaning is a part. "Participate" won't do to speak of this relation of part/whole,
because that notion tends to mean two separate things which are characterized by one thing's being in the other thing. We would have thereby begun
with a primordial separation of realities which means that the whole would
be taken as an entirety of the parts. The basic words which I shall use to
name the part/whole presence are *event* or *occur*. The advantage is that
these two words may say how we are aware of whole and part without
meaning that part and whole are separated things.

Whole is not experienced as a thing or as a part of a larger context of
experience. When Heraclitus, for example, spoke of Logos as the unity of all
change I do not think he had reference to an entity posited by intelligent
guesswork or to a particular thing in his experience. He addressed by his
notion of Logos a non-objective awareness of sameness, a wholeness which
happens as diversity happens.

This starting point is significant for us here insofar as we want to understand how therapy happens with two or more persons. We might speak of our
sharing common properties or of our participating in common process or of
our privately enjoying experiences that are similar. But such manners of
understanding assume from the outset a separateness that takes no account of
being same together in its point of departure. Such accounts make wholeness
either something to be accomplished or to be found from a particular perspective. Particulars are not received, from the beginning, as phenomena of
sameness when we speak of participating in a common process, privately
enjoying similar experiences, or sharing common properties. In such instances,
we give a virtually unchangeable primacy to particular perspective.

But meanings precede perspectives in a linear as well as in a founding
sense. When we speak as though particular perspectives are primary for
either meaning or awareness, we misstate in a deeply forgetful way the
primacy of meaning with respect to all particular points of view.

A point of view is always a meaningful part of a meaning event. Shall
we say that that event of meaning is like a body of water that contains a
particular drop of water which we note particularly? Meaning is not like a
body that holds and contains. Meaning is an event of relatedness that allows
for identification. Things are already together in certain ways such that we
may occur in particular ways regarding them. Our regard, our awareness in
our particular manner, is our being related in certain ways with things that
are already together with us in certain non-perspective ways.

"Existential analysts" such as Binswanger have located the general characteristics of human experience in the a priori structure of human experience. We, however, are following those who locate such aspects in the "world," that is, in the identifiable relatedness of things and not in an a priori structure of mind or experience. And we are noting that world-relations themselves constitute our awareness as the foundation of our perspectives. How things are together and how we are with them is the region of awareness, as distinct to a posited, interior brain structure. Further, the wholeness or the sameness of the event of many fluctuating particulars is to be found in the already together quality of the event itself. Things being apparent in their own relatedness is the region for inquiry when we want to understand our experiences of part/whole.

Meaning names an occurrence that tolerates an apparently immeasurable range of differences. Things are good, bad, indifferent, threatening, inviting, or whatever. But in any case they are present as something: they are nameable and related. Meaning seems to be an horizon that cannot be totally transcended, even in radical experiences of meaninglessness, since these experiences are founded in nameable world-relations which are experienced as disconnected or falling apart. Meaning, though not like a physical container, is pervasive, an immeasurable sameness that tolerates an infinite range of differences and opposites. And human awareness occurs as meaning event: it is at once a situation free of the individual, and individual stance in that situation, and a pervasive occurrence of meaning regardless of the contents of the meanings.

We may consequently speak of an awareness of meaning as well as of awarenesses of certain meanings. One is always found with the other, but neither is the same as the other. An awareness of meaning happens indifferently vis-à-vis which meanings occur, and that awareness is defined without regard to which desires, interests, comedies, or tragedies are going on. And yet, without an awareness of meaning as such, the world would be totally absent, i.e., "I" would have no sense of relatedness, identity, or particularity.

6. Metaphors for the Experiences of the Whole

Metaphors for the experiences of the whole are frequently ones of depth or of light; down deep, underneath, back behind, feelings of depth and descent, translucent, pervasive shades, light of lights, like the light of the sun, and so forth. Metaphors of hearing could be used just as well, if not better; pervasive sound, backdrop of silence, unsounding harmony. In any case, pervasiveness and distance without objectivity are important aspects of the meaning of the experiences of the whole.

"Whole" is being one's own event. We are never finally circumscribed by any one particular situation or by any one set of factors which identify us particularly. Being whole is, as classically seen, transcendence of that particularity which is also real. Parmenides doubted the reality of particularity and, closely related to Parmenides' doubts, Plato doubted the reality of change and changing things. None of us can share these doubts now, in the way they seemed unavoidable to Plato and Parmenides. We are more inclined to doubt whatever casts relativity on change and on a presumed absoluteness of particularity. We are more inclined to doubt the whole of being our own event than we are to doubt the idea that change is absolute.

In our classic, metaphysical tradition the reality of the whole or the one tended to be identified as a permanent kind of thing. The very notion of the whole may connote a circumscribed being which is all that and none of this: identical with itself. We must dissociate, however, the idea of the whole as something permanent or as something changing. It does not occur from the context of permanent and changing things if we are to be attuned to the experiences of wholeness. It does not occur as something permanent or as something changing. It does not occur as a thing at all. We experience the whole as an alertness that pervades and casts an horizon vis-à-vis all present things. We could call it non-voluntary readiness for experience in the midst of experiences, awareness that pervades opposites, a sense of the limitedness of identity, the mood of finiteness, alertness that goes beyond and beneath all that I reflect and know, a sense of sameness with all the differences of my experience. It is like light that illumines all lighted things as far as one can see. It is like darkness that cannot be grasped or seen through: dark into dark. It is like a tone reaching the limits of audibility and seeming not even to stop there. It is like a silence that is heard with sounds. It is like an unfathomable and unreachable source that is as it is, but does nothing in particular.

7. When I Am Afraid of the Eventfulness of My Being

My relation with my own eventfulness, my own being, always involves a sense of the limitedness of who I am in particular. When I identify my being with my particular way of going about things by crystallizing myself into patterns that I take to be absolute for me, the eventfulness of my being will be deeply and inevitably threatening at every level of my particular awarenesses. My self-understanding will need to be protected. What I possess will need to be guarded and defended. Ownership will foreshadow repeated crises of danger and attack. My sense of place will need constant reinforcement to make clear its fortification against change. Peace will seem to be the opposite of open freedom. Definition will need the enforcement of strong commitments. Fixity will need guarantee. Guarantee will need defense. My very eventfulness will be a constant taunt of the particularities of my life. My life might feel deeply and vaguely decayed, like there is something gnawing at the core. Death might feel like a hand taking away something precious. The horizons might seem like boundaries under imminent attack. The danger of loss, defeat, and perhaps poverty will pervade my successes, fulfillments, and affective riches. I will be utterly at odds with my own being.

When I am at odds with my being in that way, and when I am with you, I will be inclined to attack or defend or hide or control. But I will not be inclined to be together with you in the horizons of awareness where who I am in particular fades back of our being together. I will immediately and non-reflectively define our relation in terms of interests and intentions. I will want to build or tear down or change or keep things as they are, that is, I will want to do something. But I will not seek touch with that non-particularity of the event of being together which happens in the aims and interests of our relation, but which is itself neither aim nor interest.

Being out of touch with my eventfulness, my wholeness, is like being out of touch with any other dimension of my own reality in this sense: I cannot feel close to it even when I focus on it or think about it. It will seem distant even when I know about it. It will feel foreign in my relations with it. It will seem inappropriate or suffocating or emptying in its closeness. I will seek to protect myself from it, and in whatever protection I find I will be solidifying an opposition to dimensions of my own being.

When I am opposed to the eventfulness of my own being I will be predisposed to blocking openness and pervasiveness at all points in my existence. I will want to control my bowels as well as my children. I will feel the threat of merger and loss of identity in all dimensions of relating with others that do not involve clarity of intention and a sense of control. I will want to exercise a maximum jurisdiction over the details of my death. I will tend to define consciousness in terms of structures of knowledge, and I will tend to define my psyche in terms of volition. I will tend to find the meaning of my life solely in projects and accomplishments. I will find open and free listening difficult. I will find deep serenity, as distinct to happy relaxation, impossible, and I will seek, perhaps compulsively, confirmation of the value of the particulars of my life.

The oppositions which are part of my existence will, in this situation of refusal, tend to seem unnatural or wrong or contradictory. If my tendency is toward moral judgments, I will feel wrong and guilty to be different from the favorable aspects of my being. If my tendency is toward literalism, I will tend to deny the existence of my own self-differences. I will generally think of truth as different from contradiction and opposition, such that I will be unprepared to face the enormous range of opposites and differences that make up being human.

8. When I Welcome the Eventfulness of My Being One and Many

I am swaying back and forth among the words *oneness*, *unity*, *wholeness*, and *eventfulness* because *wholeness*, *unity*, and *oneness* traditionally have named the region of pervasive non-diversity. But I have used *event* and *eventfulness* in an effort to set our thinking apart from the traditional inclination to attach to *wholeness* or *unity* the meanings of either change-lessness or sole claim to being or the characteristic of being a separate thing in relation to other things. And I have said that *wholeness* is not an object of awareness, but is a dimension of awareness that is immediately and non-personally self-aware. The eventfulness of human being is the occurrence of awareness in its pervasive immediacy.

We have seen that this dimension of our occurrence is an experience in the sense that we live it unavoidably and with non-objective sensibility. It pervades all aspects of our lives. But we are free to assume various stances regarding it. Among those postures, we may reject it or welcome it in all manner of ways.

Therapeutically, when you address and confirm the claims of my being, you may need to remain silent regarding the claims of my personality. My particular way of being my well be opposed or hostile to how my being is. I may fear my own occurrence as whole and non-personal. I may be angry over my own inevitability of change, given my desire to keep what I like. I may deeply resent and view as evil the inevitability of my death, given my enjoyment of me and my life. I may hate the pervasiveness of loss even when loss means the growth of my children or of a friend or the maturation of possibilities in a situation which I liked in its nascence. I may not like being limited, and I may seek to defy the limits of my being. Or I may not like the intangible and indeterminate presence of possibility and seek to eliminate as much indeterminacy as possible. If any of these situations are true of me, and I am your patient, I shall want you to confirm and support me in my usually non-conceptualized refusal of my being. I shall want you to attend to my particular way of being at a distance from my being. In a word, I shall want you to support my refusal of my own occurrence. What will you, my therapist, do? Won't you hear the claims of my being, the occurrence of deathliness, limitation, possibility, indeterminacy, intangibility and change? Won't you be at peace with them and welcome them as you hear me and my disturbance? Won't you remain silent when I seek you to confirm me, in order that you may give place and time for my event, my occurrence as human?

And yet you always address me in my partiality as you address the claims of my being. I may be divided against myself in hostility to the claims of my being. I may be tight and pinched and blocked in my fear of the claims of my being. I may be so distant from those claims that I dash madly about at times in which slowness is appropriate and am hardly capable of movement when speed is most appropriate for the aims of a given situation. So as I seek your confirmation for the sake of justifying or confirming my way of being, you, whom I trust, let us say, remain silent. And yet you admit, allow, and accept me in my particularity. No resistance from you, no denial, and so forth. In admitting me freely in our way of being together, you have allowed me my denial of myself, my hostility or fear regarding how I occur, or whatever the case may be. Your non-confirming allowance of my particular way of being admits at once the claims of my being and how I am in particular. When depth therapy occurs, I am freed for my being in acceptance of how I am denying it.

Perhaps I now overplay the obvious when I say that in welcoming the eventfulness or wholeness of my being, I find myself free for diversity, difference and opposition as characteristic of my own existence in my being with others. I may now be open to be as I am in my particularity as well as to be transcendent of my identity in the very occurrence of my reality. I occur as part/whole, or—and I intend to say exactly the same thing as part/whole—I occur as an event of awareness that is in a particular way.

The wholeness of human being is not an achievement, and when I welcome it I am in that welcome free from the necessity of validation of my being by means of accomplishments. The wholeness of human being is not a specific situation; and when I welcome it, I am free from the demands, responsibilities, and opportunities which also define my place and position. As I allow it, i.e., do not resist and refuse it, the freedom for being whole pervades these demands and opportunities and is lived as my not being enslaved or destroyed or finally defined by them. I am then deeply free for change, in those particularities and consequently in my self-understanding and identity. The difference of wholeness vis-à-vis particularity is my freedom in my being from the identity of a particular way of being. This difference may be lived, for example, as hope when one's life is desperate or as the capacity to change even when one's life is happy, or as an uninhibited desire for growth when one feels generally satisfied with the particulars of his/her life or as what we name vaguely, but significantly, *soul* and the German language names *Mut*, i.e., that disposition which is the desire to be as distinct from the desire to be one thing in particular. I believe that Freud made reference to this difference made by freedom for the wholeness of one's being when he spoke with Binswanger about resistance to therapy. He noted that there is often a time in therapy when the patient may turn toward a healing process or away from it, and that, he said, is a time over which the therapist has no control. I believe that is a time when one is faced with the experiential meaning of welcoming or turning away from the eventful quality of his/her own being.

I might turn away because I am deeply and precognitively convinced that I will simply pass away if I do not affirm absolutely the *way* that I am alive. Absorption might be the primary object of my fear. Or I might be terrified of a total insignificance which might come if I do not second by second insist upon my way of being. Welcoming the wholeness of my being might well feel like opening my arms to dying or like sinking into a deep sea or flying endlessly and aimlessly with no control. These terms are founded in my immediate awareness of the difference between being partial and being whole. The positive direction of the terror is my sense that if I cease being partial in the way in which I now am, I cease to be. The meaning of the pathological direction is my ignorance of wholeness as compatible with intense partiality.

If you are my therapist and seek to respond with my terror in such instances, you will have the difficult task of hearing my being with my particularity. I will need to learn in my relation with you that I can welcome my wholeness without dying or totally losing my sense of myself. Perhaps I will make this non-intellectual discovery as I find myself repeatedly accepted by you in many diverse or opposing ways. Or in your freedom for whatever I am unfree for in myself. Surely there are uncountable ways in which such awareness occurs. But whatever its mode, I shall be able to welcome the wholeness of my being with you only as you and I touch or hear with and behind our words and silences and feelings and aims that occurrence pervasive of all that happens: the wholeness, the occurrence, the happening itself, which is always with, but never the same as what is going on.

When I welcome the happening of my being, its event, I happen with the oneness of existence. I am immediately in touch with the strangeness that there are beings, that this and this and this *is*. As Parmenides, Heraclitus, and Plato knew, the wonder of things is not found exclusively or even primarily with reference to their idiosyncrasies. Their particularity is necessary in their occurrence, i.e., that's the way these things are, but there is also an occurrence of reality, an event, the very opposite of a vacuum. It is the coming forth of what is there, its being there, not absolute dissolution, but coming out as things; not total darkness, but lighting up; not absence, but being. Welcoming the happening of my being is my being open with this unfixable region of awareness which I have named the wholeness or the event of being. When this welcoming openness is a part of my particular way of being, I suspect that I will no longer need extensive therapy with you.

With no consideration, no pity, no shame,
they've built walls around me, thick and high.
And now I sit here feeling helpless,
I can't think of anything else: this fate
                    gnaws my mind—
because I had so much to do outside.
When they were building the walls, how could I
                    not have noticed!
But I never heard the builders, not a sound,
Imperceptibly they've closed me off from the
                    outside world.

"Walls"
C. P. Cavafy

III
ACCORD AND DISCORD ON THE BORDER

There are occasions when a chorus, orchestra, and soloists come together in a communicative unity that allows the music to fill the aesthetic space among them, to bring them together, to speak to them, each, as a work in which they have their presence together for a time. I saw the emergence of such a moment reflected in Robert Shaw, as he suddenly changed the baton from his right to his left hand, relaxed with a deep sense of intense peace and involvement, and allowed the music (Mozart's *Requiem*) to take him up with the hundred and sixty people on stage into an intuitive, resonating completeness, not performing so much as knowing Mozart together. Voices everywhere, speaking and answering, rising and falling, sound upon sound, hearing and responding in the sounds and with the sounds until the attunement carried each voice toward the other, each voice welcomed the other, each movement reflected the other movements, and a glow and enthusiasm brought the individuals into an ensemble, a symphony of fleeting and full voice. Shaw said that such communication is the reason for performing, that the event of communication in the music is the thing. He called it a love that was not subject to expression except in music as one becomes a part together with the sound and dwells with the composer in the resounding event.

Such intensity is not altogether rare. It may happen around almost any kind of focus as people are aware in a state not at all their own, but belonging to the event itself. In an organizational effort, in sports, in family projects, in group and individual therapy, the wholeness or sameness happens with a sense of rightness, sometimes with ecstasy, and always with a sense of haleness or profound health. By looking at communication in which we sense our health, we may find a basis for understanding our well-being and our being ill, a discovery to which our interpretations of world, mind, oneness and diversity lead us.

The musical event with Mozart's *Requiem* was not, of course, a simple event of spontaneous ecstasy. Imagine the four soloists and the members of the orchestra and chorus together if none of them knew the music. All sight reading, missing notes and entrances, no one knowing the whole piece well and thus no one knowing how his/her part is to be played. As the first encounter with the music goes on, people are working just to manage a first step with the sounds and the way they come together. There is a common effort, but hardly a sense of being in common in the music.

Or imagine the first rehearsal with the soloists, orchestra, and chorus. Everyone has learned his/her part and each has good technical mastery of the score. The people must now work on hearing each other. Given the *celli*, the basses override the alto part. The trumpet and the tenor are a fraction off. Two of the soloists give emphasis at different places in the duet, slightly different crescendo, different stresses when deep blending is needed.

By the second joint rehearsal the orchestra and chorus have begun to remember and anticipate each other. The tenors do not only sing their part in measure fourteen; they answer the oboe. The basses find resonance to the violin's play. The violas and the altoes find each other in a developing sound. In the music, a friendship or kinship is being formed by the play of the music itself.

Even in the brooding parts. If the music has dissonance or opposition or destruction in it, the kinship is still there. This kind of communication is not only *what* is being sounded. It is sounding in resonating touch with each other through the music which no one is and which everyone together is not. The performance can be bad. Each playing merely his/her own part. Or the composer can be forgotten by a director who hears mostly him/herself as he/she interprets the music. But in this fantasy of Mozart's *Requiem*, as the music recollects death and hopes, demands, remembers, promises and pleads for endless light, the people in the music give sound in hundreds of ways, engendering stillness by sound, or finding the very walls of the auditorium and pushing them, reverberating off of them with sound, or swelling and retreating ever so slightly as they hold a heard place and give that place a single shade of meaning within the whole of the music. And, O happy fantasy, all of the work, knowledge, and talent come together in a way in which a whole occurs transparently. If you can hear what is going on, the development and the end of the event are pitched and played and sung in the first notes. Among the musicians, jealousies, criticisms, judgments, angers, lack of self-confidence, depression, manic rush, competitiveness, fear of mothers, terror over one's own death, loneliness, asthma, and gout are released in the music and retreat to an unnoticed place. In spite of themselves, the musicians, who have worked hard on this piece after years of training and thousands of hours of practice with their instruments and voices, find a fleeting commonality in the music, a kinship and communion that many of us will never find with words and that some of us would find too intense, quite intolerable if it were to occur with another person or persons outside of the music. The very indifference of the musical event with the musicians' particular states of mind, however, reflects to us something far deeper in our lives than what we usually know ourselves to worry about and struggle for, and that depth of regenerative commonality in the indifference is what we shall now discuss.

1. Accord

> " . . .and the object shall catch fire and become present. . . ."
>
> Martin Buber[2]

In Buber's language, an object, something that is presented by means of something else, such as a concept, a feeling, or any other structure of experience, is not the presence of what can be heeded and loved for its own sake.[3]

As an approach to the events of accord, consider two kinds of occurrences. First, meditation or contemplation. I have in mind those occurrences in which one ceases to participate actively with anything, but continues to be aware.[4] In that kind of awareness one's distractions will not necessarily cease, nor will pain necessarily disappear. One need not lose his/her sense of spatial and temporal orientation, and one need not lose his/her sense of "who" he/she is. But in addition to the particularities of one's personal sensibility, fantasies and notions will take on a momentary life of their own, coming into presence, ceasing, and so forth. There may be considerable intensity as one part or another of one's body relaxes and releases associations tied with that part. Or, if one is more attuned to things around him/her, he/she will find those things to be present without function and probably with directions of meaning that do not involve the contemplator at all. They may well communicate an otherness in relation to their own definition, a disclosure of happening that is not a specific thing. Or there may be a sense of nothing present at all, a sense of emptiness or of waiting, of being a clearing, a place only of light or of darkness. In any case, awareness comes more and more to be presence without attention and sense without direction, even if this state of mind occurs while one is running or working at some task. As in the case of dreaming, one can develop his/her ability to recall what happened in those aware states without impeding the awareness itself. Or one can turn off the remembering observer and be simply a state of aware passage that remembers later in immediacies and by accident, but not by design.

---

[2] Martin Buber, *I-Thou*, trans. W. Kaufman (N.Y.: Chas. Scribners' Sons, 1970), p.90.

[3] We have discussed the possibility of this kind of occurrence, viz. immediate awareness as I-Thou, in Chapter I, in terms of mind as non-subjective event. How the non-objective happens, however, is particularly elusive for description, not only because our language remembers objects and subjects more easily than what occurs as neither object nor subject, but also because we probably tend to think of "non-objective" as synonymous with feeling close or with personal intimacy. The accord of what Buber named I-Thou, however, is neither of those things.

[4] The discipline of learning how not to interfere and of how to step back of the awareness that happens as one is an agent can be particularly difficult. It involves loss of intellectual and affective control vis-à-vis whatever occurs and can consequently threaten one's identity as well as one's theories. As I shall indicate below, this kind of awareness is not what we usually think of as "humane," and yet it appears to me to be one of the most important aspects of therapeutic occurrences.

In such states, our presence with things is through our lack of interest, our indifference, and this presence through open emptiness, let us call it, is an awareness quite distinct from our awareness through and in activities. We become increasingly aware with things in their eventfulness, and more and more the non-interest of the awareness and the non-interest of things, be they ideas or automobiles, becomes the sensed region of kinship.[5] The very happening of awareness-with-things gains luminosity or audibility in this way. A sense of anonymous accord occurs, and if appropriated into one's other sensibilities, may grow into a pervasive quality in one's usual consciousness.

How things happen in this accord is itself important for our understanding of how things are and how we may be with them without maddening inappropriateness, and we shall return to this question in section three. We shall be most helped now by focusing on the event of this kind of awareness in order to see that our particularizing interests or our common desires are not our sole, perhaps not even our fundamental, linkage with the occurrence of things.

In contemplation we discover that one kind of serenity, we have called it an anonymous accord, happens with fantasies and things. Awareness in this case happens as a non-interfering region of acceptance which is not under what we ordinarily call intentional control. This very openness accords with the event of things, their coming forth or opening out, so that their happening, not so much what they are for or their contextual significance, but their happening is their kinship in awareness. Happening resonates happening, and this resonance without subject or object is the serenity of contemplation.[6]

This same awareness may also happen between people and between people and things. In this form I shall think of it as fundamental dialogue.[7] I do not have in mind those significant conversations in which I experience myself as deeply recognized and accepted by another person, who also experiences him/herself as deeply recognized and accepted by me. Such profound, personal experiences usually have the effect of affirmation and confirmation of my existence as well as of my identity. They carry with them often a quality of broad forgiveness and acceptance and are irreplaceable for personal growth and self-confidence.

[5] Ref. Chapter I, sec. VI, on indifference and Stevens's poetry.

[6] I am hesitant to call this kind of occurrence a peak experience in Maslow's sense, because it is not the experience of a subject—it is something that a conscious subject may find itself in— and because the word *peak* is itself misleading. Contemplation is not like a peak at the top of something. If anything, it is more like being the whole mountain and the valley as well, without a dominant sense of who one is.

[7] Martin Buber's *I-Thou* is a definitive, if often mis-read description of this kind of occurrence. See particularly the First Part. I shall speak of the occurrence itself without elaborating Buber, but with indebtedness to his language and insights.

The dialogue that I have in mind, however, is not a personal experience on the part of a person. It is of a different genre. The person, the one who recalls and experiences in individual ways, may remember the event with fear, appreciation, puzzlement, or whatever. This kind of dialogical event can happen in the midst of anger, strangeness, or uncertainty, as well as with friendliness and personal love. It seems relatively independent of what specifically is going on, although it does not appear to be totally independent of a person's predisposition.

A few examples. Sitting at the base of a large tree in Denmark, where he was studying, a friend of mine became aware, as he put it, "of the tree's being alive." Not in the sense that it was about to speak to him or do something to him or with him. Just alive, my friend said. He remained sitting and allowed the awareness. He became oblivious to the park, the people, the day, the environing sounds. "It sounds silly out of context," he said, "but I was in and with the tree's life. I felt the strangest kinship. As though we were somehow alike in being alive." The intensity of the awareness lasted a short while, less than an hour. But it was a new kind of occurrence for my friend, and he spent many months trying to allow what that experience meant, this sense of anonymous kinship, to seep into the way he understood and related with things. It made respect and love of living things easier, he said.

Another person glanced up in a boring conversation at the man speaking across the table. Their eyes met, not in a bond of intimacy or even personal recognition, but in a simple moment of seeing without defense or interest. He found the entire context of boredom/interest to dissolve for a moment, to open back into a more fundamental way of being together and alive. A short event that canceled the boredom in the passing awareness, but which revealed an unexpected and non-personal commonality.

In a discussion a teacher and student unexpectedly fell silent. Each found the student/teacher difference to dissolve, each allowed a commonality of living that was their common bond without regard for role or personal differences. Then, free of embarrassment, they laughed with surprised happiness and resumed the conversation.

Each of these occurrences involved a suspension of intellection, directed affection, and identity, although not in opposition to them. One way to deny these kinds of events is to turn them into special communications from each other or from someone or something else. They come from no one in particular. They are little disclosures beyond the boundaries of interest and concept that are by no means extraordinary, unless the ordinary be defined in such a way as to exclude them. My guess is that they are the ordinary fare of most therapies, although they are probably infrequently recognized. In such events, says Buber, "no purpose intervenes between I and you, no greed and no anticipation; and longing itself is changed as it plunges from the dream into appearance. Every means is an obstacle. Only where all means have disintegrated do encounters occur."[8]

One of the remarkable characteristics of fundamental dialogue is that as it goes on one has a sense of inexhaustibleness, like endless air or a clear, bottomless pool, like ever. It often seems, in its moment, so completely right to one as personal observer. Yet it cannot be volitionally generated. One may search for it by generating intimate encounters, sexual passion, personal warmth, cooperativeness, or that particular seriousness of being in earnest about life and people. But that kind of searching misses the domain. It is non-voluntary and never happens as the end of a search. Like the barely perceptible spider on the leg of the table in a dream in which two men are loudly fighting, fundamental dialogue usually happens incidentally with our interests and desires. It fulfills something in our being that will be neither subject nor object, a dimension that is untranslatable into passion, piety, or personal fulfillment.

These happenings of accord appear to reflect to us our non-personal being in common, like the aurora borealis reflects the polar ice in bright sun. They are approachable by way of stepping back that I shall call intending not to intend. We shall first reflect on the notion that consciousness is a state of desire and then suggest alternate language in order to set a framework for thinking about intending not to intend.

2. Intending Not to Intend

(a) Is our consciousness always a state of desire?

The idea that consciousness is intentionality is founded in the tradition which interprets human being as essentially willful.[9] There is good reason for that perspective. The frustration and fulfillment of desire is central for human existence. Longing, craving, seeking, protecting, keeping, hiding, bestowing, asking—these words name ways people are, and taken together they mark out a region in which we hurt and thrive in basic ways. The issue within the tradition that gives primacy to the will has to do with the nature of the will. Does the created energy of people seek union or harmony with its source? Why would it veer away from the origin of its very life? Is it deathless in nature? And so forth. But whether will is conceived as spiritual or fleshly, it occurs as desiring. Desiring means that one is a direction that can be affirmed or denied. Desiring may or may not be reflectively aware, but in any case it issues immediately in meanings for human beings and is to some degree accessible for understanding and interpretation. Things happen

---

[8] Ibid., pp. 62-63.

[9] Although intentionality is often used in terms restricted to a theory of knowledge, I want now to use it within an ontological context and mean by it the name for how human consciousness universally happens.

for us, according to this tradition, always in a context of human direction and that means, broadly within the context of human interest, even though that interest be transcendentally grounded.

The form of desiring may be immanent to another order of reality as argued by Plato and believed by Kant. Or its essence may be blind, as it is for Freud; its object may be power, as it is for Nietzsche and Adler; or God, as it is for Augustine; or control, as it is for a modern technologist (implicitly at least); or harmony, as it is for Leibnitz. In all these cases, however, human consciousness is conceived as a tension of directions. The elements within the tension may not be complimentary, but we experience pain or dissatisfaction nonetheless when the directions are not fulfilled. If the direction of consciousness is basically spiritual in nature, we would expect it to be fulfilled in ways we traditionally call religious. If it is rational in nature, we would expect it to be fulfilled in knowing. And if it is strictly biological in nature, we would expect it to be fulfilled in certain bodily states.

I have put all these highly variant positions together and overlooked the importance and subtlety of their differences because I want to call into question the fundamental and remarkably pervasive idea that awareness is basically directional or intentional in nature. I want to emphasize that "awareness" is not to be taken as synonymous with "knowledge" and that "will" or "desire" does not necessarily imply "knowing what I want." Awareness and desire may or may not be accountable to themselves. But when desiring is primary for awareness, awareness is always structuring in nature, and the structure of awareness will be meaning. In short, awareness will be interpreted appropriately as intentionality.

I am persuaded that no one, either classical or modern, has understood the nature of awareness as desiring better than Jean-Paul Sartre. If one begins with desiring as such, and frees himself in his description from both scientific and religious commitments; if, that is, one takes the phenomenon of desire on its own terms, he finds the urge to be. Sartre's description of this urge as immediately self-aware and totally flexible as to how it finds expression in individual instances separates him decisively, for example, from Freud's theory of the libido. His understanding of conscious immediacy as pre-thematic or preconceptual distinguishes him from those who limit awareness to discursive states. His insight is that human awareness is the immediate desire to be. As desire it lacks fullness or completeness of being, and its aim is to overcome this lack, to satisfy its own urge to be itself fully and wholly. The satisfaction of desire means the overcoming of its own inadequacy or incompleteness. Desiring consequently happens as the appropriation or grasping of whatever seems to promise its completion. But what is grasped is an object of desiring awareness, and qua object it is festered with the very insufficiency of being that characterizes its subject. Human desire cannot overcome its lack in its appropriative action because its own limits define the perimeters of the reality that it can own. We always find incompleteness in whatever we seek as the fulfillment of desire.

Sartre's further claim that nothingness is characteristic of being is well known. He identified human being with awareness and consequently with desiring. Desire occurs as the hungering lack of its goal, and this lack is intrinsic to human being. And since the goal of human being is to be without the absence of being, without lack, we are driven to see that the desire to be happens as an upsurge toward what being is not: complete and without fissure.

The other element of Sartre's thought which helps for our purposes is his insight into the nature of objectivity. Desiring is not objective. It is sheer immediacy that is aware. It is awareness, pre-conceptual direction that is appropriative in nature. In its search for fulfillment it always goes for the "not": the Other that is not I and thus casts me in vulnerable contingency, the past that is not the desiring moment but conditions that moment, the restfulness of unconscious beings that cast into inhuman relief the human process. If I can only grasp these beings, overwhelm the "not" that separates me from them in my being, I can be full, non-contingent, serenely absolute: I can be the goal that I lack. Human being thus seeks its goal by conscious reach and grasp. Like watery sand slipping through my fingers, completeness evades me in the form of a creation of consciousness: an object. I am in the presence of non-objects, beings that are there without my awareness, but I engender yet another "not" in appropriating them. As objects they are not of the immediacy of my being. They are not I. Human being inevitably makes objects. So it is in Giacometti's sculpture that we discover, for example, the meaning of objectivity: a being that recedes in the very process of my being aware of it, a thing invaded by an immediate emptiness and separateness as I come into relation with it, an unsatisfaction that makes plenitude impossible and disappoints my desire for objectless union or completed harmony. Desire creates out of what it is, not objects that it is not. Where there is desire, there is always contingency and separation.

Sartre is clear that human being is not all the same as personal identity, that personal identity is founded in the urge to be. He has a remarkable resonance for the ways in which we deceive ourselves into thinking that how we are in particular has some primacy for our being. He listens with the particular way of being to the fundamental urge and frequently hears with unnerving accuracy how we hide our fear of our own being, of our contingency, of the nothing-quality of our particular projects. He allows the being of desire to tell us how pretentious and deceptive our ways of being are when we leave them unrelated to our fundamental state. He shows accurately that desire means inevitable non-completion because it always objectifies and can never be fulfilled by an object. That position shows the existential impact of the two claims that human being is consciousness and consciousness is desiring. It is one appropriate way to complete the claim that will is primary for human awareness.

The spirituality that is appropriate for Sartre—and he is certainly not a materialist—has less to do with honesty than many commentators lead us to think. Were are to avoid that seriousness born of identifying ourselves with our roles or talents or positions or ideals, and that does indeed mean undeceived acceptance of our being. But the stress for Sartre falls on making and creating. Passionately pursuing one's particular fundamental project, even if that project be moral purity or social acceptance, while being fully aware that there is no final justification for the project—that is the region of appropriateness for Sartre. We are to be our urge to be however we find it with intensity, to make and engender out of that urge, without illusions that hide from us the unjustifiableness of our urge and our project and with the wisdom of knowing that creating, and no finished creation, is the expression of our unfulfillable aim. We are to be as we are. There is a strength of soul demanded by that acceptance that would be hard to overstate.

But both the description and its implications for living seem to me to set too narrowly the boundaries for description and insight. To go beyond these boundaries we must free ourselves of the conviction that will in any form defines the region of awareness and being.

(b) Awareness is "world-openness"

My own conviction is that the language of volition, so prominent in their concepts, is inadequate for the insights to be found in such diverse figures as Plato, Augustine, or Freud. They saw far beyond the limits of their metaphysics and to my mind their experiences are more to be heard than some of their dominant assumptions. Rather than work through the inadequacies of their thinking for the range of their insight, however, I want to turn to a region for description that is far more promising for our purposes than desiring.

I shall call this region world-openness, which reflects the ontological turn of Heidegger away from both the classical and the Cartesian manners of thinking. The emphasis now falls on the coming forth of things, on disclosiveness, and not on a speculative realm of being or on the creating human subject.

Hiddenness is as good a phenomenon as any for our attention. It is a breaking-point in many ways. Non-lucidity, impenetrableness, non-reflectivity, not-like-us—this dimension of reality has long been the testing point for interpretations of what is real. We all know from the start that much is dark to us. Intuitively we are convinced of being in the presence of what does not succumb to our way of being. Earth, nature, darkness, mystery, and so forth have named this dimension in literature that carries human memory to its historical limits. We know this awareness is pervasive. It is found reflected in gods and heroes, practices and philosophies throughout civilization. Most of us probably feel indebted to Freud for recalling us out of the silly prejudice that our minds are phenomena only of

light when we are good as well as rational. If we are unable to account for
hiddenness or for the experience of darkness, we know that we have made a
bad mistake along the way.

In recent interpretations, at least, hiddenness is usually conceived in
terms of unconsciousness. We have seen the reason for this characteristic
turn of thought. In a variety of ways consciousness, conceived as basically
volitional, has been taken as the origin of meaning: man the maker, human
consciousness the progenitor of the world. We are aware nonetheless that
meanings, like dreams, arise in relation to what we do not know. We have
an "almost sense," an awareness that the other side of what we know and
how we know is given, but is not apprehendable. It is almost within our
reach, but like a shadow, keeps its distance however we move in relation to
it. We also know that there are conditions for our consciousness, such as
nerves and their activity, the other physical aspects of the brain, and the
like. We are consequently inclined to believe that the hidden, the unconscious, is what never appears and that out of which comes what does appear.
Although the process of transformation from the unconscious to conscious is
a vexing one that is usually considered best ignored, and although the
unconscious is in principle a speculative object because it cannot be
described, it has had the attractive and influential impact of noting the
hidden dimension of human experience and the limits of human reflection.

But hiddenness in fact appears. That appearance is the basis for our
judgment about its importance. If we take "appearance" to mean "subject to
my will" or "fitting my logic" (which are variations of the same thing), then
the appearance of hiddenness seems counter-intuitive. On that basis it would
seem more reasonable to say that everything that appears "fits" either in my
scheme of desire or in my system of clarification. Appearance would be
taken to mean "subject to my desire" or "subject to clarity," and consequently hiddenness and appearance would appear to be opposites. Hiddenness
would be taken to mean not appearing. But if we pay attention to hiddenness, we find it quite present indeed.

When we walk along a beach at night, for example, we can think of the
dark distance, from which the waves come rolling, as like the unconscious.
We don't know what is out there. We can only guess at it. And we may be
inclined to say that the dark distance of the sea does not appear. The waves
that we do see and feel are like the appearance of things that emerge from
an invisible realm. But the dark distance does in fact come forth as dark
distance, as dark space without light from which waves come rolling in. The
dark sea is not something I create or posit. It is there as it is, quite available
for experience and description. In the dark distance we are startled or
pleased or unconcerned by the light that suddenly appears. We see an
aspect of what previously appeared only as darkness. A different way of
coming forth has occurred. We may think, "There was a boat there all the
time, and I didn't know it." Yes, of course. But by paying attention to how

things come forth, we are able to see that our not knowing what might be there in no way means that hiddenness was unapparent. We see, rather, the profound difference between being in the dark and being in light, and we are able to interpret this difference without basing our description upon either knowing or willing.

World-openness, which I have taken as the key, rather than will, for understanding our being, names the region of appearing.[10] It does not mean the absence of hiddenness, but our openness for the forthcoming of hiddenness as well as of other ways of being. Hiddenness is there in the sense of being uncovered in this way as distinct to ways other phenomena occur. The term, world-openness, seems more appropriate to me than words of desire because it makes way for the bestowal or given nature of things. Instead of being motivated to look speculatively behind phenomena for a reasonable cause, be it a finite thing or God, we are inclined to allow things to stand as they come forth. Rather than describing primarily human activity, we are inclined to attend to how things occur on their own terms, to how we stand in the open with them. We are then free to see that we act with things that are already apparent, and that their apparentness does not occur like knowing or willing occur. Knowing and willing are phenomena to be taken solely on their terms and not as a metaphysical substrate or as explanatory principles.

The meaning of this language comes to bear for us when we note that hiddenness (and we could take any other disclosure) is neither a function of intending nor a dialectical opposite of intending. Hiddenness is there to be dealt with, unposited, unhoped for, a given for reflection, but not a structural element of reflection. The coming forth of things is their availability for reflection and desire, however reflecting and desiring occur.

The appropriateness of the term "world-openness" for human being will stand out more clearly when we consider the difference between intending and letting go. We have taken will to mean the immediate and not necessarily egological upsurge of human awareness. The claim has been that human awareness, whether or not it is accountable to an individual's specific choices, is desirous by nature. We have thus named conscious activity, as it is presented in this account, desiring. I have said to the contrary of this position that phenomena are not found as pre-egological modes of desiring, that the descriptive categories of phenomena are not structures of immediate intentions, but that they are names for the ways things are immediately disclosed such that they are available for intentional activity. I have thus taken disclosure to name the non-egological and non-willful presence of beings. The

[10] I am using this term in a Heideggerian way, and specifically I take if from Medard Boss's term *vernehmende Weltoffenheit*. Cf. *Grundriss zu Medizin* (Zurich: H. Huber, 1971), part II. But since I am using the term in a context that departs considerably from them both, I shall not rely on a complicating exposition of its meaning outside of my use of it.

region of appearing, I have said, is better named world-openness than
intentionality, because world-openness means that things are available to us
primordially without a reflection of desiring. Desiring in its most fundamental
sense is founded in the givenness of things on their own terms, i.e., in their
disclosure or coming forth as the way they are. Hence the emphasis on
describing how things happen instead of on necessary conditions for their
being present. Things do not happen as necessary conditions and consequently
an account of those conditions, such as brains, a priori structures, law-abiding
regularity, etc., is abstract in relation to the concrete phenomenon.

How are we to be individually attuned to this fundamental and pre-
egological state of disclosure? By allowing the phenomena to be as they
come forth. By deeply letting go of our interests regarding things we may
find ourselves both aware and in the immediacy of what comes forth. If I
were convinced that the meaning of reality is in some sense volitional, this
kind of language would sound absurd. I would rather attempt to find ways
of willing that are appropriate for the volitional direction of what is present.
I would attempt to conform my own individual desires to the interests that
give order to the world as I encounter it. We saw that for Sartre that meant
giving up my desires for justification, completeness, wholeness, and finality
and seeking rather to express that fundamental desire that defines my own
life in a way appropriate to my contingency and finiteness. Or in a specifically religious, non-Sartrean context I might attempt to mold my desires
after the will that gives essential direction for my life and the world. But
when I see that my being occurs as situated openness for how things are,
when I find that disclosure is the interpretive key for human being, I see
that appropriate awareness on my part does not necessarily involve activity.
I find that disclosure does not occur like the activity of a subject occurs.
Rather, my activity is aimed at release from activity. I seek to allow world-
openness without interference. I intend not to intend.

I hope that it is clear that when one lets go his/her intentions and desires
he/she does not encounter an undifferentiated nothingness or a seamless
plenitude of being, which is the same as nothingness. The distinctiveness and
particularity of beings are fundamental for our being. Things are given in
the world-openness of human being as particular things. Letting go of my
intentions means that I am a living allowance and trust of the forth-coming
of things in world-openness. This non-interested and non-judgmental state is
well exemplified in a therapeutic process that is characterized by profound
honesty and the allowance of whatever happens to be as it is. One may resist
this process because of the deep conviction that if he/she allows the world to
be as it is, he/she will be engulfed or overwhelmed by it. He/she feels the
need to hide aspects of the world by an intentional order with which he
identifies him/herself. Perhaps his/her own inclination to destroy and hurt is
too threatening to allow (as distinct, of course, to an intentional carrying
out), and his/her way of life becomes a denial of those aspects of the world

that mean destruction on his/her part. He/she cannot face those people toward whom he/she feels destructive. But once he/she is free to allow what is there to be as it is—in this case, people whom he/she wants to hurt— he/she finds him/herself not only in touch with him/herself in a new way. He/she also finds him/herself released to his/her own world-openness, his/ her not having to feel as he/she does in the face of people whom he/she feels inclined to destroy. The non-intentional nature of world-openness means freedom in a double sense: allowance of beings as they are and no necessity that they be that way.

There is a double-cut to this realization. Our friend who has accepted people as contingently, but enjoyably hurtable also discovers that his/her own identity is not necessary. As he/she begins to respond to what he/she has now allowed, he/she changes. He/she does not have to be this way. Is there any way that he/she must be? Probably not. Release to world-openness is at once release to the mortality of beings, to the finiteness of disclosures. This uncoveredness of unguaranteed things means an allowance of disclosiveness without prescription. Or, the non-intentional nature of human being means the finiteness, the pervasive aborning and dying aspect of beings in their either fearful or attractive particularity.

The disclosiveness of human being is the ontological possibility for a state of non-intending awareness. Intending not to intend is one's releasing him/herself to the non-intentionality of world-openness. Not intending is allowing things to be as they are, free of all interests, desires, or concerns.

Intending not to intend is an activity. One desires to respond appropriately with his/her own being. He she cultivates his/her attitudes toward him/herself as creator, user, and knower. He/she works at retaining a sense for the ontological limits of knowing in the very process of knowing. He/she builds into his/her active perspectives on him/herself and others the awareness that his/her way of viewing recedes into a non-perspectival state of immediate awareness. He/she finds those mental gates and doors that shut off the uncoveredness of others into whose realm he/she fears to enter with undefended immediacy. He/she develops a sensibility for the givenness of things around him/her, for their simple thereness as they are. He/she attempts to allow things to be on their terms and to give way to the openness in whose element things happen prior to knowledge, use, or further creation. He/she disciplines him/herself to attend to the concreteness of things rather than to what presumably lies beyond them as conditions for their presence. He/she finds ways to cultivate and enlighten his/her interpretation of how things happen when they are unclouded by intentional matrices. Above all he/she works at an uncluttered allowance of immediacy.

This kind of activity aims at the dissolution of its aim. For whatever reasons, we have to work at being with things without aim or interest. Our friend in the previous example may say, "Well, I'm destructively inclined because I was severely restricted when I was young." And that may be correct. But in this case correctness is the expression of the desire to escape the immediacy of how he is. By dissolving his aim to be protected from the attractiveness of people-to-be-hurt he can find release to the world-openness of his own being, i.e., he can be free for how beings come forth. Intending not to intend has its fulfillment in release from aim in the disclosiveness of human being.

Intending not to intend may be taken to mean preparing oneself for communion. I have already indicated that I find no basis for claiming that this state is itself intentionality or a "higher" form of intending. We prepare for communing as we struggle for release to world-openness, which is the region of disclosures.

Communing happens as an awareness of things free of intent. This openness does not posit anything. How I in particular live, how the tree comes forth, how my neighbor is—all beings may be as they are. Like in a deep dream, no deception is necessary, because nothing is guarded or kept. Communion happens as the disclosure of beings without prescription in the clear openness of human being. One is then free for the occurrence of mundane things, spiritual things, life-giving events and life-destroying events; he is free for struggle and serenity, for whatever. And he/she finds that all things happen primordially in a non-projected dimension of allowance which neither defends nor opposes the wishes and interests of a particular identity or of subjectivity in general.

If we were to understand these statements within a humanistic context, our thinking would be centered on the phenomena of self-integration. Communing would mean a fulfilling achievement of human existence. I do not find such an interpretation adequate for the meaning of world-openness. The central issue has to do with our allowance of disclosiveness. As we are free for world-openness, we find ourselves also free for what in particular happens. That primary freedom—i.e., of world-openness—is not a self-relation or like a self-relation. And it is clearly not a subject-object relation or a subject-subject relation. It is release to the realm of appearances, a release in which one's own particular identity fades back and awareness occurs without desire or interest. The otherness that is constitutive of wonder and awe in the presence of an overpowering but compellingly attractive other is left behind. One is then released in the free and uninhibited disclosiveness that is openness for whatever comes forth. That disclosiveness is not one's own. It is the world-openness that pervades all occurrences which one discovers him/herself to be in and with and of. Communion is accord in disclosiveness.

"And all things shall be returned to him." Kierkegaard brooded long on this statement. He interpreted it to mean that one finds that all he/she has given up in obedience to God is returned to him/her with much in addition by God's response to his/her trust and love. My reflections are by no means in agreement with Søren Kierkegaard's own faith. But that sentence does

point to an aspect of transformation that is wrought by communion. Individually one does not necessarily cease loving his/her friends and seeking their
good. He/she does not stop needing money for food and shelter, or needing
the support of tradition and community. But when one's life is influenced by
communing, there is a change of place which desire occupies. The once
overriding nature of projects and interests changes to contingent possibilities
for relative fulfillment. They become options for action and judgment rather
than consuming demands upon which one's life seems to hang. One is not so
much driven as he/she is free to choose vis-à-vis what is allowed. His/her
choices are present, modified by a sense of openness and by attunement of
his/her being which grounds, but does not guarantee who he/she is. He/she
does not expect a fulfillment of his/her being by the accomplishment of
desires. He/she is aware that both the desires and their accomplishment find
their ontological meaning in being relinquished in non-volitional communion rather than in objective, momentary self-satisfactions. His/her intending is fulfilled, paradoxically, in the non-intending state of communing.

One is free to long and crave and hope in addition to his communing.
He/she is free to seek desired states. Nothing is taken away, but the
dimension of non-volitional depth is added to one's particular sense for
him/herself and the world, and he/she is also free to find his/her inclination
to entreat modified or vanished. This range of allowance cannot occur
within the perimeters of desire or intention, and it is the foundation, the
primordial region, for all occurrences. This import of communing, is that
when we are attuned to the non-agent or non-subjective disclosiveness of
being we are receptive to the non-subjective dimension reachable in awareness. That dimension impresses me as the pervasive aspect present in all
experiences. In a word, communing, not desiring in a particular way, is a
common aspect among people.

I have noted the "return" that comes of communing in order to emphasize that it is a way of being in the world. It happens as one becomes free
for the disclosiveness of things, and it gives occasion for one to broaden
his/her way of seeing to include the foundation of that seeing. Communing
is dependent on no object and no subject. It is the world-openness of human
being accorded to itself and released for what comes forth.

3. Discord and Difference

Differences abound in our being, not only in our individual lives. If we
bring the Hermes experiences together with the events of accord, we see
that "the friendliest of the gods to men" crosses a major border as stepping
back of intentions and desires occurs. Just as crossing the perpetual border of
being one and being many does not eradicate the difference, intending not
to intend does not eliminate intentional relations or subjects and objects.
Fundamental dialogue no more eliminates the inevitability of personal

sharing or objectifying discourse than contemplation eliminates the unavoid-ableness of discursive and pragmatic involvements. By being open in the differences of our being, we are open to the continual dislocating of all the inevitable fates of being human and to the pretensions that each dimension holds for one who, being dominated by it, forgets the others in their differences.

By "inevitable fates of human being" I mean the non-reducible dimen-sions that happen as "borders in mind," e.g., fantasy and literalisms, part and whole, willing and non-willing, order and absence of order, person and non-person, identity and absence of identity, etc. We have seen that awareness is the event of mind, not only a conscious activity of a person or a subject. Differences that are not reducible to anything else constitute that awareness. Awareness happens in difference. We have noted one kind of accord that happens between an individual and the non-individual dimension of aware-ness. There is a kinship between these two regions. But there is also differ-ence, and the accordability of the difference is reflected, for example, when a person lives as though personal interest totally defined the world around him/her. It gains a flat, pragmatic, vaguely boring, surface, and often compelled or obsessed quality. It then reflects, in its straight-arrow literal-ness, the absence of an appropriated, pervasive ambiguity granted by the whole of the parts or by the whole of the elevating and non-literal event of non-personal I-Thou. The discord of the difference is reflected when one attempts a wholly contemplative life or a life free of the miseries and com-plications of practicality: sometimes a sweet irrelevance develops, or a profound incapacity to cope with the ordinary, or ethereal disrelation, and so forth.

The discord of the difference lies in the non-reducibleness and the simultaneity of the dimensions and aspects of our being. The aspects of our happening, i.e., our mind, will not dissolve into a final chord of harmony. Each appears differently from within the domain of each. Our awareness may be dominantly bellicose, dominantly redemptive, pervasively cold, always tending toward invention and novelty, highly ethereal, basically dominating, and so on probably *ad infinitum*. Further, any region of familiarity has basic sympathies and antipathies. Stated in one way, Hephaestus, the earthy forger and inventive genius, and Ares, passionate spirited warrior, are probably always at odds with each other. But they are both attractive to Aphrodite, the eternal lady of love, and they are both taken by her. Stated another way, the awareness in earthy, slow, deep, strong and inventive building and the awareness in spirited, aggressive-defensive hostility seem to be commonly at odds and yet commonally aligned in the passions of attraction and physical intimacy. Saturn and Poseidon, however, are not attracted to Aphrodite and are not akin through her domain. Hephaestus and Ares are not profoundly compatable awarenesses, although the intensity and physical quality of love brings them into proximity. What is distant to them? Calculation without spirit or warm passion, like Saturn or Faulkner's Popeye and the family Snopes. Or the ocean quality of Poseidon (which is certainly distant to Hephaestus), i.e., the flowing depths of feeling without aim or inventive interest, the unfathomable currents, alternately cold and warm, alternately serene and awful in storm, the fluidity that continuously unmakes structure, and the harbor of as much decay as generation.

We, as individuals who must cope and be some "who" or other, cannot reside at once in all the dimensions of our being. Nor can we perpetually cross borders without losing our particularity. We are dwellers. We are each aligned with some aspects of our being while we are distanced and even alien to others. To try to be in all of them is like trying to be a god, and destruction of person appears to be inevitable if one persistantly, with some success, denies the limits of his/her rootage and dwelling place. The differences in our being, with our limits as individuals, mean discord, perhaps in the form of deep and insatiable longing, or having regularly to cope with dimensions of reality that become familiar to us only as alien and pesky or dangerous. As sexuality was for St. Bernard (on one occasion he jumped through the ice of the monastery's fish pond to extinguish his sexual desire), as self-sacrificial love is for someone who is young and building expansively with a genuine sense for his/her importance, as contemplation is for an entrenched identity. As we saw in the last chapter, the very reality of identity involves difference with our own being. The serene indifference of wholeness and the differentiation of identity will always be different from each other. There is a consequent discord, an absence of total sameness, an absence of total difference, a need for extensive differentiation in one's mind. There is always a possible openness to shadow, to the alien, to the threat of disintegration in one's own being, to the mortal danger of ideal, seamless accord. There is the inevitability of other and stranger, and the possibility of final chaos. Nothing resolves the fundamental differences.[11]

To be open in the differences of mind means openness to discord by virtue of our accords and other possible ways of being in accord. Within the context of his meditation, Buber notes the inevitability of the I-It, of total loss of I-Thou. I-Thou actually heightens dissatisfaction with most ways of being with people and things. And I-It always calls into question I-Thou,

[11] Michel Foucault speaks of "transgression" in a way similar to my meaning of being on borders and crossing them. "Trangression is an action which involves the limit, the narrow zone of a line where it displays the flash of its passage, but perhaps also its entire trajectory, even its origin; it is likely that transgression has its entire space in the line it crosses." Further, "the limit opens violently onto the limitless, finds itself suddenly carried away by the content it had rejected and fulfilled by this alien plenitude which invades it to the core of its being. Transgression carries the limit right to the limit of its being; transgression forces the limit to face the fact of its immanent disappearance. . . ." *Language, Counter-Memory, Practice*, ed. Donald F. Bouchard (Ithaca, N.Y.: Cornell University Press, 1977), pp. 33-34.

because I-It, no matter how understanding, is not an I-Thou awareness. I-Thou's own way of happening is its difference vis-à-vis I-It, and that difference means that I-It awareness loses I-Thou awareness by recognizing that I-Thou is. As I speak or think about I-Thou, for example, the awareness of and in this way of speaking and thinking exclude the reality that is addressed. And in I-Thou occurrences, I-It leaves off, passes away, and is absent so that the normal world of understanding may seem mad, perverse, and unnecessary.

Given the apparent inevitability of difference in mind, we can never appropriately expect the opposite of madness to be accord with discord, nor can we expect our best communication among ourselves to be solely that of profound serenity and agreement. Differences of awareness, as we have been speaking of them, are not founded in personal experience and are not, as we usually think of the word, perspectives. They are regions in the happening of mind, spoken of richly and indirectly in mythology, characterized by awareness, and regions in which an individual consciousness can dwell. Where one dwells is usually not a matter of choice. But as I begin to see how my dominant awareness occurs, where its natural alliances and antagonisms are, I begin to find both self-awareness and tolerance for difference.

One implication of this claim is that a significant loss of mind occurs when one communicates out of a region without a sense for its place with differences. Dogmatism is usually thought of as a kind of personal insistence on one's own boundaries, as though they were final for all reality. Insistence on the absoluteness of a region is not simply a personal action. Periods of time, eras, epochs, and ways of speaking may also carry with them a trans-personal insistence. I doubt that a thirteenth century male of noble birth could thoroughly doubt chivalry as a code of right conduct. He could also probably not feel remorse over destruction of people and property in war, unless his own or a relative's or some person's of sympathy were involved. The chivalric code as well as cruelty were a part of his dwelling and had an insistence that few could transcend. Most of us probably experience the same insistence in the reality of individuality and in the quantitative structure of things.

This insistence, whether personal or trans-personal, means at least a tacit refusal of equally real, yet utter differences and an incipient hope for accord in one region to be the defining character of all reality. The hope of eternal peace in the way of the Holy Mother Church in the thirteenth century, for example, appeared to be without challenge at the level of utopian ideal. Yet it clashed totally with the chivalric hope of glory in battle, which carried with it, for all practical purposes, the hope for continuous war, a barely acceptable substitute for which was the Tournament. And the Tournament functioned only as a substitute between battles, never in total lieu of them. The two different regions, one of perpetual, ecclesiastically structured peace and the other, of perpetual code-structured battle, exerted total demands, insisted on a complete view of the end of all things, and yet many people then and probably now attempted to live in the insistence of both regions. That occasioned awful foolishness, madness of a particularly destructive sort, as people tried to live in both regions at once, oblivious of their insisting differences. The Crusades and the One Hundred Years' War are good illustrations of the madness that infected this century through nonreducible insistences.

Among individuals—and I shall draw the differences radically for the sake of making a point, although subtle differences of regions are equally important and more difficult to perceive—a person whose consciousness is dominated by abstract relations and one whose consciousness is dominated by concrete relations can each cause guilt in the other, in addition to virtually inevitable misunderstandings. Each will find the other in some sense strange and probably deeply irritating. If one region is overgeneralized the concrete relational person will find the other's abstractness pathological and vice versa. Endless struggles over intellectualization and muddling, and so forth. That hostility is avoidable if one allows the differences of dominate ways of perceiving, particularly if one can name the differences and not seek reduction of one to the other, tht is, not insist on the extra-regional dominance of one over the other.

Alphons Lingis has developed the polymorphous character of mind in relation to sensuality.[12] Lingis quotes Aristotle's observation that "man's soul by its nature is destined to open upon, and to somehow be, all things. It is the universe as such that is the proper object of the craving in man's nature."[13] The enormity of the universe, vaguely craved by us, is reflected in the polymorphus openness of the human soul when it is not controlled by highly individualized limits. The immediacy of soul as longing, and universal reality as the longed-for may be lived as sensual innocence, as distinct to conceptual comprehension. Dancing, entwining, penetrating and receiving, leaving and reuniting with little or no individual recognition or choice is one way in which human beings acted out and celebrated. In this case, individuality is a threat to participatory immediacy, celebration, and one kind of knowledge of how one is real. Eroticism of this sort, says Lingis, is a way of knowing far removed from our dominant understanding in the West, but one that was apparently in at least one pocket of civilization in India, called the Chandalla Kingdoms, a thousand years ago.

"The temples are intricate assemblages of porticos, cones, drums, towers, stalagtites, across which the mind is invited to follow the surprising derivations and correlations between a vast number of abstract forms which a sovereign logico-mathematical intelligence has elaborated here. But this abstract geometry embraces within itself layer upon layer of friezes where

[12] "Khajuraho," *Soundings* (Summer 1979).
[13] Ibid.

what seems to be a sort of universal combinatorium of carnal positions is brought to the same explicitness and precision. Auto-erotic stimulation, dual and multiple cunnilinctio, penilinctio, copulation, homosexual and bestial intercourse circulate about the temple walls, without primacy of place or of artistry given to any mode. There is nowhere suggestion of audacity or provocation, the leers that would suggest civic taboos being violated in the sacred precincts. Within the erotic there is not selection of with whom and for what being taught, but an extensive intelligence exploring all the possibilities and an artist sensibility perfecting the form and equilibrium of each mode, such that nothing is sanctioned and nothing ignoble, imperfect in an eroticism universalized. The temples tell us of a society that existed among men where sexual repression was once, but completely, unknown.

. . . .

"These then are veritable temples of love—but in what sense? They are not incitements to sex-civic-magical inculcations of fertility or palaces where phallocratic power is glorified. For the statuary depicts neither procreation nor even orgasm; on the contrary it is a blissful state of erotic charge that is maintained in a stasis of suspension, contemplated and displayed, that we especially see. The artistic exaggeration of genitalia proper to pregnancy and fertility cults does not occur here, and many of the tableaux depict non-impregnating manipulations. And the dyssymetry of the sexes does not become a practice of power and dependency. Penile erection is not generalized into male ascendency—as in the art that casts secondary gender characteristics—male chest and male musculature—into the image of tumescence, nor does it become the concrete symbol, the very concretion of verticality and value.[14] Khajuraho shows men receiving female initiative, lying upside down beneath women, and the male figure, supple and pliant, coils and breathes rather than hardens into muscular erection, or into pillars about which the female would twine, seeking phallic support.

. . . .

"The unity of purpose of the site, the highest standards of craft maintained in all details, and the prodigality of the effort—there were 85 temples!—tell us that the Chandalla kings who ruled here maintained an exceptionally powerful, and exceptionally noble political order. But these are not monuments to secular power, and these are not carvings of divinized rulers; they are works of religion, of that supremely theoretically and metaphysically elaborated religion, Hinduism. We cannot look at these

[14] The relationship between phallocentric culture and the institution of the dimension of vertically and value in metaphysical thought was first perceived by Jacques Lacan (cf. *Ecrits* [Paris: Seuil, 1966], pp. 685-86) and Jacques Derrida (cf. *La dissemination* [Paris: Seuil, 1972], pp. 56-57).

temples without being convinced that the society that built them was one of exceptional pragmatic and technical achievement, of intense social purpose not maintained through divinization of secular power, of widely diffused abstract and gratuitous intelligence. But what is singular here is that craft, engineering, architecture, social organization, mathematical intelligence, religious mysticism opened up wholly new domains for eroticism and were not inaugurated over the censorship of sensuality. These are not temples of love in that the culture knew nothing higher to enshrine than biological functions; they are temples in which sensuality itself reaches a supreme degree of intelligence, thoughfulness, beauty, and assumes cosmic and salvific dimensions.

"Indeed rarely has man assumed a more ennobled visage than in this rock. These men and women closed in passionate embraces have brows poised with respect and gazes emanating intelligence, mouths trembling with susceptibility and lips benevolent and responsive, fingers ungrasping and reverent. Here there is nothing guilty or crafty, nothing disfigured with leering and duplicity, nothing self-indulgent or self-ashamed. There is nothing servile. They are blissful with the freedom of gods who have understood everything.

"These bodies are not just writhing about like a tangle of worms. Each tableau is in fact yoga; this gymnastic copulation of Shiva with six women is not an orgy but an asana. Is not nobility a physiological, vital, rather than civic, virtue? In these hundreds of figures we see all that men have noticed to be noble in the wingspread of eagles, in the languor of a cat, in the coiling of scorpion, in the watery freedom of fish, in the intensity of a cobra ready to strike.

"And the human body here does not only, in its orgasmic intensity, contract every organic form, it does so to the point of carnal intercourse with every form of body. The temple frieze is the place where a carnal visage of all things is divined, is caressed. In animals: there is not in the yoga that seeks to know and to stand, soar or creep with animal perfection, the sense that one debases oneself to make love with animals. In things: the sanctuary finds a carnal visage to vines, to trees, to flowers, to mountains and fields; men release their white liquids in the holy Ganga, cosmic river which, in what we have named the Milky Way, is seen to flow across the night, to descend upon the celestial Himalayas in what we see as its snow, to pour across the plains where man's most ancient civilization was elaborated, to carry the ashes of its generations to the oceans, to descend too into a subterranean Ganga to flow across the underworld before it re-emerges again in the most remote heavens. Men pour their semen into this white sidereal river; women open their wombs to the moon, to the sun, to the lonely and perfect stars. The carnal yearning embraces not only all terrestrial, but also the heavenly bodies. At Konarak it is thousands of lovers that form the chariot of Surya, the sun, whose movement across the heavens engenders all

chariot of Surya, the sun, whose movement across the heavens engenders all
that is carnal, but is itself composed of the thousand movements of carnal
desire. Here one neither descends, when one makes love with animals, nor
ascends, when one makes love with the moon, the rivers, the stars, one
travels aimlessly or circularly about a universe eroticized.

. . . .

"Here pleasure is not being conceived in the psychoanalytic way, as the
immediacy of sense gratification, and tension release. On all the tableaux of
Khajuraho the intensity of the serpent charge is being maintained. It is sustained because what is immediately disclosed in carnal contact is the most
remote and most strange things, scorpion, sea anemone, comet in oneself.
'Here (within this body) is the Ganges and the Jumna . . . here are Prayaga
and Benares—here the sun and the moon. Here are the sacred places, here
the Pithas and the Upa-pithas—I have not seen a place of pilgrimage and an
abode of bliss like my body.'[15] As the Apsaras contemplates her own body,
the Kundalini rises; her body coils with its own ardor. This gaze that finds
the holy Benares and the Ganges, the sun and the moon in her body, this
gaze deflected across the rivers and down the astral orbits, is dispersed and
scattered not by frustration of a primary sense pleasure, but by its very
intensity. And the subterranean rivers and celestial constellations, the places
of pilgrimage and the wandering planets are not dissimulations of a carnal
libido, but discoveries of the Kundalini fire itself which renders them carnal;
this is then why awakening of the serpent power culminates in this poised
gaze and no longer issues in orgasmic tension release. . . .
      "What the eroticized gaze contemplates is not the splendor of the intelli-
gible order, appropriated by a comprehensive contemplation. Here the
beauty of the partner is dismembered into an unending sequence of animal
and vegetative and crystalline forms, each closed in its own perfection. It is
at once the enchanted discovery that the singularity of each strange form of
nature is perfect. The beauty of this face is the beauty of the sesammum
bud, of the swelling gourds, of the fluttering water birds, of the floating
polyps discovered in it, by the disconcerted gaze, by these fish eyes delight-
ing in these dark waters. Where what delights is the flash of the ephemeral,
the evanescent. These eyes do not see in the necklace the Apsaras bound by
the chain of ageless stones; they see a flight of water birds.

. . . .

"And what then is this artist will, that has carved this bliss forgotten
centuries ago in the jungles of Madhya Pradesh as our civilization
constructed its cenotaphs? Why carve this glandular and fluid sensuality in

[15] Shashi Bhusan Dasgupta, *Obscure Religious Cults as Background of Bengali Literature*
(Calcutta, 1946), pp. 103-4.

this rock? Why this petrification, if not out of a will to eternalize the ever so fugitive spasm of carnal love?

"But very likely the question also expresses our Platonico-metaphysical nostalgias. Is not the supreme feat of eroticism here—that which demanded these carvings, these temples—to render the stone itself passionate—rather than passion petrified? Hindu sculpture does not, like Hellenistic art, bring the petrified into life by carving out tensions and counter-tensions in musculature, in the mechanism of bones and sinews, as though life is force or will power. Rather here the chest, torso and limbs are smooth and loose like glands, accentuated by the sharp carving of ornament against the smoothness of skin—chains and necklaces, water birds taking flight. They breathe; it is *aspiration* that the sculpturing genius has engraved in the stone, that and not force and self-movement is the gravity of life that afflicts and weighs in the mineral substances out of which it is composed. And that is also why this carving is passionate, all the coils and smooth surfaces of the forms invite the touch of the sighing lips and the breath-like touch of the caress. But of course the carving is especially a vision. To be looked at, with eyes. With eyes of fish, of happiness."

Lingis's remarkable observations allow us to focus radical differences in mind, differences that offer enormously varied possibilities for the basic dwelling of people. Our inclination to judge or to explain this Indian life gives us occasion also to allow the difference and to see non-individualized sensuality juxtaposed with our person-centered lives. And yet who has not felt the tension between innocence, Eden-like, and the responsibility of a struggling, surviving individual? And perhaps the people of Khajuraho, as they planned and built their temples, felt the possibility of a life founded in decision and individualization. It probably seemed, vaguely, like a threatening and destructive madness to them, arising from the dark openness of their own souls. To differentiate or not to differentiate means discord as one region insists, no matter how quietly and peacefully, that it be here and now.

4. Accord and Discord: In-difference

I have pointed out that accords and discords are inevitable in mind, primarily in order to give a basis for understanding how both together form a basis for human well-being and illness. How accord and discord are allowed constitutes a most important aspect of depth therapy. Therapeutic eros, true to the classical heritage of eros, involves profound contradictions, and allowing those contradictions, which are basic in human being for character formation, is one of the most difficult and over-looked aspects of what in fact ordinarily goes on in psychotherapy. One implication of the discussion so far is that human being needs to be interpreted by primary reference to the differences in mind and not by primary reference to a dominant aspect. Otherwise we shall be inclined to think of human being as identical with a certain constellation of characteristics and lose our sense for the whole. Nothing that we are prepared to live for and die for sufficiently defines our being, and only if we have a sense for the reality and ontological legitimacy of opposition, borders, contradictions, and shadows will we be able to remain open to the wholeness of our own event.

In the rifts of our occurrence vis-à-vis our being and who we are individually and culturally, not in the firmness or satisfactoriness of character, will be found the regions for our most profound well-being and serenity. As beings we are the differences that are set against our identities. In those differences our awareness happens as dream, fantasy, intuition, and break of common sense. Those awarenesses often seem foreign to us. Our awareness at first seems vast to us in comparison to the consciousness that we own as ours in particular. We tend to disown our extended awareness, to refuse the otherness of our own being by trivializing it or by attributing the awareness in difference to other beings, to dark outer regions, or whatever. But we are the dreams and fantasies and breakages that happen in mind. Their excess of our identity and character does not deny the living nature of their event. Only the absoluteness of the limits of identity, individual and cultural, for our own being is denied. The creation of fantasy in all its forms, the aware engendering of further awareness, testifies to the excess of awareness in relation to identity and points out that in difference, not in identity, a different order of accord may be found in comparison to that of personal peace of mind.

I shall continue to use the word *in-difference* to name our awareness as it happens outside the bounds and control of who we happen to be, but I shall use the hyphenated form in order to emphasize that in differences, i.e., on borders, the indifference of mind is manifest, but not as any one difference or the totality of differences. It is meant to note that our being happens in the rifts, the differences that mark mind, as well as in the domains in which we are habitated. I stress in-difference because we are prone to think of awareness more in limited setting than in borders among settings. These borders, marking the difference, are the places where we transcend the identities of mind and are able to be aware and free of the limitations of identity as such. It is a vis-à-vis situation: borders are always of places, and differences are relational events. As we are as we are, we also transcend those limits in the differences of mind. Not only because we can take another standpoint or to some degree come to perceive very differently, but because we happen as border and as difference vis-à-vis all possible identity. Our being occurs also as in-difference.

We have seen that being in-difference vis-à-vis our selves, who we happen to be, is a type of discord, if accord be seen from the place of identity and person. We have also seen that the deep accord of I-Thou happens without the mediation or active presence of identity and person.

In-difference may be taken to name awareness without naming any one place or set of places, no one's domain, in which this remarkable accord of being happens. We pass through it in a pronounced way as we undergo significant transition, although we are always, at least in principle, in the presence of the borders of mind and always happen with in-difference.

5. In-difference and Dying

I imagine that the accounts of Hermes leading dead souls to Hades reflects some of the experiences that we have in times of deep change or catastrophe. The underworld realm of the dead, quite the opposite of the coming of spring, is very much like depression in its dark and gloom. It was surrounded by the rivers of woe, fire, wailing, and forgetfulness. Certainly not all fundamental transitions of human life need this imagery. Yet few of us go through deep change of character, even in the normal processes of growth, without considerable deep, perhaps quiet travail. What is close and important to the child grows more and more distant to the emerging youth. The child, as a place of experience, dies away. What cannot be forgotten by the child cannot be remembered by the youth. Often only fantasy or hypnosis can return the forgotten. And so on through the fundamental changes of life. One comes to feel differently if growth is successful. During such transitions there are times of unusual suspension, loneliness, senses of being vaguely out of joint, heightened sensitivity to pain and loss, symptoms of grief. Such states are exaggerated, of course, in traumatic transitions and are the daily fare of effective therapy.

As one lives through transitions in closeness with in-difference and has no clear place to indwell, he/she goes through a situation remarkably similar to that of a terminal illness. In working with terminally ill people a team of caregivers found repeatedly that a person dies in a way continuous with how he/she has lived through other difficult situations.[16] The known terminal nature of the person's disease is an important difference, but how the person lives through this "last" illness will usually be quite the same as he/she lived through threats and uncertainties in the past. Some with Stoic defiance, others looking for ways to maximize gains and with little inclination to deal with the hardships or pain, some with hope and good cheer in full acceptance of the "realities," some with depression and withdrawal, and so forth. The point of interest presently is that there is a continuity with life-transitions and terminal illness. Part of that continuity appears to involve the suspension of what one takes for granted, and a predominate awareness of loss, fragility, the preciousness of what is good, an uncertain future. Significant transitions are experiences of dying in which in-difference shines through most of what otherwise appears solid, durable, and certain.

---

[16] At Vanderbilt Hospital, begun in 1970.

I suspect that one could hardly overestimate the importance of understanding grief as well as the affections of loss when he/she wishes to
understand the experience of psychotherapy. Dying and grief are experiences in which not only my and your domains are cast into relief against a
backdrop of no-place and nothing. They are nearing contacts with the in-
difference of our awareness, which makes deathly all dwelling places by
being itself aware and yet no place, nowhere, no thing. Relatively few
people who have not opened to their own dying and in-difference are ready
to allow the dying, grieving occurrences of in-difference in others.

When we soften the I-Thou event by interpretations which turn it into
personal intimacy or times of warm affection, we lose the close relation the
I-Thou occurrences have with dying. Just as a moment of unguarded
intimacy may frighten a highly defended person, a recognized occurrence
of I-Thou may threaten a person's sense of him/herself. A stream of words
may suddenly invade the event. Or a person may turn to a safer or at least
more familiar sexual orientation, or one may become assertive or simply
withdraw to reconnoiter the resources of personal identity. I have seen
physicians raise their voices to a virtual shout in ordinary conversation with
patients after a moment of silent encounter without benefit of role-
character-mediation. In therapy people have wanted to hold on to
something, and therapists have turned quickly interpretive after similar
events. They are not so dramatic, these I-Thou occurrences. To the contrary,
they usually are wholly lacking in drama or movement. It's their silence,
their immediacy, their lacking definition, and, in our time, their
unexpectedness and extra-ordinariness that makes them frightening for
many of us. Our responses to them are frequently dramatic, I suspect,
because in them we are aware of in-difference and in that awareness we
experience a dying away of who we are.

That dying away happens partially as who we are falls away and no
longer is reflected in the occurrence. In I-Thou I do not find out who I am. I
lose hold of my capacities, my acceptabilities, my failures, my place, my
history, and so forth. On the border all that is left behind. If I welcome the
event, 'leaving behind' feels more like being free than losing something
essential. No one takes my identity. I die to it and reinherit it, and it is
alright. But that "alright" means that I am free for the unbounded openness
of being in-difference, not in place, not a different being related with other
beings, but open as no place in particular, no "who" in particular, no single
this. Coming to this "alright" is like dying in the sense that losing my child-
hood-with-my-parents was like dying and in the sense that letting go a
compulsion that has pervaded most of my actions is like dying. In-difference
often means a sense of dying for the person, but it is also "where" being
meets being free of baggage, without cover, without difference, without
threat of loss or promise of gain. It is awareness in being, naked and alive,
perceptive without stakes.

6. Awareness In Silence

When we recall that aesthetics comes from *aisthanesthai*, which means to perceive or to feel, we may reasonably speak of the aesthetics of communication as we attempt to understand how things come together to disclose this or to hide that. We may come to recognize in-difference, like we may recognize that I-Thou occurs whether or not we are in conscious touch with the awareness. Being together therapeutically involves in-difference as awareness and can be a focus for an account of how perceiving goes on in the communication, regardless whether we recognize it. This awareness in in-difference probably happens most usually in silence and as silence.

Aesthetic silence (silence which is itself immediate perception) is an occurrence of awareness, very much like the silence of a total pause in music or absence of form and color in a painting. You hear my not speaking for a moment when you have communicated your desire for my response. Not responding for a moment means at least hesitation (over your request) on my part. Or I fall utterly silent in the face of your plea and talk about something different. You hear the rupture. Or in the midst of talking irrelevantly and avoiding our intensifying interest with each other, we fall silent and the silence communicates the relevant, present involvement with each other. I cannot imagine a meaningless silence in therapy, in which the not said and the unsayable are as important as the said.

One form of aesthetic silence is not saying while much saying is going on: silence in the form of what is present and ignored, the oppressed back-ground feeling, the relatedness that is going on, the unsaid but remembered, the underlined not-to-be-said between us, the not-remembered but apparent event. Another form is a sense of absence that occurs under however things are going on. I do not mean depression, necessarily. Simply the sense of absence or emptiness or non-place that may be with or behind presence, plenitude, and location. Sometimes it might be an exhaustion, like that that can accompany sexual satisfaction. Or it might be a quiet sense of void, of death, limitation, indeterminateness, loseableness.

Behind our roles and postures and identities in dialogue we may sense, let's say with increasing intensity, a sameness with us, a likeness, a non-name quality that is merely us together, increasingly, regardless of how we are. In this silent awareness, the importance of our roles diminishes, we have a growing sense of living, possessions decrease in significance, prudence is not a procedural issue, intensification of perceptivity probably goes on. All this without specific recognition on our part.[17]

[17] A young man and I once had a long and difficult series of conversations in which I, as teacher, refused a proposal from him which I took to be a way of passing my course with virtually no work on his part. That led to a conversation about his intention to drop out of school. His goal was "to love" his parents into a reconciliation and reunion out of their spiteful

The image I have is of a depth that underlies and accompanies surface events. That depth is frequently silent in our usual sounds. It is a depth that changes the appearances of things as one goes into it. A therapist may hear, "I only occasionally have this quality of relationship, and mostly when I am with you." Or a person may find that with a few persons is he/she able to have "touch" with a silent depth in him/herself. In that touch, values often change significantly. A person may become more selfish with his/her time. Or more self-giving. Or disgusted over what he/she spends most of his/her money for. Or deeply happy in spite of physical pain. And so forth. Often an adult who becomes newly accustomed to this 'depth' will change jobs and life-style. And usually the more attuned a person is with it, the less he/she says of it. It happens as a kind of silence in the way one makes decisions, receives pain, hears others, "picks up" a quality of relation, accepts failure and success, lives with loneliness, lets go of dependencies, and nurtures goods and loves.

The silence of in-difference may appear more noticeably as a therapist (or a friend) allows a person's move out of familiarity into the indeterminacy of transition, or as the two (or several) people find themselves in an unsure area, unmaped by previous experiences. If the therapist can stay with this uncertainty, free of his/her school's guidebook and rules and interpretations, without rushing into names, concepts, and words, he/she may be successful in letting in-difference come into the therapy as a no-place in which one may find how to be without maps, customs, and landmarks as one also lives with certainties, and knowledge and social norms. That allows a person's utter contingency to come to bear, a bearing no more comfortable for the therapist than for the rest of us. In that bearing silence, one is free to find that he/she may change in no wise or in multiple ways. One is then open for the indeterminant, for I-Thou, dying, the discord of not being who we also are, and for the accord that happens as the discord is allowed in the differences of borders.

In one instance, in the midst of silence, a young man looked up and laughed and said, "I see, I see." He said later that he meant that he saw a silence and indeterminacy and what it meant for his life. In another case, a dying woman held a friend's hand, while her two grown sons bickered over her bed, reaching for him with her eyes, and the two went beyond their friendship to the silence of absence and death and stayed there together for a moment, as the sounds, room, and occasion receded from their consciousness. In a third instance an obsessional woman saw this region of indeterminate silence at a distance and said, "No, no! Stop! Stop!" She said that she would not "go that far" although she did not know why. Later she said that she was sure that she would die if she let go of the little that she had.

---

separation. I had said nothing for fifteen or twenty minutes as he spoke. A silence fell between us, and I became intensely aware of the young man in his pain, which was severe, but hidden behind an oddly humorous exterior. He looked at me and said, "For the first time you are coming through to me."

None of these instances involved prior discussion of silence, depth, or death. We are dealing with a region of awareness that lacks definiteness and location, with awareness that is different from particularity of any kind. This awareness appears to occur with our own events, to be one dimension of our happening. Its presence means that total reliance on particularity or sets of particular things, on familiarity, certainty, location, and identity is a kind of madness that is a tacit refusal of a dimension of our happening, a profound contradiction in our being of our being.

7. Suffusions

By "suffusions" I mean the ways that different dimensions of events or of an event are simultaneously present with each other. Suffusions are types of immediate awareness when the event is an aware occurrence. This can be border awareness in the sense that it is an alertness composed of the immediate adjacancy of regions. The border, however, is pervasive presence in the region and composes a special kind of immediacy. Or it can be the enmeshing of various, nameable elements in the composition of an aware event.

We tend to separate regions, such as that of I-Thou and objective relations. Buber thought, for example, that I-Thou and I-It could not happen simultaneously and probably our most frequent experience involves the loss of great areas of experience because of the limits of the present experience. I once asked a young man how he managed to stay in a highly racist situation where he worked, since he was an activist in desegregation causes in the early '60s. He said that he kept his bags packed, at least in his mind. His preparedness to leave pervaded his day to day decisions so that he was able to resist being absorbed into the mentality around him for the sake of security and acceptance. That image can also apply in a broader framework.

In a hard conflict between two people who love each other, their love may be apparent to each in what appears to an outsider as merely a terrible disagreement. And agreement over things can certainly open out into a fundamental lack of accord among people. The non-literal depth of any lively ritual is usually not available to aliens, but is obviously and experientially present in the ritual actions and things to those well within the tradition. An apparently trivial conversation about what happened yesterday between a therapist and patient can be charged by a depth of meaning and relatedness founded in their quality of trust and familiarity with each other. A sense of respect can pervade a mortal conflict between enemies. An awareness of mystery can suffuse a person's daily cognitions. A high degree of ambiguity can be present in simple actions of support or opposition. I suspect that a literal reading of anything in the world is a mistake of abbreviation anytime claims of adequacy are made for the literal rendering.

Highly different regions of awareness suffuse each other. The issue usually is not whether such suffusion is going on, but how much of it a person can stand. Can we tolerate our awareness in the temporariness and transitoriness of all things to suffuse our experience of a most beloved person? Or can we allow this awareness in contingency to permeate our sense of ourselves and our intentions for our own destinies as we act with certainty and security? Or can we allow our awareness in cruelty to be open with our awareness in nature? Each region of awareness may threaten the dominance and "place" of other regions. However the threat might have come about— by birth trauma, through parental anxiety, or through some other trauma of very early life—my awareness in parental presence may seek to block, for example, my awareness in radical change. Anything that opens a present moment to this feared region, that breaches the border as it were, may engender a high degree of anxiety in me. I may faint, become hyperactive, go into depression, or whatever. My guess is that a great deal of therapy happens as people learn to allow feared regions of awareness to suffuse with other familiar and allowed regions.

I can think of no reason why any region of awareness could not suffuse any other region. Reasons why they in fact do not are clear enough: prohibitions with life-stakes, ingrained habits of cultural character, and so forth. But one may be alert in radical difference as he/she pursues a favored or virtually inevitable direction of consciousness. A thorough-going monotheist and western Judeo-Christian moralist, for example, can be open to the vegetative, promiscuous, and innocent sensuality discussed above. He/she can opt away from it without denying its presence and knowing it as he/she knows things and people in a context of personal responsibility and ego-centeredness. It can be a quiet, subsidiary quality of recognition and understanding. The same can be said of our criminal aspects, and all our other aspects that are different or opposite vis-à-vis who we are in particular.

In our openness to open borders of awareness, in our freedom for our differences in awareness, we discover openness in the world without the need for closure to any particular dimension of specific happening. This openness itself can suffuse our involvements. Being open in the border, we find a dissolution of specific discords, and the very discord of difference between in-difference and particular character gains a quality of deep accord, an openness in mind that can suffuse our intense involvements and associations without denying fundamental differences. It is like a depth or height that accompanies what happens, an extensiveness, even enormity that never defines things in their particularity, but quietly persists as another, present dimension of awareness. One may sway with tensions between these great domains. He/she may lose touch with one or the other. Senses of presence and qualities of alertness may change considerably. Or one may find extended times of undisturbed suffusion. In any case, openness with difference in in-difference means a kind of simultaneity that allows, without interference, parts and particulars that are suffused with the alertness of being on the border.

8. Wilderness

I have been thinking primarily of light and oepnness in the experience in in-difference. A person tends to open to the world in its huge diversity and lack of single identity when his/her consciousness is suffused with openness to the borders in mind. Another dimension of this occurrence, however, is best thought of with the metaphors of wilderness and wildness. I do not have in mind the wildness of a bacchanian revel or of an adolescent who is out of control. I have in mind the wildness of uncultivated prairie, untamed forests, and other regions alien to the survival of people and also the wildness of wolves in the wilderness.

Barry Lopez has described this metaphor with unusual insight.[18] Who or what do we kill when we kill a wolf? he asks. I noted in our Introduction the closeness of the Nunamint Eskimos with wolves, their kinship which constituted a remarkable, intuitive understanding, marked by a perceptiveness, anticipation, and style of mind that is not available to most other people. Quite the opposite relation to wolves has characterized the lore of European and American whites. Instead of finding the wolf a great hunter and a skilled survivor in the wilderness, the western "civilized" myths have presented the wolf as a bloodthirsty predator. It was a beast to be feared with passion, a killer with inhibition, the embodiment of much that we fear greatly in ourselves. Wolves are to be hated. They have been hunted with a self-righteousness and sense of duty like few other animals, slaughtered by poisoned meat that also killed thousands of other meat-eating creatures who got to the bait first. Thousands have been killed from airplanes that circle a pack, caught on the tundra or prairie while someone shoots them. Thousands have been allowed to die slowly in traps. Lopez chronicles the history of torture and destruction directed toward wolves, a history probably best reflected in the history of human punishment for major crimes such as theft, murder and heresy.

If we grant Lopez his well documented thesis, that wolves mean to western civilized whites something that they want to stamp out in themselves, the metaphor begins to have the power we need to see the "dark" side of in-difference.

Two instances from Lopez's discussion will suffice.

> The wolf (to the Pawnee) was a symbol of renewal, just as the willow, the sacred tree of the southeast, was a symbol of death and rebirth. When the willow was cut down it grew back quickly, just as the wolf who was the first to be killed became the first to return from the dead. At that time, in the heyday of the Pawnee, anyone could look out on the prairie and know these things were true. He could hear the songs of the wolf, like the songs that took up a man's life from birth, he could see the wolf trotting, trotting, trotting, like a warrior, like people moving camp in the great coming and going that was life. . . .

[18] Barry Lopez, *Of Wolves and Men*, particularly Chapter III in relation to Chapter II.

One morning in Montana I sat in the home of an old man named Raven Bear, a
Crow. He had made a trip to Seattle a few years before to see his family. One day he
took his grandson and drove to the Olympic peninsula where he had heard there was a
commercial zoo with a number of wolves. He found the place, paid six dollars, and
went it. In a while he was ashamed he had brought his grandson there. The wolves
were all in small pens, obese animals suffering from diseases, he thought. The people
running the zoo told him the wolves were the last remnants of the Great Plains wolf,
canis lupus nubilis. "I wanted to tell the man he didn't know what he was saying,"
said Raven Bear, "but I didn't know how to do that. I just took the boy and left."

It was late at night. Raven Bear was sitting on top of a bunk bed with his stocking
feet hanging over the edge. After a while he said, "It hurts like hell, you know, to see
it finished. . . ."[19]

And the testimony of an Alaskan trapper, Lawrence Carson. He had
trailed a wolf, Lopez says, for twenty miles and "found him hung upside
down by the dragline on a steep hillside. He disentangled the wolf for the
purpose of taking pictures, then shot him in the head." "Lobo died as he had
lived," Carson wrote in his journal, "in defiance of all things that would dare
to conquer him. His bloody career was ended, but even in death his fiery
eyes and truculent jaws opened in a look of unremitting hate. Lobo, king of
his domain—and rightly a king he was called—was dead."

But Carson's thoughts reveal the ambivalence of some of these wolf
hunters, for he continues:

As I looked at his lifeless form, a feeling of condonation came over me. Even
though he had been a wanton destroyer of wild life and ill-deserving of mercy, somehow I felt sorry that he was gone. . . . Something has been taken away that would
never be put back in the scheme of things. Somehow I felt as if there was an irrepair-
able loss. The well-known axiom had again asserted itself; the sport and fun were not
in the kill, but in the chase.[20]

Another hunter, however, said after killing a pack of wolves from an
airplane, "Everytime I kill one it makes me feel good."[21] He spoke for many
others who have written and spoken on cleaning up the wilderness to make
it decent and habitable.

On the one hand, I think of the freedom of the wolf, a mortal freedom
that gave it slim chance of living a decade, but a freedom to be its nature,
highly adapted, not at all human, an easy survivor where most people could
find nothing to survive by unless the terrain were rapidly and radically
changed and reduced to human size. On the other hand, I think of people
wantonly killing wolves because they (the wolves) were "wanton destroyers
of wild life." I think of the thousands of wolves killed in order to allow deer,
elk, and moose to increase so that more hunters would come to shoot them. I

[19] Ibid., p. 134.
[20] Ibid., p. 163.
[21] Ibid., p. 162.

think of the wolf seen as a very evil person and therefore as free game for every killing lust that it symbolized and was killed for.

The psychological point is easily stated: we live out the very aspects of mind that we do not personally countenance and integrate; our destruction of wilderness in the name of human need, commercial survival, the rights of property, and the insistence of civilized identity can lead to the creation of another kind of wilderness, a barren wasteland of civilized successes, often lacking a sense for ritual, mystery, certainly disinclined to awe or wonder, excited by invention and advances of cultivated controls, a region of boredom, with little depth and richness of meaning, manic struggle for more and more of whatever is to be had, disabling anxiety, destructiveness far beyond the capacity or will of most creatures of the wild, and more sensibility for behavior than for freedom. We need to be equally clear, I believe, that in mind there are places like wildernesses, places that are not fit for personal habitation in which something like a wolf's howl is often the sound of the place, as well as the silence of a frozen night in which nothing happens perceptible to our eyes. It is a place without morality or our spoken word, without legislation, where jurisdiction is an issue of strength or numbers or stealth. There is no sentiment, no human right, no cultivation of taste except for the sake of survival. It is a place of bestial struggle, not mere urge, but wild desires to live in many forms, wild flights of owls and eagles and song birds, wild, quiet grazing, and wild-hiding in burrow. Where the accords and discords of personal relations cease, in the wilderness of mind, nothing personal is sought or preserved. But that place is very alive and subject to death.

The metaphors of wilderness allow us to focus the non-civilized aspects of the unpossessable openness of mind. If we absolutize our civilization, our collective work, and human reflection in everything around us, like gardens, we lose touch with non-human vastness, with life free of our imprint, with the wolf trotting and trotting and trotting, with the silence of the desire to be, with openness for being however it happens, with creation. The non-human also reflects to us huge dimensions of our own occurrence, which if not countenanced, can become deeply threatening to us. And in our fear of the non-humanity of mind, we can destroy our humanity by our own human effort to humanize, tame and cultivate everything. There is much that we should never touch and that we may look at only with humility and indirection.

Lopez describes the eye contact between wolves and their prey:

> They walk on the perimeter of caribou herds seemingly giving warning of their intent to kill. And the prey signals back. The moose trots toward them and the wolves leave. The pronghorn throws up his white rump as a sign to follow. A wounded cow stands up to be seen. And the prey behave strangely. . . . I called this exchange in which the animals appear to lock eyes and make a decision the conversation of death. It is a ceremonial exchange, the flesh of both animals, not the predator alone, choose

for the encounter to end in death. There is, at least, a sacred order in this. There is nobility.[22]

This "conversation" goes on only among wild animals, observes Lopez, not between wild and domestic animals. There is a quality of perception that indwells wild animals, that is part of their wildness. Wildness has autonomy. It is an irreplacable region of occurrence.

When dark and unapproachable wilderness is allowed, a suffusion can happen in which the density of light is freely allowed as being also like impenetrable darkness. Wolfish and elkish wildness grants a certain, almost eerie nobleness to life and death struggle. Light and dark interplay in shades which, when allowed their distance, can be as beautiful as they are unhuman. A strange kinship with the wild may be found that frees us from unalert repetition of it. As we allow it we step away from it in its great difference from our region of identity. An accord rings through discords. Indifference is again apparent.

[22] Ibid., p. 94.

The question about the essence of man is not a question about man.

Heidegger

IV

UTTER DARKNESS AND UTTER LIGHT

We turn to the immediacy of darkness and light in awareness. These dimensions are usually overlooked both as we think about awareness and as we think about myths. In both instances, we tend to focus on the character found in the milieu, on, for example, the Queen of Night or on the Creator of Light. But awareness occurs in immediate shades, in basic "elements" that are part of the awareness—not parts that come to being as we note them, but parts that are constitutive of awareness, that are aware as such. To be free with such elements is an important aspect of allowing our own awareness in a responsive and appropriate way. Utter darkness may be thought of as imprisonment. But it may also be found as the backdrop of an obscure freedom, wild and primordial, foreign to us, yet vaguely compelling.[1] And the freedom of pure light may threaten a freedom and madness no less than darkness without light. Both "elements" have been narrated in early Greek mythology, and that mythology may be taken as chronicling regions of alertness, beyond our ordinary grasp of reality, elements that are of our own being. Their geneology and ways of happening speak of how non-objective and non-particular alertness occurs, of the immediacy of mind un-circumscribed by any domain of identity.

1. The Elements of Hades and Zeus

Zeus and Hades are brothers. After they and their allies defeated Cronos and the Titans, Hades received the Underworld as a gift, and Zeus found his sway and aegis at Olympus. The element of Hades is darkness, not the moon-lit kind or even a moonless, starry kind, but a pitch darkness, a lightless realm of divinity that is impenetrable for living mortals. His realm is not at all like the Isles of the Blessed, that were to appear later in Greek imagery, where heroes find timeless fellowship together. Hades' place, a residence of the dead, is more like a prison and being taken there is like violent capture or rape. It's a heavy place—down, down, down—and is probably more akin to Saturn's element than it is even to Hades' spawning mother, Gaea, whose children replaced empty chaos. Saturn freezes and

---

[1] This is a freedom Foucault has detailed particularly in the later pages of *Madness and Civilization*, cf. chapter IX and Conclusion.

rigidifies. But Hades captures too, in darkness and invisibility, if with greater warmth.

Hades, in fact, took Erebus's place. Erebus was not spawned from Gaea, but from Chaos alone. Chaos "was" total emptiness until Gaea founded and gave forth the world. Erebus was a void under the earth, a vast emptiness in which nothing came together or happened: no spawning, no growth, no harvesting, no speaking, no sound, no decay, not a soul there: nothing. With Hades came place, darkness over against light, death, condemnation, imprisonment. The goddess Night, also the child of Chaos and not of Gaea, is closely related to Hades' place. She gave forth both Aether and Daylight, as well as Fate, Destiny, Death, Sleep, Dreams, Memesis, Old Age, and Strife, among others. (She is also the Grandmother of Strife's children which include Murder, Lying Words, Lawlessness, Famine, and Ruin).

Hades' place is no womb. But the place happens nonetheless: it is manifest in its darkness, and therein is Gaea's heritage and victory over Erebus. She enjoys part of her victory in the occurrence of death—death too, like all else, was absent in Erebus. And the misery and fate and con-demnations and violence and putrid hatreds and all that is dark and ugly and deathly have their place in Gaea's son's region, in which much that is awful and lifeless *happens*. This awful place means life.

Invisibility happens there too. Hades' gift from Gaea's monsters, the Cyclopes, was a helmet that made its wearer invisible. He received it at the same time that Zeus received the gift of lighting and thunderbolts from the Cyclopes, as they all prepared to defeat Cronos and send him and the Titans to the Underworld, to be guarded by the monsters of Gaea. Darkness for Hades means invisibility: not seeing, not coming out into the light, no can-celation of Lethe, no truth. One might wonder if Erebus isn't to be preferred, if one might choose, given the totally evasive and ungraspable region of Hades in all its terror. But Hades is there, quite utter and divine, forever canceling absence in his dark and elusive way.

Zeus's element is Aether. That is not to be forgotten. Aether, daughter of Night, grand-daughter of Chaos, not the child of Gaea or of Uranus or of Cronos. As far as I know Erebus and Night were the only children of Chaos. For Nothing at All, Chaos did a lot, giving as It did the element of Hades and, through Night, the element of Zeus. But Zeus's element is once removed from Chaos, and the distance between Aether and utter darkness must itself be considered divine. Aether is not mortal light, and though related to Day, is not the same as the light of Day. That light vanishes and comes back, it is suffused with Night, circumscribed by It, and reflects the mortality of human beings. Aether, to the contrary, is as pure as Hades' darkness is utter. Clear luminosity, ever light, total absence of darkness, clean separation from Mother Night. But grandchild of Chaos nonetheless. As awful for people in its purity as Darkness in its density, but in a totally different way. Zeus could see as far as he wanted in it. Vision was not obstructed. It neither held things up nor weighted them down. All that is in Aether appears. Its touch is manifestness. No closure, no hiddenness, no necessity, no requirements, not even one principle of order. Old and condemned Chaos, once removed, smiles absently in the no order, no destiny, no history, no person, no good, no evil, luminous and absolute indifference of Aether, Zeus's element.

But Zeus is also Gaea's son, who defeated Cronos, the victor over Chaos's victor. He gathers and produces wonderfully. Eos, Helius, Silene, and Caephalus, the dawn's cold wind, are evoked and ordered divinely to keep people in light. And Eos and Caephalus together gave people the morning star of hope, in the direction of light, as the cooling breeze announces the rising, cloud-reddening illumination. But Zeus also brought together, in Aether, gods and goddesses, not for the sake of people, but for divine fellowship. In Aether, where there is no dawn or darkness, there was no natural order at Zeus's arrival at Olympus. Only absolutely uncompromised light. Chaos gave no order.

Zeus's situation is not enviable, given its history. Uranus angered and over-worked Gaea. Cronos was a tyrant, selfish and alone, and Gaea would not tolerate his self-protective, ingesting refusal of a chancey kingdom and of growth and expansion. She did not like for her begotten to be closed off and held captive, and she was already giving Zeus, who had the Titans imprisoned, trouble when he emerged as King of heaven. Aether gave the conditions for divine sight, but nothing else. No guidelines or protection. In this unimpeded luminosity, the gods, now great and wonderful in their victory, gathered. And Zeus had to figure out how to rule with no precedent and with considerable danger.

What did the gods do in their element? Among many other things, they: partied, counseled, were angered, were envious, sang, danced, had entertainment by the Graces, made love, gave birth, ate, listened to the Muses sing, thought, held games, were worried, were eloquent, recalled things, built, were jealous, cultivated, tended, were violent, were deceitful, were creative, were fearful. Olympus was not an abstract place, but a place where much that we think of as finite and fallible went on. Limited orders were forever forming, new alliances were made. There were reconciliations and agreements, friendships and complicated forms of opposites. And through all this ran old Chaos's indestructible heritage through the parentage of Night: immutable, mysterious, marble-like, unbending Fate that Zeus had to live with and respect. Grandfather of Fate, Chaos, was omnipresent, imprisoned or not. Zeus might have control of mortal's lives, but he was in a universe he did not make with an element that was foreign to his own lineage, with a company of deathless, headstrong gods who would pay him only so much attention. The element, Aether, and the company of gods were absolutely present with anything Zeus might do in the direction of order, and we must not forget that Fate and Aether combine at Olympus to mean that orders of divinity, and consequently of mortals, occur in directions and in luminosity that are absolutely indifferent to even the god of sky, contracts, oaths, and the protection of guests. What Cronos set in motion, Fate and the Light spawned of Night, are immutable in the place where Zeus rules.

The elements of the brothers, Hades and Zeus, have the same parentage and are not related at all to Hades and Zeus. I suppose one could think of mortal light, Day, as between Darkness and Aether. But however they relate, they are in the same cosmos, and we have to think of this cosmos as one with their radical difference. Their sameness needs also to be noted. It is named as absence of order, as impenetrableness, as mystery, as most utterly other vis-à-vis the human. And they are both where the gods are, even though they are not related to those gods who indwell Darkness and Aether. They are each elements of the presence of life. They each cancel their Grandfather Chaos by defining places. They occur as the depth and vault of Gaea. In Aether Zeus could see to Hades, who dwelled in a kingdom which eliminated all Aether. Aether always made visible—the opposite of forgetfulness. They are the same in the sense that neither is mortal, neither is kind of energy, and that the immortality of both together is reflected in the mortality of a Day's passage.

When we interpret this situation of the gods and the difference and sameness of Darkness and Aether as expressing aspects of the realm of awareness, we are put in touch with a world of a remarkably wide and variant range. Particularly when we do not collapse the situation into an order dominated by any one part or group of the parts. Chaos is remembered in both concealment and illunination. Being alive is remembered in being deathly. Totally incomprehensible movement (Fate) is remembered in the highest and most divine orders, of which we are not the authors. The non-partiality of growth, nurturance, fecundity, and life itself is remembered in the process of continual emergence and overthrow of the greatest of powers. Even sleep, forgetfulness and deterioration recall death, loss of brightness, passage of all lumination. The non-order of simple, unpolluted clarity for sight means also the strength of ordering, the community of divines, the escapades, fights, and lives of the greatest powers, the present distance of utter darkness. The very presence of Hades (as well as Persephone, Charon, and particularly Dionysus) means that Darkness is endurable and dwellable. We are in a cosmos, a region in which the whole is implicated in the parts and in which the parts immediately reflect each other in their relations and discontinuities. Above all, in the situation of the gods, we are able to see that awareness is a region of relations, organically related, and not subject finally to explanation, but subject to description.

I am paying particular attention to the presence of Aether and Darkness in this account of cosmological extremities. I am assuming that these mythological elements reflect fundamental and given states of the realm of awareness, and that by reflecting these reflections we draw closer to our own immediacies and see them more clearly. Our therapeutic sensibility will also be affected as we find out what is at stake in an invididual life as one lives out denials and acceptances of these outer regions of the human cosmos.

2. Aether and Darkness are the Progeny of Chaos, Once Removed

They are not engendered by Uranus, Cronos or Gaea.

This most remarkable insight in the myths shows that hiddenness and luminosity, in their utterness, are not produced by any ordering direction. They do not reflect personality or intentionality or a cosmic plan. Although Uranus, with his power of generation, overcame Chaos, Night and her children remained, unrelated to all powers of decay and growth that were to emerge. Manifestness and hiddenness do not mean anything, although they constitute the boundaries of the world and are the elements associated with the highest and deepest dimensions of reality. They are both timeless in the sense that they have no structure or movement. That does not mean that they occur without reference to time or movement or structure. It means that with all time and differentiation occurs an element or aspect, pervasive and ever and utter, that is not the same as what goes on or as the going on itself, a freedom, if you will, that is no choice, no identity, and no history.

These regions are violated as I make anything of any sort finally definitive of my being or the being of the world, such as: identity, substance, what-I-want, definiteness itself, a virtue or all virtues, or volition. Aether and Darkness are present as non-identity, not-substance, not-what-I-want, not-definiteness, not-a-virtue, not-all-virtues, not-volition. They are what I fear most if I define my life by identities. Aether is where I can seem to fly endlessly and worldlessly. Darkness is where I can cease to see, grow, remember, etc. Each, in other words, can be remembered or forgotten in how I live. And each can mean absorption and loss of world. But together they are the regions that give place for all that is divine and free of human constriction. They are present as the awful regions that mean awe, wonder, self-transcendence, depth, profundity, inspiration for us in our particular ways of being aware. As the grand-progeny of Chaos they are free of everything that happens in their realm. They are never seen as objects or subjects or things or images. They are utter. And they mean for human identities an incomprehensible endlessness that has not begun and that is present, but on no terms, exactly.

3. Aether is the Element Related to Fate in Which Zeus Takes Counsel

Zeus is the father of the Fates of human being. As the grandchildren of Cronos they draw thread from a distaff, wind it, and cut it off. They have control over the time of birth, life, and death. But Fate is someone else. It was born of Night, too. It decrees, and Zeus has nothing to do with that. Fate does not mean anything that mortal minds can grasp. Fate is the "It is done" or "It is to be done" quality of experience in which one knows that he/she has no say, and not because someone else is more powerful, but because others are in the same decree. Surely a descendent of Chaos, with no perceptible over-arching intuition or wish, but ever-present in human experience. It both pervades structures of life and passes out of human comprehension, and it is not informed by the interests of human personality and character.

Zeus has interests and can be influenced by particular, human concerns and gifts, as well as by human beauty. He protects, and I suppose that he needs to protect, divine prerogatives. He is terrible in his power as far as individual mortals are concerned, but he is always having to do something. Aether has nothing to do. Fate does things, but without interest as far as I can tell. But Zeus is a ruler—a passionate, working, protecting, seeking god. He establishes. He is capricious and irrational. But he wants order among the gods. He wants order among people (he *will* have hospitality, for example). Even when he is doing just what he feels like doing, for no good reason, a person can see what he is up to and what is going on. His order is fallible, and he is always punishing, shoring up, taking sides, and repairing the damages. His divinity is found in his ordering power.

That power occurs in Aether, which is not a power, and is compromised by Fate, which has no known relation to ordering and generating powers and has plenty of relation to Chaos. The very element of Zeus's sight (and hearing too, I assume) offers no nurturance for what he sees, wants or plans. And Fate's iron decrees do not reflect his capacity for planning, much less his interestedness and passion. Fate and Aether do reflect each other in the absence of purpose, concern, personal meaning, and character. I suppose that means that in the acceptance of inevitability one draws closer to the pure light of divinity in Its lack of all personal intent.

In this absence Zeus also finds an unestablished region that means that the very condition of his divine perceptivity and sensibility make inevitable the contingency of all specific (divine) relations and situations. His unending activity reflects this non-familiar element that does nothing and thereby relativizes all his doings. Pure luminosity, in Its absence of meaning, means to us the light of everything as it is and the non-necessity of all orders. Just as Fate does with its ungrounded decrees.

4. Day, the Light of Mortals, Alternates with Night, Her Mother

Night, reclaims her regency regularly vis-à-vis her daughter. Day, aligned with Helios, Eos, and many other deities, has a daughter's power. But she is never free of her mother. Aether seems to have total freedom in Its unaltering, pervasive luminosity. It is constant and reflects Night in Its absence of content and Its incomprehensibility. That is a reflection of total independence. But Day dawns and dies. Her light, which gives us our perceptivity, comes and goes. She and Night together are the elements of mortality. Day means that our sight fails, even as she means that all things are visible for us only for a time. She gives no order except in being born and dying. She always means Night, who has an encompassing power: Night is not born; she is found there in the depth of day—always there, a primordial absence. Night is in an order, but she escapes it in the sense that she will be present when this order ceases or when Order is gone. Even Gaea has no power over Night.

Being in Day and Night, mortals are limited moments in the progeny of Chaos. Best not look for meaning in that. Meaning happens in Day and Night with their support, to the extent that one is not ensnared in Fate. Mortals reflect, limitedly, the directions of the gods, in the weaker sister of Aether. Being free is being in light and darkness and doing what one finds worth doing in living reference to the company and history of those who are to die. If I expect Aether in Day, I shall be terribly confused by dawn and twilight. No joy, no serenity. If I live as though day leads to Aether and not to Night, I shall be repeatedly confounded by Night (and by Day as well): I shall be depressed in Night, instead of living with her daughters Sleep and Dream before Day reborns in the gift of Caephelus and in the bright distance of the morning star. The hopes and rests and directions and meanings of mortals happen only in the realm of no-hope, no-rest, no-direction, and no-meaning.

The elements are not to be denied in our being. They are our place, our region, even when they are not our specific place and have no meaning in particular.

5. The Elements of Hades and Zeus do not Weep or Laugh

Through the myths I have been hearing aspects of awareness, which go far beyond personality, character, and individual identity. The elements of Utter Darkness and Aether are not objects of speculation or names for something outside the range of awareness. They name kinds of occurrences that are outside the range of our creating, ordering abilities. They name dimensions of all events which can not be had, objectified, or comprehended. With all orders—ontological, social, or psychological—Utter Darkness and Aether are density and clarity that cannot be achieved or lost or incorporated by an order. They name those most awesome dimensions, usually forgotten and avoided, that are with, but totally free of the most intense and important passions and powers of reality. They name the non-powers of awareness that are ever and utter and appear to us as boundless in themselves, but bounded by each other. They refuse resolution or reduction. They are the elements of pure sight and pure hiddenness with which we share intimacy in being utterly different from them. They are reflected in the light of day and the darkness of night, in circumscribed insights and nightmares, in thinking and confusion, in elucidation and oblivion. On our owning their presence depends our alertness with divinity and with the mortal freedom of our being. I shall not be free to live and die until I countenance the utter differences of Hades' and Zeus's elements.

We have already noted some of the things that go on in these elements or regions of occurrence. We have noted too that the Cosmos involves them both in their radical difference. If I fail to live out of this difference I shall most probably 'humanize' everything, even Night (into relative darkness, missing the quality of darkness itself), Chaos (into uncooperativeness, ignorance, bad upbringing, and so forth). Cronos (tick-tock, tape measures, and dots on a line), and Lethe (repression, bad memory, or psychological blockage). If I give one dominance over the other, losing again part of Old Chaos's progeny, I will not see the manifestness of darkness or the hiddenness of Aether. Either the underworld or the highest regions will dominate my way of being with things, such that Gaea tends to mean to me total obscurity or mystic luminosity. She is both at once and will not be without sky-horizon or inner darkness.

This at-onceness is the center of our final emphasis. The difference of the elements of Zeus and Hades is not the last word. Hades and Zeus are great gods in elements not of their own making. How they are together is part of how (the meaning of) being human is in Day and Night, and these elements of the soul are not affective or intuitional or passionate at all. They are Utter Darkness and Pure Light, without tears and without a smile.

6. Hades and Zeus Are Brothers; Darkness and Aether
   Have the Same Parentage

The oneness of the Greek Cosmos, with its overpowering diversity of divinities, each of whom is far greater than human character, will not be denied. The pervasive Darkness that is Hades' realm, and the pervasive Light that is Zeus's realm are as related as we are Zeus and Hades. Coming from two different parentages, the four relate like royal, intermarried families. They are related deeply in their histories—their being, as we know it, involves a tellable story of power, reign, murder, conspiracy, defeat, creation of kingdoms, and peaceable conjunction. That Chaos, through Erebus, becomes a place through Hades, and that Chaos, through Night, becomes a region of sight through Zeus is terribly remarkable. As remarkable as seeing that is never resolved into what is seen, as light that is so deeply related to darkness that in being light darkness is revealed, and in being darkness light is revealed.

The cosmic nature of the whole story means that each of the dinivities, and the place of each, manifests all the others in their relatedness. And the reflection of these divinities and realms in all our lives means at once a cosmos of infinitely related differences. Nietzsche, teacher of classic literature, forever in service of Dionysus and Apollo, speaks out of this world of the soul:

> You higher men, what do you think? Am I a soothsayer? A dreamer? A drunkard? An interpreter of dreams? A midnight bell? A drop of dew? A haze and fragrance of eternity? Do you hear it? Do you not smell it? Just now my world became perfect; midnight too is noon; pain too is a joy; curses too are a blessing; night too is a sun—go away or you will learn: a sage too is a fool.
>
> Have you ever said Yes to a single joy? O my friends, then you said Yes too to *all* woe. All things are entangled, ensnared, enamored; if ever you wanted one thing twice, if ever you said, "You please me, happiness! Abide, moment!" Then you wanted *all* back. All anew, all eternity, all entangled, ensnared, enamored—ah, then you *loved* the world. Eternal ones, love it eternally and evermore; and to woe too, you say: go, but return! *For all joy wants—eternity.*[2]

Chaos with definiteness. Night with light. Aether with Utter Darkness. And always at once.

The at-onceness of the Cosmos of related eternal differences means that we are with each other always in the reflection of the whole. When the whole is not reflected in a dominance by one of or more of the parts, a usurpation occurs that will not long be tolerated by the Cosmos itself.

7. Freedom and Fantasy

I have read these mythical relations as an account of how human being happens in a related universe far beyond its compass or meaning. Their power is in their indirectness: to be literal with them is always to miss them as myths. Their power to describe how things are, as well as their evocative and suggestive power, is in their non-literal manner. They give account of the happening of things in an "at once" that pervades even the most fundamental elements of all real things. Myths consequently have their meaning for human understanding in how they are appropriated, never in literal application. One must live with them, as one might live with a dream, until the gods begin to interact, as in a waking dream, alive and present without our guidance. Only then, I believe, will the full power of the myths of our tradition become consciously efficacious for the philosopher or therapist: not as a pattern for pathology or health, but as a region of powers with which we dwell, sane or not, as we interpret ourselves and our world.

Freedom with such powerful determinants? Hades found his freedom and his space of life in his element, Utter Darkness. And Zeus, in Aether. These non-orders, non-matters were the regions, the place-qualities in which

[2] Friedrich Nietzsche, *Thus spoke Zarathustra*, trans. W. Kaufman (N.Y.: Viking, 1966), p. 323.

these gods could make their mistakes, establish their domains, suffer, and perhaps even die. I do not mean to suggest that we are like Hades or Zeus or both together. They are not like persons. They are powers considerably in excess of all human character. I do mean to suggest that Utter Darkness and Aether, in the lineage of Chaos who countenanced no order, named the freedom of these two gods, and that like them we humans have our freedom, our "element." It is found in, shall I say "mything"? Or in free imagining? Or in countenancing with fantasy? Or in naming things as they have to be? I mean to say all those things. Our "element" is the orderless region of dreaming, fantasizing, concocting, seeing, imagining, intuiting. I say 'orderless' because the range of orders and worlds that can take place in this most awesome region appears unlimited. Who has counted the number of dream-orders that happen in dreaming? Does the region of fantasy tell us how to put things together? Do myths, as such, teach us right and wrong? They thrive on contradiction, battles of orders, differences among gods.

What is my life like when there is little imaginative psychic movement? Intelligent, perhaps, distracting, involved with things, but banal. Attentive to detail or spacy, responsible or separated from claims, but flat behind the surface. The absence of much psychic movement is like an absence of enlivening meaning or lively images in addition to everything that is going on. At an extreme, it is that dead sense that gives backdrop to whatever a suicidal person does. In a more ordinary way, the absence of psychic movement is lived as an absence of imagination, as a vague boredom with everything, as a feeling that nothing is deeply arresting, as not being very moved by anything. In that absence I do not get inside different ways of seeing or different ways of being and find how to be in those differences. I live a straight out identity of my own, no matter how devious or how upright, without being able to experience that identity from different postures and in different ways of being. I tend to be literal about everything. I like the finality of certainty. I want non-ambiguity. Fantasy seems the opposite of truth. Dreams seem the opposite of reality. And you seem vaguely distant behind whatever closeness we may achieve. When there is little imaginative, psychic movement in my life, I live as though I were not free.

Our freedom is found as we open to the region of fantasy without guarantees of stability, of life with multiple teloi, this region of fecundity that supports nothing for long that we hold dear, but engenders yet dearer, as well as more dreaded, things. We may also come to our element as we dwell with the myths, finding ourselves strangely free as we imagine the inevitable and discover that we are ourselves of an element that casts doubt on even the most inevitable things of all.

"Among the generations (in my past) there have probably been madmen, and their voices must be heard," Betty went on. "I'm not only a cemetery—in my brain there's an insane asylum, too. I hear the lunatics shriek their wild laughter. They pull at the bars and try to escape. Heredity cells aren't lost. If man is descended from an ape, he carries the genes of an ape in him, and if from a fish, there is something of the fish in him. Isn't it funny and frightening the same time?

Shosha, Isaac B. Singer

. . . . the action of an always incomplete knowledge, responding to an always unslaked passion to be known . . . .

Henry Corbin

I hear callers in the trees
but I stay in one place,
knowing motion is nothing
if I can't stand like this
hour after hour.

In this immobility a fire inflates,
and so much turbulence within the static—
the owls call, still in their tree.
They can see in the night, they don't need to move.
I don't move myself—the river moves

somewhere, the clouds without sound
move and move. They drift and disband.
The dogs are still, except for their jaws,
which click in the night.
They smell the darkness, they don't need to move.

My work is to stand still and see everything.
My work is to rethink the immobile,
the owl and dog, and without moving release them,
release myself, let everything live again,
recalled into movement and loved, wholly still.

"Still"
David Halpern

V

BEING AWARE

1. Immediate Awareness

Our account of immediate awareness has involved us in a variety of indirections: the metaphors and myths of Hermes, the happening of fantasy, the simultaneity of being one and being many, an interpretation of mind as world-event, finding ways to speak of being aware without subjective interest, attending to depth occurrences of polyvalences, remaining in touch with a dimension of happening free of identity and sense of self, the myths of light and dark, and so forth. We are cultivating a direction of interpretation that expects an awareness free of our particular interpretative interests as well as free of our conscious values and intentions. This kind of interpreting expects, sooner or later, to step back before awareness that is alert with itself in its own happening and that is not an activity of a knowing or desiring subject. We are dealing with that region of awareness that is neither moral nor immoral, that is not fixed by an overarching law, but that is nonetheless alert and alive as the occurrence of many relations of regions and things variously and finitely constituted.

A major blockage to expecting this alert immediacy is a conviction that the occurrence of being is always under subjective guidance. That guidance may be thought of idealistically as the subjectivity of mind, or intellectualistically as the ontological priority of conceptual and logical intelligence. It may be thought of theologically as the control of an intelligent or desiring being analogous to our identity-consciousness. These expectations constitute blockage to the immediate awareness that I have in mind if they are experienced as ultimate principles that describe being however it occurs.

We are opened to immediacy of awareness, however, if we let emptiness or openness or disclosure or transcience center our thinking. For example, when I allow each moment to dissolve as it happens, when I let things be without insisting on anything regarding them, no matter how much I insist and own my preferences for me in my own actions. I, in this freedom for transcience, may find a translucence and lightness in things quite the opposite of dense solidity and "material" heaviness. But whenever I impose desires on the occurrence of things, solidity usually dominates and the experiences of insistence and holding come to the fore. Insistence and holding are by no means necessarily bad or to be avoided, but they are not composed of translucent and light beings nonetheless. This solidity seems to be composed of the mediations of desires, which provide connections and continuities that otherwise do not happen. We make things that way. We make environments for ourselves that reflect our desires and the history of a complex of interests. These environments are mediated realities on which our survival depends. Their goal should be the nurture of the subject who desired them. We may give them such intensity of attention, however, that we forget the unmediated regions, often wild places in comparison to environments.

If I am able to empty myself of activity, however, and be utterly simple, alertness happens in the occurrence of whatever comes, not in my own activity. That kind of communion and nearness, which can be terrible if what comes is terrible, as well as lovely or awesome, simply does not happen when things occur heavily modified by conscious and unconscious directions inherent in my activity.

The shadow of any form of subjective guidance is guilt in the form of falling short of ideals imbedded in the person's desires and in the form of inability to meet the full scope of some demand or expectation, or other senses of inadequacy. If I am relieved of guilt by forgiveness I shall be joyful. But if I come in touch with a place where subjective guidance cannot occur, this very indifference threatens the whole scope of my expectations, both forgiven and unforgiven. I will feel my life to be threatened. Yet such a threat originates in the simple, immediate openness of mind for whatever happens. That openness is our availability for the presence of any happening of life. It is our being. Our being happens as immediate alertness, always capable of reflecting itself to itself and reflecting itself in the happening of things, always open in the presence of whatever happens, and also always capable, in its openness, of shutting itself off from parts of itself. In its simple immediacy our awareness is neither guilty nor justified nor forgiven. That simple, non-justifiable, non-subjective happening is extremely difficult for most of us to allow. We probably feel more at home with ourselves and more related to the world when we cover up this indifferent anonymous awareness. And we are thus inclined to cultivate forms of subtle holding-on, prescribing, directing, managing, and structuring. These are ways of perpetuating, with the skill of the desire to survive, the primacy of personal identity in relation to all being. Our well-being, however, depends also on our becoming free for the simple openness of immediate awareness.

Fichte and Schelling, following directions set by Kant's notions of imagination and the unity of reason, thought of immediate awareness as inherent in reflective acitvity. Immediate insight accompanies our knowledge of things, which knowledge depends on rational, mediational action. Schleiermacher used this same form of thought in showing that the feeling of absolute dependence accompanies our feelings of autonomy and freedom.[1]

Both Plato's account of *noesis* and Aristotle's of activity are in the background of the wide varieties of observations about intuition, insight, and immediate awareness. The dimension of immediacy that is usually missing, however, is history.

Immediate awareness is often taken as non-historical and hence as not reflective. In modern times we have been under the dominance of Leibnitz's, Descartes's, and Kant's notions of rational activity. Each of them saw that mental certainty is immediately alert, but none of them thought of awareness as happening in the world in ways that are self-aware and not subjective, conceptual, or "rational." Immediate awareness for them, as well as for Fichte, Schelling, and Schleiermacher is *intrinsically* non-historical, because it is intrinsically conscious. Schleiermacher was particularly astute in showing that immediate awareness is found always in historical circumstances. But as a capacity or *Vermögen*, he, like Kant, could not think of immediate awareness itself as historically generated and subject to eradication and replacement by historical events.[2] They have led us to think of awareness itself as being non-historical presence with historical happenings. Even Hegel, who generated the disciplines of the history of philosophy and the history of ideas, could not think of consciousness except by reference to timeless essences which constitute consciousness.[3]

This conviction that awareness itself is not historical has meant that we are prone to think of immediate awareness as non-reflective and consequently as blind and incapable of becoming self-aware. We might think of the basis of consciousness as libidinous urge, as timeless essences, or as an essence of our being. In any case the essential qualitative difference between the two realms of timeless and temporal means that symbols or images are

[1] I have in mind most particularly Fichte's later thought, which reached unparalleled expression in his *Wissenschaftslehre* of 1810 (although his notion of intuition is already quite present in WL of 1794), and both Schelling's early essays on aesthetics and his later ones on mythology and revelation. See Schleiermacher's *Speeches*, his Introduction to *The Christian Faith*, and his *Lectures in Ethics*.

[2] See my "Schleiermacher and the Problem of Divine Immediacy," *Religious Studies*, (Winter 1969).

[3] Immediate awareness, according to Hegel, is absurd in the sense that there is no perceiving subject in pure immediacy. There must be relation for there to be consciousness. There is, however, in his thought the immediacy of being dialectically conscious. The very occurrence of dialectic is immediate, and in that immediacy of the whole an individual consciousness is impelled to the development that its place and time demand through contradiction. The inevitabilities of development, i.e., the principles of dialectic, however, are not themselves historical. Hegel is still very much in the Greek web of thinking of non-temporal things as gaining space and time through an incarnational process. That means that the notion of two worlds, one timeless and the other temporal, invests his thought at every point with the consequence that he thinks of consciousness as the constant conjunction of both worlds, like Mary's womb.

necessary before meaningful relation can be established between the "Unconscious," or other forms of primordial awareness, and the person. In such ways of thinking, history has to do only with the mediating symbols—that is, different images have symbolic power at different times for traceable reasons—and with appropriating personal consciousness, for example how people have heard and come to terms with the non-symbolic through the symbolic. Re-presentations form the center of this attention, and the cultivation of immediacies seems foreign and counter-intuitive.

In the course of this chapter, we shall pay particular attention to those occurrences which point out the development and self-awareness of immediate states of mind. The growth of immediate self-awareness is an aspect of the emergence of human well-being.

2. An Instance of the Growth of Immediate Self-Awareness
   in a Series of Dreams

A man had a series of dreams over a seven year period in which, first, an older therapist appeared. This older man was in waking life a therapist in another country known to the dreamer, but the dreamer has not been in therapy with him. In those dreams, the therapist appeared as a guide who showed the dreamer helpful things, as a comforter who brought solace, and as a presence who was unambiguously supportive in a way that felt healing to the dreamer. These dreams brought with them a vague sense of growth and development in ways the dreamer could not describe.

After four years, involving half a dozen dreams of the older therapist, the therapist in the dreams changed. He was now younger than the first one, but older than the dreamer. He lived in the same country as the first therapist, but was a citizen of the dreamer's country. He was a less comforting figure and more active. He was aggressive, though supportive. He appeared creative and dynamic, somewhat skeptical, a little distant. The dreamer knew him in waking life primarily in working situations in which the two men were often in disagreement. He was also a therapist in waking life, and the dreamer felt "younger and behind" the older man. In the dreams the therapist was nonetheless a healer, one who showed ways and lent a most nurturing presence.

In three years, this therapist appeared in eight dreams. Then the dreamer dreamt himself giving solace to a huge, clumsy, weeping younger man. In another dream he guided a confused young man. In a third dream he supported the mother of a young child. In other dreams, coming in a short period of time, he allowed a tiny, ant-sized infant to die and withstood its mother's displeasure with a sense that the infant's death was appropriate. He befriended a suffering man, listened to another man's troubles, and stood quietly firm in the presence of a troubled woman's rage.

The therapist in this man had become self-aware over a period of time. One could say that the dreamer had become more autonomous and independent, but that is a misleading way to describe the development if "autonomous and independent" refer to his waking consciousness. He was indeed stronger and more autonomous in his waking life. But the development in his dreams expressed a non-voluntary process of growth in which the healing, guiding, and nurturing abilities in his awareness came slowly to a sense of themselves as they fancied themselves first as an old, foreign man (with whom the dreamer sometimes spoke the therapist's native language in the dreams), then as a bridging man, and finally as the dreamer himself. All this is in the fancy of dreaming, over which the dreamer exercised no conscious control. In waking life, the dreamer experienced the last awareness of the dreams as a quiet sense, a stillness, he said, that was the opposite of anxiety. He was more open to affection. He did not look away, he reported, when feelings became intense at times when he did not choose to feel intense. He said that he had a sense of openness to whatever came to him in deeply communicative ways. The immediate awarenesses of both those mental aspects, viz., the aspects that needed help and the given capacities for response to those needs, developed into senses of themselves which could relate to each other as they were in a region of alertness that was not the same as the dreamer's personal, waking consciousness.[4]

3. An Instance of Self-Awareness as a World-Event

We begin with an excerpt from a therapy situation, about two minutes into the session. A forty year-old woman, who is in a professional training program, and who has been in therapy for one and a half years, comes to a break-through:

A: I am late because I . . . because I am not worthy to take your time.

T: You do not feel worthy to take my time?

A: (crying) No. I have to give you something to deserve this. I have nothing to give. I'm not changing fast enough. I'm letting you down . . . I defend myself by feeling responsible for you. . . .

Pause

T: And if you did not defend yourself?

A: I would feel so unguarded. I would be unguarded. I would receive and not be worthy. . . .

If I did not follow my commitments I would be so open to hurt. If I am unguarded here, I will want this kind of relation all the time, and I won't have it. I've never had it before. If I am unguarded with you, I will want to receive like I receive here and. . . .

[4] For examples of similar developments of immediate self-awareness in waking dreams, see Gerald Epstein, *Waking Dream Therapy*.

A long silence. A. continues to cry.

T: If you are open to receiving, perhaps you will find that you receive more.

A: Maybe . . . But I would . . . I don't know . . . I feel a commitment to you to improve. I will let you down if I don't improve.

T: To me? And to yourself?

A: Yes. But, I've promised myself to improve because you have given me this.

T: It sounds like your commitment to improve for my sake guards you.

A: Yes, it does. It protects me from receiving when I'm not worthy. But I *have* to change.

T: If you allowed yourself to receive, say this hour, without regard to being worthy or not worthy, would you have changed?

A: (After crying and a long silence) Yes.

This issue continued for the hour as A. moved back and forth among her feeling committed to changing, being guarded against open reception of anything, and using her commitment to change in therapy as a bloc against the therapy itself. She found that her sense of unworthiness was part of the meaning of her "not changing, not working hard enough." She said, "When I stopped trying to do things for my brother all the time, we began to relate well for the first time." She focused repeatedly on the therapy itself as what was problematic, because she would have to be free simply for herself, regardless her merit or lack of it, and give up hold even on the ballast of feeling unworthy. She wanted to be punished severly, to be beaten, for her unworthiness. She wanted to escape it. She did not want to let it go. She found the beginning of what became a dissolution of her blockage vis-à-vis receptiveness and non-defensive openness. That worked a beginning for a significant change in her life.

I use this example to put us in touch with the kind of therapeutic happening in words in which a period of work culminates in a person's finding his/her "issue" in an intense, experiential way and also finding at least the possibility of an acceptable way to live with or through the problem. We speak of a growth of awareness, of changing structures, of new ways of being.

In this particular situation, A. had been moving toward this discovery for some time. She had finally, unconsciously pushed the issue by uncharacteristic and repeated lateness to therapy. At one level of relation she was friendly, apologetic, and had reasonable excuses. At another level she was intense, hard, and angry. In the immediate background were her hard early life, filled with threat and psychological violence, her survival by responsible, self-giving kindness (particularly toward her parents, both of whom were psychologically unstable), her sense of being nothing of value, her collapsing marriage, her care for her child, and her desire to be able to love and be loved. She knew about all of these and other relevant things. But taken together, in the therapy situation, they were part of a much larger immediate awareness that was pushing for resolution in a growing tension among a sense of being without love, a desire for love, an experience of love in therapy, and a sense that openness for love and loving would cause her unbearable pain. Her link to this awareness was the strength of her commitments, short of fully open love, but full of care, and her deep dissatisfaction with the limits of relation only by dedication. She was, of course, deeply shaken as this immediate awareness became increasingly self-aware. Not that she knew about it. That tense relation of factors became itself more and more aware and her own relation to that growing awareness had fewer and fewer defenses, until she was able at once to be aware and to accept consciously that awareness, to dwell in it and to survive. Self-awareness in this context is not the same experience as that of knowing about oneself, any more than being able to participate actively in a fantasy is the same as knowing about the fantasy.

Words in the therapeutic relation bore A. to and into her emerging, depth self-awareness. At an earlier time she did not know about the components of her state of being that had begun to emerge. Nor could she "go" there or dwell there. She was not aware of herself in herself there. Over many hours she spoke of experiences with her husband, child, friends, brothers, sisters, and parents. As she spoke in dialogue with the therapist she felt the experiences of which she spoke, saw things she had not seen, changed her opinions about some things, felt differently about other things. She found that she need hide nothing, that she could allow the therapist to share with her her experiences. She came to remember forgotten parts of her life. Over and over again words bore her into unknown parts of her life, or bore these parts to her, and these parts glowed like illuminated scenes in which she came to participate and to recall as she experienced other things. Awareness too dim to look at pushed her without her knowing it as she chose topics in therapy hours, as she followed associations, as she encountered the therapist. These dim awarenesses are what came to light. She found herself in awarenesses about which she did not know. She became able to live out of awarenesses that she learned to recognize and allow to be present in how she was conscious with things.

This lengthy process itself grew to self-alertness. She came to know about herself through a process of emerging awareness that was not itself a knowledge about anything. It became immediately self-aware, this therapeutic process, and she was changing not through deprivation, oppression, and denial, as had been customary in her life, but by a growth of awareness through the relations of trust, allowance, and acceptance that felt healing rather than injurious, regardless the pain. She was not doing the process but, as a person, she underwent the process, cooperating, responding, resisting, refusing, and so forth. For her in particular, her personal receptivity with a non-voluntary process was closely linked to the suffering she sought to eliminate. As she gave way to the growth of awareness, a significant part of the therapy happened. The awarenesses that grew in the therapeutic relation influenced her and changed her. Her thoughts, desires, and attitudes all shifted. She opened to growth that took place in a region that transcended who she was.

Her desire for change, her developing trust of the therapeutic situation and of the therapist, and her verbalizing all appear to be conditions for the process. But the process itself was not the same as the conditions. Her mind was changed by a growth of immediate self-alertness in the therapeutic experiences, and that change allowed the person, A., to appropriate new ways of being and to be appropriated by them. She in particular found that she had to free herself from one of her dominant traits, her predisposition for stern commitment that carried the meaning of survival, but the absence of love, as she drew closer to the experiences of open trusting, and being trusted openly. She began to learn a different orientation for commitment. Above all she was able to give up her preoccupation with being worthy or unworthy as awareness of open acceptance and allowance grew in her.

I note particularly the remarkable ability of words to carry hidden and forgotten meanings and experiences. They appeared to function as mediators or messengers for A. between awarenesses, as yet unknown, and consciously intended meanings. She wanted to be *independent*, she said. At first she thought that meant freedom from her husband's income, although it came to mean her being responsive to her own soul without external justification (from the therapist or someone else). She wanted to be able to *love*, she said. At first that seemed to mean for her primarily orgasmic sex with someone to whom she was wholly given. It came to mean non-defensive and non-judgmental reception of the people in the world around her, less search for love, and more openness to free givens: it came to mean openness to her own being without justifications. All the time, words. Words that bore drifts of awareness about which she had no notion, viz. that she could be without justifications. Words that bore the awarenesses in the therapy, the new situation of allowance that she at first could not recognize even though she was in it. Words that formed meanings which surprised her and caught her off-guard, revealing that she was too defensive to allow the love she wanted. Words that said what she had not intended to say. Words that brought her to what she could not say. Words spun images, just as images spun words. But in her case, words carried her more often than non-verbal images to the places of hidden and unknown awareness. Her words not only communicated to her the hidden and allowed the illumination of the hidden. They communicated her to the hidden and facilitated the remarkable process of growth in awareness in which unknown regions became able to communicate themselves before she came to know them.

4. Words in Mind: Immediate Awareness In Words

Words bear awareness. We become who we are through the language we come to speak. Different manners of speech bring different ways of feeling, relating, and thinking. A highly stylized way of speaking, for example, engenders relational attitudes that are almost unthinkable in a naturally informal society.[5] Negotiators are familiar with the importance of changing hostile rhetoric in order to create "the right atmosphere" for positive compromise. A language dominated by verbs and gerunds engenders a different sensibility than a language dominated by substantives. Taken in usage-groups words form pre-judgments about relevance, acceptability, and other values. We are disinclined, for good reason, to use the language of music in computer engineering. "Universe of discourse" we say, when we talk about regions of words that carry their own interests and standards. "Freedom" and "dignity" are archaic signs of a dead past in B. F. Skinner's verbal region. But those words carry deep emotion and relevance in the language of humanistic psychology and among people newly emerged from an oppressive dictatorship.

Words may name experiences and beings that tend to be forgotten at a given time. The simple meaning of *is*, for example, is far more difficult to recall presently than the meaning of *apply*. We saw in chapter one that *mind* names far more than intellection, and the word, fully recalled, helps to establish contact with a remarkable, often forgotten kind of occurrence. Forgetfulness of mind as well as the forgotten are born with the word's being spoken. Because of the meaning that the word bears, we are able to recall what we forget in the way we remember the word. The word itself carries this ability or capacity for remembering.

Gaston Bachelard has shown how words bear awareness in reverie.[6] By *reverie* he means a state of mind in which words come to presence bearing experiences and depth of meaning that originate outside of our region of consciousness and identity. As our control of language gives way to the words themselves, a state of mind develops in which mind occurs in awareness of itself as words come forth. The feminine dimension of mind, for example, becomes more and more apparent and simultaneously, more and more alive as one simply allows the issuance of words and sounds. A space—a spaciousness—emerges that nurtures words and relations of words, not for a purpose other than the nurturing itself. "A feminine silence" is another phrase Bachelard uses, in which communication goes on as whatever process

[5] Manners of speech can also be developed out of emerging forms of behavior, but presently my concern is with the creative and formative power of words.

[6] The following remarks are based on *The Poetics of Reverie* (Boston: Beacon, 1971). Bachelard's account is often in a language that means that awareness is in fundamental separation from world. This Cartesian drift on his part is unfortunate, but his account of reverie is often helpful and original in spite of the detriment of his ontological legacy.

takes place in the space of allowance. Fantasies grow, take on lives of their own through words in the states of reverie he describes. One lives through the sounds of a poem or simply hears the gender *in* words or hears sound upon sound that create word-images which merge and relate with other images. Awareness without concepts and a deep unfolding of mind's engendering go on. One may then witness the mind's reflecting itself to itself in words of creation, images of dancing water welling up from a spring and over the tiered grotto. We do not speak the words or images. We learn, in reverie, to hear what we do not speak and often at first do not understand.

A profound androgyny takes place in this immediacy in which masculine and feminine elements interplay, sometimes like a dream of a couple in intercourse without clear distinction of who is male and who is female, sometimes like the coming of light into a receptive darkness, sometimes like a project born of hearing words previously unknown.

Any situation of open trust, alertness, and hearing is like reverie in the sense that a person is in a state of mind in which heeding and the disclosure of things outside our own identities are the prominent characteristics. Such situations are themselves androgynous, regardless the physical sex of the participants. Generative space for the incoming, the coming of incipient powers for development, coupling of meanings, and presences: a male/ female happens in such events. In that kind of situation, words themselves may carry the non-voluntary, immediate meanings. I may become frightened when the words "he bore me away" come suddenly to mind. Or when you say, "Is that what you mean," I may begin to cry. In such instances, the words bear experiences that come to presence with the words. By association, we say. But *association* can be an occurrence in which words immediately bear experiences and meaning and I am moved by them.

When words happen as events that come on their own, bearing whatever, we can be particularly attuned to their awareness, much affected with them. They can provide structures of relations, networks, in which we may come to see what was outside of our consciousness. They can grow and develop awarenesses outside of our instrumentation. Born in mind, they can be also mind aborning.

5. Meaning and Awareness Without Agency:
Immediate Awareness in Communicative Events

We are familiar with the experience of hearing what is not said explicitly, and we are familiar with the statement, "he/she means that . . . ," when the meaning is expressed, but not stated explicitly. We are familiar with hearing what we cannot say explicitly in a poem, personal experience, music, or other events. H. G. Gadamer has shown how language itself occurs as an expressive unity that communicates more than any set of literal statements could say.[7] *Meaning* is neither exclusively literal nor always susceptible to direct statement, and if one tries to "boil down" or render literal most communications, one simply does not understand the meaning of what is said. The understanding of meaning is found primarily in the language, in the communication, and not in "mere" observations about the communication after the communication has taken place. Language happens as an enormous, and probably infinite from any one point of view, context of communication. This context is always communicated to some degree in particular uses of language. The very event of words, of coming to word, bears meaning, as well as meanings, that grant place for relation and reference, that make claim on people, and that open up as an occurrence of reality. Learning to understand is developing an immediate sense in one's communications for the meanings of communication and for the larger whole within which a communication takes place.

One such intuitive understanding happens as sympathy for communicative occurrence. A person may be with others communicatively, but be so fixed on the details of what is communicated that he/she has no apparent sense of the larger communicative unity that is happening with the particulars. I knew a young therapist, for example, who seemed to me to be right in most of what he said about the patients with whom he worked, but who had very little sense for the communication as such that went on. Another therapist, whose credentials were less impressive, and who had worked with disturbed people for some time, had a remarkable therapeutic ability. She seemed always to hear how and who a person was with an almost unnerving sense for the unstated meaning of statements, postures, moods, and so forth. She had a sympathy for the being of a particular person, an ability to be in touch, that was itself an understanding of the person. She could "go with" the person, "stay with him/her," and above all allow the person's depth issues to be expressed without interference. She could allow the larger communicative event to be her understanding in the sense that she was in tune with it, reflected it on its terms, and allowed it to mold her words and postures. Her intellect and prejudices and interests followed the communications, allowing them their claim and the expressive place they engendered, and giving way to the fantasies they called up. She allowed the meaning of a given situation to occur. The other, less experienced therapist tended to lose meaning and understanding by finding signs and references exclusive of the larger expressive occurrence. He saw "compulsion," for example, but failed to be alert with the meaning of the compulsive awareness *in* its happening.

The ungraspable, reflective dimensions of communicating are the very communicative happening. These dimensions are words, when *words* means

[7] H. G. Gadamer, *Truth and Method* (N.Y., Seabury Press, 1971). See particularly p. 449, although the book as a whole develops and establishes this claim.

communicative expressions. And they are lost in their meaning by reductions which focus on the parts of what is said or expressed exclusive of the communicative event itself. As Gadamer puts it, "To say what one means, to make oneself understood . . . is to hold what is said together with an infinity of what is unsaid in the unity of meaning and to let it be understood as such."[8]

In many cases therapy occurs by virtue of the communication that develops between two or more people rather than because of what is discussed. Often in such instances, nothing in particular is resolved, or if some resolutions of problems occur, they are incidental to the therapy. In one instance, a young African man went through a year of therapy speaking in his own tongue with a therapist who did not understand one word of that language. The young man lay on a couch and in his monologue told his father everything that he had ever wanted to say to him. The therapist was a considerably older European man who listened attentively to the affections, moods, feelings. He was totally supportive, and he expressed open sympathy for the young man's struggle. The older therapist's loving presence and the young man's freedom to be unrestrained and open in his conversations with his father developed into a freeing experience that he later described as irreplaceable in his own development. Open, free communication in relation to the oppressive limits that his father meant to him appear to have been at the center of the healing. His awareness came to word in a situation that reflected central issues, such as an old, well-established man's sympathy with a young man's rejection of his fathers's traditional authority, the old man's allowance of the young man's own language, the affective tie between the young and old men, independent of exactnesses or literalisms, etc.[9]

Communicating as such is the way in which multiple regions of awareness that are foreign to a person come to word. These regions can be owned, allowed, and appropriated in the communicative situation, rather than primarily through a specifically cognizing or recognizing act. I may

[8] Ibid., p. 445. This translation is by Robert Orr in an unpublished dissertation, *The Meaning of Transcendence*, Vanderbilt University, 1979. Related to our present interests, Orr writes, "Gadamer's 'infinity of meaning' is not to be understood as intelligible presence. And because it is not so understood, the meaning of any linguistic expression can never be fulfilled eidetically, nor by implication can it ever be exhausted by any set of strictly univocal, exact representations. Language in essence is neither univocal nor exact" (p. 48).

[9] In Freudian analysis, *transference* and *countertransference* are the names often used for this kind of communication. I am not using these words because of their heavy dependence on a tradition whose assumptions and language regarding human being need alteration. The relations that are named by "transference" and "countertransference," however, are crucial therapeutic events, and they should be used as phenomena of reflective communication. The notion of "projection" also has usually involved an assumption of isolated projective consciousness, with little or no sense for the historical commonality of human awareness and existence, and consequently the word is also best dropped.

countenance my bestiality, my hatred of my sister, or my religious passion in deep interaction with you long before I can report accurately on what I have experienced. Responsibility is not first and foremost an issue of voluntary choice. It is an issue of responding with how things are. Being responsible is the opposite of being deceived in the sense that as responsible I am free for what happens without insisting that occurrences be other than how they are or that they bear meanings other than their own or that they communicate themselves differently. Then I am free to say yes or no in relation with things. I may despise them or love them or be indifferent with them, but in any case I will be in communication with them, responsible with them. I will allow them as the part of world and awareness that they inhabit. I will be free for their commonality as meaning with all in the world, whether or not I have dealt with them intellectually.

That kind of freedom and responsibility may well develop as I learn to be open with my awareness by being with your openness with me and my openness with you. Perhaps I am factually mistaken in what I tell you about my father's behavior when I was three. You and I both may mistake what is the meaning of my constricted way of being. We might not even recognize the issue when it is expressed in a dream or in my reticence with you one day. But we do allow the development of fantasy, openness between us, and the rightfulness of any awareness. The meaning of what comes out in this communicating is not dependent on recognition. My own particular way of being becomes available for modification by my being open to whatever is present. That openness is itself responsive with the openness of awareness and with the freedom for many differences that characterize awareness. The meaning of events as giving place, relation, and existence is heard and resonated in the openness itself. Availability for things as they happen in this openness reflects the indifference of awareness, its hospitality and elemental regard for opposites, differences, and radical contradictions. In my openness for whatever appears, the meanings of things, as well as the meaning of the openness itself, provide a growth and development of personal consciousness. Just as my consciousness grows as I learn to speak a language because of the language, my consciousness grows as fantasies, feelings, and relations are allowed. "He is a different person," we say, "since he fell in love." Or, "since her death, he has not been the same." Fundamental changes occur in consciousness and identity through non-voluntary events that make their first difference through their presence, not through an agent's intentional appropriation of them.

Things grow consciousness through their presence, because they are aware events, happening in relation with this conscious identity, providing intrinsic difference, diversity, new dimensions within which other experiences occur. As I experience your hostility in the presence of her new, and, let us say, unexpected love of me, I transcend your negativity in my happy, life-affirming surprise. In a significant therapeutic breakthrough, people often are immediately attuned to the surprising and creative dimension of things. They enjoy a sense of well-being that their therapists can share only at a distance because that sense is the experience of the other things of their environment with their own break-through. When I allow the contradictoriness and deathliness of my awareness, optimism founded on simple identity and insistence on the positive-for-me becomes impossible. In these and countless other instances, the presence of allowed experiences and things changes one's conscious identity whether or not one does something special with them.

Therapeutic interpretation appears to occur in a similar way. When a person is deeply and trustingly in touch with another, and when their communication is therapeutically oriented, interpretations alter who one is whether or not one intellectually grasps the interpretation. Your words disclose the overlooked and forgotten in my awareness. They engender recall in me; they allow me to see relations and presences. Your interpretive words happen as disclosing messengers that bear the context of our relation, the quality of your insight, the meaning of our presence together, my own disclosure, and some of the relations of what you say with other parts of me.

This conversation occurred in the session following the one quoted above in section one:

"I neither give nor receive," said A. "I withold myself." The therapist reflected those words back to her, in the context of her long struggle to come to the point of being able to see her self-withholding. She then said that she had nothing to give. The therapist pointed out that giving and receiving of herself were the issue she had brought up. She said that she could only give and receive with one (unavailable) man. Then, through further talk, she saw that she was again hiding from what she had seen moments earlier. She raised her guilt and self-hatred, her selfishness, and experiences in her early life. Each time she appeared to be hiding from what was most difficult for her, giving and receiving instead of withdrawing. The therapist was interpreting as he kept those issues in the forefront and as he saw the other issues, in this context, as ways of withdrawing from the dominant issue. But A. found at each round of obfuscation a way in which she had in fact justified her withdrawal from people, a way of withdrawing which perpetuated the suffering that had brought her to therapy. The therapist's interpretive communication occasioned continued contact with a most dreaded set of possibilities and recognitions.

In such therapeutic events, the openness of people together, the openness of their language together, the openness of awareness, and the openness of the world as horizon and history of all happening form a remarkable resonance. The resonance may take many hours to develop. Trust and fear are always issues. Learning to allow closures to fall away may be impossible for many people. The demands for alert and free simplicity on the part of the therapist can be extremely difficult if he/she is partially closed to the awareness that is coming out. But when it happens: release, a sense of world-openness, kinship beyond any specific identity, meaning with death, preparedness to be, identity without blockage or insisting refusal of the boundaries in mind. Such open simplicity might come only in a moment or two. Or it might form into a continuing background state of mind. It might happen as an intimation of how things might be. Or it might happen as a sense of something lost, as a deepening nostalgia. However it happens, it carries with it a sense of being well and being human. This kind of occurrence suggests to me that openness for disclosure, hiddenness, and difference is the essence of human being and that language, world, and human being are of the same openness, a perpetual mystery that grants, allows, and engenders without ever making a choice or doing a deed. Individually we seek to articulate ourselves in an openness that gives itself as availability for things to occur on their own terms, free to be, and thus things that give themselves forth as free occurrence.

6. The Presentation of Awareness and Agency

In the preceding section I have noted how growth in the consciousness of identity may happen without specific actions on the part of one's agency, but with open allowance of words, fantasies, relations, and things. Awareness in particular is presented by fantasies, words, relations, and things, and a good analogy for such a presentation is a work of art.[10] A painting, for example, presents something that is already present in some fashion. The idea of re-presentation, however, carries the sense of mere repetition and often accuracy of presentation becomes the pre-occupation of those interpreting the work under the influence of the notion of re-presentation. A painting presents in the sense that it brings something forth in its own way. On the one hand, the painting is autonomous; it communicates itself, engenders possibilities, bears a history, provides its place, and may be a center of attention. It can influence, communicate, and be taken on its own terms. Yet it also bears its subject matter—the mountain, the prince, the battle. It is a view of something else which presents what is viewed or experienced. Even if one tries merely to copy something, the painting still presents the painted, without, in this case, appreciable self-consciousness in the presentation. We can say that a painting brings something to presence, that it makes a difference by being a presentation, and that what is presented, how it is in the world, is modified by the presentation.

Analogously, when a fantasy occurs in an individuals's particular alertness, the fantasy, as an autonomous event, presents something. A state of awareness, erotic desire for example, is borne by the window through which

---

[10] I draw heavily from H. G. Gadamer's *Truth and Method* in the following notion of artistic presentation.

a coupling of naked bodies is vaguely apparent. The traffic outside the window carries meaning in the relation of the observer and the window. The red-headed woman who moves away from the scene, taking the observer with her, the long path to the left with the laughing young women, the buildings around them, and the puzzled young girl in their midst—they each present awarenesses. And the fantasy as a whole is itself an awareness. Presenting is going on. The remembered fantasy (or words in other instances) modifies the person, is an event which immediately reflects the person in a larger region of awareness, and thereby engenders new possibilities and a broadened sense of self.

The autonomy of fantasies and words carries an intrinsic relation with what is presented. As presenting, a fantasy brings something forth, i.e., something occurs in the fantasy. The presented is not merely pointed to or pointed out; it happens in the fantasy event. As self-presenting things, beings happen as communications. We are familiar with the significance of presentations in highly formed situations, such as in diplomatic arrangements in which the timing, setting, background, etc. make the presentation. Readjust the Vice President's seat to the other side of the Prime Minister's, and you present the Prime Minister's office as "below" the Vice President's. The Prime Minister is degraded *in* the situation. He and his office are insulted in their presentation in this instance, but they happen in it, are part of the presentation, and they are in consequence vulnerable in the presentational occurrence.

Awareness happening as word and fantasy is in the presentation. The presentation's own history—its language, the tradition borne by the fantasy, the space of presentation, the other factors envisioning it—intrinsically affects the presented. When the awareness of sexual desire, for example, happens as an image of naked, free, and happy abandon in an expansive, green park, the desire itself occurs. It is not identical with the fantasy, but it is in the fantasy and part of it. It is vulnerable to its presentational expression. In this case it blossoms out. Coming to fantasy and word modifies the presented. Creation and destruction of awareness can occur through their presentation, as well as elaboration and diminution.

I think of a child whose new stepfather was highly jealous of her. She was in a situation that developed into cruel hatred, a situation in which she deteriorated psychologically, found no good sense of herself and became a vacant-eyed, crumpled little girl. She was not identical with the situation that presented her to society and society to her. She could have developed differently. She could still be helped. But she was certainly a part of her situation.

A man lived through a fantasy of falling, taking a part in it through a waking dream. He felt the fall. He endured the intense anxiety. He felt the crushing end as he hit the ground. He panted and moaned and lived. The awareness presented in the fantasy was changed, weakened, brought to light.

A woman in active imagination found a huge cross on a beach to which she held while the sea raged and pulled at her. The cross withstood the storm and became a focus of growing strength for the woman. The awareness presented in the cross grew and developed.

As awarenesses come to further expression, some of their possibilities and limitations are accentuated. They gain a definiteness in a person's setting. They share meanings with other attitudes, identities, and horizons of possibilities. They take shape in highly complex histories. How the awareness of spirited aggression finds itself in this timid person's personal life accentuated its possibilities for destruction, intense self-presentation, and aggravation. But in your life, perhaps, this awareness is presented as a striding man, full of energy and ready to work for his goals in the face of opposition and hardship. In such presentations a merger of possibilities and definite limitations occurs to form the event, the coming forth, of what is presented.

As people exchange words all manner of presentations go on. Not only I happen in my words, but awarenesses far beyond my knowledge also happen. The words themselves carry awareness and give world-forms in ways of which I am at best vaguely conscious. Only by intense and informed investigation will I come to see what was happening in a few of the words I used. The history of peoples is invested in them, and those people's ways of being in the world, i.e., their culture, is borne in words. As I non-voluntarily pick words, my own destinies and possibilities are presented. You notice that I am using words of victimization or words of generosity. Other kinds of words would have said the literal things I had in mind. But my style of speech and choice of words articulated more than I knew at the moment. You pick up a range of feelings in my words. They express comfort and at-easeness or something else. Perhaps conflicting feelings. Perhaps profound tensions. And your words, too, present a great deal. In the communication something is created, an exchange, a momentary, particular place of relation with many dimensions of awareness, a quality of commonality and difference. The communication itself is a region of awareness. Later, when we see each other again and engage each other, we may immediately remember each other in the engagement, like people remember each other in a dance. What awarenesses come out and guide various dimensions of the conversation? What fantasies are close and distant with our interaction? How does the interaction itself communicate with other parts of my awareness and character? In a threatening way? Attractively? And to which parts of my awareness does our interaction communicate most directly and with least relevance?

In any case, words and fantasies as presentational events bear awarenesses and together in exchange constitute a place of awareness. A great deal is presented as communication goes on, and the conversation itself affects and carries out in particular ways what is presented in it, like Rodin's sculptures expressed and affected a culture's awareness of condemnation and love. Although there are agents all around, the events of presentation themselves transcend the agents and are not the same as the activity of subjects who intentionally do things.

7. Awareness and Indeterminacy

Allowing fantasy and words to come into one's region of identity and to present themselves in that context brings awareness to bear in the identity and brings a particular or determinate identity to bear with the awareness. A presentational event occurs in which various possibilities and ways of being happen together in mutually affecting ways.[11] One dimension of these occurrences is an ungraspable and unreachable quality. Heidegger speaks helpfully of "withdrawal." In an event, the very eventfulness of what is going on recedes from encompassing particularity or determination. If possession, ownership, and avoidance of loss are big issues for me, for example, the indeterminacy of all events will be deeply unsettling. I will *overdetermine* an occurrence in order to eliminate its elusive and finally mysterious freedom from all forms of holding, identification, and limitation. I may try to boil events down to their essence. I may absolutize categories of experience regarding events. I may pay attention only to parts and aspects, avoiding strenuously the occurrence of the whole.

The dimension of withdrawal in an event, however, can be allowed. Heidegger speaks of not jumping in and taking over and of stepping back. Both phrases are efforts to name how a person can be alert in the ungraspable indeterminacy of events. The happening of fantasies, for example, with their emergence and departure in our presence, are remarkable reminders that all occurrences escape our holds and that continuity is not necessarily the best guide for understanding how human being occurs. As we step back of the event and allow it its happening, its presenting, communicating occurrence, we undergo a subtle experience of fundamentally not being in control. We feel passage, horizon without resolution, inconstancy, an excess of the particulars in their totality. We are aware in indeterminacy. In this awareness we tend to grant the ungraspableness in the simplest and most complex things in the sense that we expect not to be able to encompass even what is most valuable. We probably become more sensitive to hearing things with a predisposition not to tell things how to be. We will use things with a sense for what cannot be used in things, with a sense of the limits of using in living with things. We will be attuned to the coming, presenting quality of things, to the awareness they bring with them and engender in our consciousness.

The immediacy of awareness in events means that indeterminacy is available to us as the event's withdrawal, as its refusal of the consciousness of

---

[11] In therapy, how a person self-consciously appropriates a fantasy or conversational event is usually crucial for lasting change, but my issue presently is not with one's taking over an event, but with the immediate awareness of the event.

particularity, as withdrawal from particularizing intentions, and as the occurrence of the happening itself. Awareness (or mind) happens. And we can be alert with that awareness when we learn how to step back of intentional consciousness and to allow the awareness of events to take place in our presence. We then see that we can be involved in the awareness that transcends our own particular consciousness.

Both Freud and Jung thought of consciousness as residing in the "ego" and its peripheries, such as the personal unconscious. They had, however, no way of understanding the conversion from the "Unconscious" to consciousness, from the absolutely non-ego to the ego. Consequently each in his own way worked with fantasies that he thought were founded in a "place" of no awareness at all, a place without history and time. The origin of fantasies had to be guessed about because each man's ideas claimed a total break between consciousness and the place of origination for fantasies. This absence of the world in the "Unconscious" means that Freud's and Jung's theories of the "Unconscious," although importantly different in many ways, perpetuate the ancient ideas of time and timelessness. Freud's version of the timeless is materialistic, while Jung's is spiritualistic, in the classical modes of bifurcating the universe. We have seen, however, that in fact awareness is the non-reducible given in all events, that awareness is intrinsically worldly and historical. Fantasies begin in awareness. Awareness is common for the known and unknown, the remembered and the forgotten. It is the universe of happening with the intrinsic capacity for self-consciousness and self-forgetfulness. In particular instances of awareness, it may look at itself or it may glow with an immediate sense of itself, like a self-aware anxiety anxiously finding things in the world or a self-aware joy joyously celebrating things.

Freud particularly thought that a dream is remembered only by the conscious agent. In his notions, that was the only way conscious memory happened, by the action of a conscious ego. A dream, however, may repeat itself or remain present with the sleeping person. The act of remembering dreams involves learning how to be awake with the dream, although one is in other ways asleep. This alertness is not necessarily a personal agency. A clearing is a closer analog than agency is. The sleeping person may continue sleeping while the dream is given a retentive place, like a clear opening in a dark forest. The person awakens and finds the dream retained and present. Doubtless many factors in the dream as well as in the person influence which dreams are given hospitality. Some dreams seem to insist on being retained. Sometimes a person awakens to find that a struggle has been going on to retain a dream that is tending to slip away. But one attainable ability is to retain the dream, much as a narrative is retained, without judgment or appreciable affect outside the dream's own affect. One gives way to the dream in an immediate and alert allowance of the dream's own immediate occurrence. It is like that kind of dialogue in which a person steps back of personal encounter and receives and hospitably entertains another person with that kind of indifference to one's own preferences that allows unjudged freedom for the other's individuality. Later one can be shocked by what he/she allowed in such a hospitable clearing.

When awareness is not reduced and is recounted in its many guises, we find it always present. The idea that conscious agency and a total absence of consciousness define mentality is the notion that has led us away from the continuousness of awareness in all occurrences. The idea of the "Unconscious" seems to be based on this idea rather than on the occurrence of awareness. When we see that self-awareness does not necessarily mean knowledge about . . . or intention toward . . . , we can see that descriptive accounts of immediate awareness as it presents itself are quite possible. *The* issue is the cultivated discipline of developing self-awareness so that it in its immediacy becomes available to a person. My guess is that to the extent that immediate self-awareness is developed, the central and primary importance of knowedge declines. Knowledge is not to be lost. But it is a poor replacement for that immediate self-awareness that is presently so seldom sought.

8. Heeding

We have seen that as we learn to step back of directing consciousness we may intensify and find access to a different kind of alertness in which the ungraspableness of events is immediately apparent. In that kind of alertness the pervasiveness and fundamental sameness of awareness, in spite of the huge range of different kinds of awareness, stand out, and one is disinclined to use a speculative idea like that of an "unconscious" to understand the meaning of words and fantasies. Awarenesses relate to each other in their happening: they may become self-aware in their happening; they are communicative; they have histories and places; they are presentations in which one way of being aware is modified by another way of being aware that presents the first way. We have shown that self-awareness is not always knowledge about oneself. And we have seen that the communicative presence of awareness is immediately affective for the particular state of mind in which the communication occurs. We shall elaborate now some of the ways in which the growth and deterioration of fantasies go on in therapy in order to see one aspect of immediate awareness in the context of mental health.

When myths or other fantasies (e.g., basic ideals, self-images, religious symbols) decline, people usually become confused, lose energy, experience hopelessness and aimlessness, and become susceptible to disease. One can see such phenomena in some native Americans and immigrants and in other situations of a people's rapid amalgamation into another culture.

I spoke with a man who had become a captain, at nineteen, in a suicide panzer squad on the Eastern Front during World War II, after lying about his age in order to be able to join the army. He had been an enthusiastic member of the Hitlerjugend. It fell to his squad, made up of particularly dedicated men, to hold a segment of the Russians back while the German troops retreated. He survived to walk back to Germany and later to stand trial as a Nazi. He pled guilty to the charges, served two years in prison, lost his civil rights, and became an insurance salesman. He told me that he was convinced that Hitler was wrong and evil, that his own involvement was not to be excused, that the Third Reich was a nightmare. "But," he said, "no young people that I now see know the meaning and passion I felt when I was a young man. Hitler was a god for me. It's crazy. I don't want to go back. But why don't they find that intensity of meaning in the church or somewhere else? I have lost it. I thought it was the end of the world when Hitler was defeated. I wandered around and didn't know where to go or what to do. I'll never feel like I felt then." He was one of the most considerate and one of the kindest men I have known, actively working for international understanding.

The "what's left?" sense appears to be a common factor in individuals who have lost intensity of commitments and involvements. They feel bereft and bereaved, dispossessed of part of their lives.

Meaning in life may also grow: the man who "never had much of anything" and who found a lasting, loving relationship with a woman and happiness with his children. "Surprised the hell out of me and still does," he said. The symbols of family life were for him symbols of divine grace and a benevolent universe. The woman who discovered communism and felt "the most intense glow in my life, an excitement I can't describe," in relation to Marx and Stalin in 1938. The man for whom a dream of a golden ring, shining in an airy blueness, became a steady presence, meaning hope, creation, and growth in his life.

All of these deteriorative and growing fantasies "come to" individuals. There is a non-voluntary quality about them that is characteristic of fantasies that mold people regardless of their choices of ways of life.

In therapy people often find it necessary to give a special kind of autonomy to the hour. "I can not reach the feeling I have here except here," one woman said. Her therapeutic goal was to have touch with those dimensions of herself that came in reach in the therapeutic hour. A therapist described the hour as a "housing." She said that she and her clients often built a relational house in which a different person could begin to grow without the threats and oppression that one otherwise experienced in his/her non-therapeutic society. In that housing, non-voluntary things begin to emerge within an otherwise unnatural security. It is a place in which occurs what Medard Boss describes a therapeutic eros:

> Psychotherapists would perhaps be wise to do away altogether with the misleading term "countertransference" and to replace it with the term "psychotherapeutic

eros." This "psychotherapeutic eros" is different from the love of parents for their children, different from the love between two friends, different from the love of the priest for his flock, decidedly different from the extremely variable love between the sexes, and differennt from the matter-of-fact indifference of purely conventional kindness. Genuine psychotherapeutic eros, in other words, must be an otherwise never-practiced selflessness, self-restraint, and reverence before the partner's existence and uniqueness. These qualities must not be shaken or perturbed by cooperative, indifferent, or hostile behavior on the part of the patient. Psychotherapeutic eros must go beyond even Christian humility in its selflessness, its modesty, and its triumph over egotism, in that it must not intervene even in the interest of the therapist's own God to seek to guide the partner's life.[12]

The fantasies may bear not only the health-retarding fears and blockages. They often bear awareness of the missing, the needed, the healing: "she held a key to the gate. If only I had that key! The field beyond was open and free. And she was so lovely." "The man was kind and gentle. He held his arms open to me." "He was awful in his distance. But when I got closer, shaking all over, he looked at me and it was alright. It was good. I felt so good and I didn't shake any more."

In the special housing of effective therapy, fantasies, words, and presence are heeded. *Heed,* related to the German *Hut,* which means cabin or small dwelling, has the sense of special care and attention. As one heeds, one takes notice. In therapy, a dwelling of care takes place in which fantasies, words, and presence are heeded. They may consequently bear out whatever they present and mean. They may take their own measure in this dwelling. One heeds them as one steps back from them to give them their room, their place, their recalling mindedness.

A person may well experience decline and destruction as fantasies of loss, death, and deterioration take place. Things are being let go and are going away. An emptying may occur. A dark night may fall. Depression and discouragement, a sense of loss and aimlessness may emerge. Often what dies that way needs dying, but have been the best holds on life that a person has had. They have been the fantasies of both meaningful place and survival, and blockages to other needed awarenesses and possibilities like a persistent, but bad marriage. "I cried and cried as the shriveled old woman died. She was ugly and mean, but I tried to find her hand to hold. I felt so alone." "Why did my father die in that dream?" a patient asked. "Isn't it time for him to die?" the therapist answered.

As one abides with the fantasies that occur in therapeutic heeding, one waits for them to mean whatever they mean in their presence with one's consciousness. One waits for developing horizons that at first often appear irrelevant for one's non-therapeutic existence. Later they may become dominant for one's everyday sense of the future. In therapeutic heeding one learns to indwell the fantasies, at least in the hour's housing. *Dwell* has the

---

[12] *Psychoanalysis and Daseinanalysis* (N.Y.: Basic Books,1963), p. 259.

meaning of *linger, delay, abide, inhabit*; and in light of its root, the Anglo-Saxon dẅellan, it also has the resonance of *mislead* and *wander* as well as *tarry*. To indwell a fantasy may be to be misled from the perspective of one's non-therapeutic consciousness. Tarrying with the fantasy is living with another dimension of awareness that has wayward direction in comparison to one's usual sense of him/herself. Boundaries are being crossed in the immediacy of fantasies which, when heeded, engender new senses, directions, and possibilities that often lead to well-being. That is a state that we seldom are able to create for ourselves if we are blocked to the non-voluntary presentations of mind.

9. When Therapy Fails

A seasoned and well known therapist publicly recounted the following experience. His patient was a highly obsessive woman. He maintained a non-directive, open and supportive relation with her over a period of several years. She "obsessed" for hours on end during that time. She was obsessed over his approaching marriage, over family situations, and on and on. She gradually became "quieter." She was able to work with other people for the first time in many years, and she successfully held a job. After periods of greater and lesser obsessive behavior, she had to all appearances worked through her obsessiveness. She judged herself to be happier than she had been in her memory. But within three years, when she was in her mid-fifties, she fell ill with a sickness that doctors were unable to diagnose and died. The therapist, who had occasional contact with her after the years of regular therapy, speculated that perhaps when she lost her obsessiveness she had no deep desire to live. He wondered if open freedom for the world were deathly for some people.

Other therapists have puzzled over some people's refusal to let a therapeutic process follow its own course. Many of us cling to suffering modes of awareness as though our lives depended on them. Binswanger remarked to Freud that there is a time in analysis, over which the therapist has no control, when the patient "decides" whether to follow the healing process.[13] In Binswanger's and Freud's eyes, it was a question of heart and courage. Jung often noted patients who were under the control of "archetypes" that destroyed their autonomy and sense of identity. Boss speaks of people's falling prey to the very openness that for others is the origin of unusual insight, and well-being.[14] We might speak of inadequate ego-strength or of character deficiency. We might also speak of the immediate power of fantasy and of mind which overcomes a person or, in other situations, of emptiness in which nothing salutary comes to dwell. The immediacy of awarenesses and of

[13] Ludwig Binswanger, *Being-in-the-World*, trans. J. Needleman (N.Y.: Harper, 1968), pp. 182–83.
[14] Medard Boss, *Grundriss der Medizin*, Section III, III. d, especially pp. 496–511.

openness as such seems to have potentialities that bring to mind possession
and vacuum. Death and destruction follow, leaving a vacancy as mysterious
as healing in the face of seemingly hopeless odds. Nothing to hear and
nothing to heed.

10. Transcendence

Transcendence happens in our experience as the immediately communicated presence of particular identities and awarenesses. The kinship of all
awarenesses and meanings means the pervasive unity or sameness that we
have often noted. Identity, person, self, and so on name an experience of
differences in the sameness of the world. We are transcended in immediacies, in the words, fantasies, and silences that make up the happening of the
world. We, as particular beings, are taken up in events that are not
governed by our particularity, but in the presence of which we are alert as
who we are *and* also alert in awarenesses that are not particularly ours.

The artist, Frederick Franck, says that when he draws *in* seeing a leaf,
for example, "No longer do I 'look' at a leaf, but enter into direct contact
with its life process. . . ."[15] He means, he says, that he shares this life with
them. He transcends whatever isolation he might be experiencing and finds
himself in the leaf's event. He is not at all fragmented. He does not lose a
sense of who he is. His consciousness as the one who draws intensifies: "I
become not less, but more myself."[16] His attention, however, is intrinsically
informed by the thing he heeds (he calls his approach a "discipline
of . . . unwavering attention.") Transcendence occurs as his alertness when it
is infused by the other event, by his own being in the other being's way of
coming to presence.

Transcendence names immediate alertness in both one's own consciousness and in the awareness constituted as the presence of something. A therapist who was working with disturbed children commented that she found
that her task was to hear and to speak with whomever or whatever communicated itself. She said that many "characters" occurred in her therapeutic
dialogues, i.e., many different awarenesses spoke in the process of the
conversation with one individual. She tried to enter into dialogue with them
as they occurred. In the dialogue she was deeply affected by those presences.
And as she responded, heeding their presence in the very way she spoke and
reflecting their presence in her language, she formed part of the dialogical
reality. She helped to mold the address in the direction of further addressing, rather than in the direction of flight or inattention. She attempted not to
interfere with the aware presences that were also forming the dialogue. Her
language transcended her intentions, interests, personality, and knowledge in

[15] Frederick Franck, *The Zen of Seeing* (N.Y.: Vintage Books, 1973), p. 7.
[16] Ibid.

the awareness of the dialogue itself, and in that dialogue the meaning of her language was in part constituted by the meanings of the other awarenesses. *Transcendence* means dialogical contact, address, and claim. Awareness and consciousnesses are events in which transcending continually and immediately goes on. Any state of awareness or consciousness is beyond its singularity in the immediate presence of other awarenesses and consciousnesses.

Being in touch in the immediacy should not carry primarily the overtone of emergence into light or of happy ecstasy. Darkness and destruction are immediate too. Transcendence is a continuing way of occurrence, regardless what is going on. A therapist may need to back away, to withdraw from some dialogues, not because the issues themselves are too threatening, but because a deep tiredness threatens over-exposure and absorption. One can always fall prey to the immediate presence of something. Possession, loss of a sense of identity, a failed capacity to be one's own answer are always possibilities. Inattention and not heeding in the presence of things often means that one is taken up by them, that he/she bespeaks these awarenesses and is absorbed into awarenesses unappropriated by this person.

The happening of transcendence is not only threatening to the person for whom separate and radically autonomous individuality is a life-issue; it is a problem for all of us when our own place and identity are in doubt. I suspect that one power of schizophrenic consciousness is in the unblocked disclosure of omnipresent transcendence. In the presence of such consciousness, we see immediately the non-necessity of all particulars, most particularly ourselves. My identity is most in doubt when I want it to be unthreatened, essentially unchanging, basically stable. The occurrence of transcendence is a threat in this self-doubt, and I very likely will respond by trying to deny transcendence in myriad ways without knowing what I am doing. I, threatened, will tend to look for non-porous boundaries, fixed and unchanging limits, invariant reliableness, and always identity without shadow, unfathomable depth or darkness. While I might say intellectually that all things change, when threatened I seek certainty and clarity without ambiguity or disorderly inner contradiction. Or if my sense of myself is shaky in the sense that I am not at all sure about who I am or if my experience tends to lack a self-aware continuity, transcendence will probably come guised as an enemy, threatenting to add power to the already excessive lack of boundary that I experience. I will tend to want to eliminate transcendence as such with a consequent flat and superficial, compelled perception of things in isolation from each other, without depth of meaning, and without intrinsic reflectivity. I will lose the possible consciousness of profound kinship in the world because of my fear of transcendence.

Transcending can also name a fundamental way in which awarenesses relate with each other without the presence of a personal subject. A., who has already appeared in this chapter, had a dream in which a young woman brought a signed, blank check to A. A. was standing outside the house from inside which the young woman came. A. would not take the check and woke up furious with the young woman. After working with the dream, she found that the young woman felt condescending to her, that A. was "not about" to take anything from her, that A. was jealous of the young woman's ease, affluence, and security. A. in waking life could hardly bring herself to buy herself anything. She could give herself something pleasurable or nice only with the greatest difficulty. She found that her awarenesses of giving and receiving, unknown to her, were taken up in the awarenesses of condescension and pride. When she experienced either giving in relation to herself or receiving, she experienced one aspect of herself as condescending with another very upright and proud (and dominant) part of herself. In this case, awarenesses were probably absorbed by other awareness in such a way that receiving and giving awarenesses inevitably and uncontrollably meant condescension and pride in conflict with each other. Consequently A. felt rigid, defensive, and suspicious whenever she received something, and she was almost unable to be generous and kind with herself, although she did not know why. By coming to experience the dreamed young woman with sympathy and openness, A. helped the development of immediate presence among these awarenesses without absorption. Awareness tends to grow when it is receptively and nurturingly focused and allowed. Therapeutically the issue is to allow with focus and to choose which awarenesses to nurture to growth. The therapist in this case was able to address and hear the absorbed awarenesses and thereby also to help to overcome the partial absorption in these awarenesses. Immediate presence with each in this difference, i.e., transcendence, is the possibility of absorption. The word names the presence of awarenesses with a conscious person and awarenesses with each other without the effective presence of a conscious person.

    Transcendence, in its immediacy, is also the region of a particular kind of awareness. When a person is able to allow events to be akin and open with each other, their immediate presence in their differences seems to grow in awareness. One not only undergoes increased awareness in the particular awareness, he/she also develops an increased sense of difference in commonality and commonality in difference. George Sheehan often describes this sense as he writes of his experience in running.[17] As he runs, Sheehan reports, his body, intelligence, will, and environment happen in accord at the same time that his sense of being only and utterly who he is as an individual is intensified. This kind of experience of sameness and difference is frequently spoken of also by people in traditions as variant as Kabbalistic Judaism and Native American religion. One comes across it in accounts of personal intimacy, new freedom from old blockages, death experiences, artistic inspiration, and so forth. A common factor in such occurrences is the

---

[17] George Sheehan, *Running and Being* (N.Y.: Warner, 1978).

person's sense of being aware in a state of mind not identical with his own person. Another factor is the person's strong sense of him/herself. The duration, intensity, and meaning for an individual's life vary considerably. But common to the difference is a growth of awareness as transcending any one location of awareness or consciousness.

This "no-one-place" quality often gives a person a sense of freedom from simple identity and location that I have identified as a primary, desirable quality for mental health. Openness with the world, like that we described in chapter 1, becomes a natural accompaniment with individual desire, and mind grows and maintains itself with a sense of being appropriate with its own way of happening, free for its many boundaries, and free from the total, blocking domination of one of them.

11. Thinking

When we think we may formulate, seek out notions, think about something, think our way to conclusions. But the kind of thinking we shall presently note occurs as one is centered *on* something, such as when one has one's mind on the trees or on his/her problems, although one is not trying to think about them or formulate them or do anything mental regarding them. We also speak of thinking in the sense of being filled with something or preoccupied by something: he things only football, etc. Thinking can also be a state of comprehension: she thinks Black, and so forth. These dictionary definitions point to the kind of thinking that Heidegger calls meditative.[18] He has developed the close affinity of *think* with *thank*. *Thank* used to mean a kind of thinking that is grateful and that expresses gratitude. Something borne in mind as thanking was welcomed and held in favor. It was worthy of praise and its goodnesses were particularly evident.

When thinking is noted in these sense of consciously abiding or tarrying with something, the work *thing* can also help to clarify the non-subjective aspect of thinking. *Thing* has the old Anglo-Saxon meaning of assembly. In that language, *thingan* meant to negotiate and *thingian* meant to reconcile or conciliate. In both Old Saxon and Old Norse a *thing* was an assembly, judicial court, or legislative assembly. These root meanings can help to show the thing as a happening in which many elements are gathered. A thing—any thing—is like an assembly in which people come together and conciliate, deliberate, set courses for action, eliminate undesirables, and so forth. We have already seen how things come together non-voluntarily as events that bring histories, affinities, rivalries, and destinies, like the gods of Greece. Things are gathering and excluding occurrences. When this thing, say the loved, suffering child, is foremost in my mind, the state of my garden or the problems of government

---

[18] I am indebted to his essays, particularly in *Vorträge and Aufsätze*, in the following observations.

are probably distant and unimportant. But caring and my own small part in the scheme of things may be very close. Things have their atmospheres, their elements, their milieu. They bear possibilities and horizons and constitute postures of perception. Things appear differently in a cave, for example, in comparison to how they appear in another thing, say a circus tent.

Thinking as an alert state of being conscious and as centered with something or other allows the thing its immediacy, its posture, its ways of including and excluding, its directions and bearing. That is indeed similar to thanking, even though I am ill disposed to the thing: I may think the suffering person, the wonder of a face, or the joy of a sunrise in the sense that I entertain those things, allow them to be their own presentation. When I think about and respond to what I have meditated, however, I may be depressed and angry over suffering, non-plussed by the face and not particularly interested in the sunrise. Thinking them in the meditative sense gave them "welcome" by letting them be, but that kind of welcome is not a judgment about them or a stance towards them.

Thinking can happen as alert release to the immediacy of things, a non-interferring predisposition that allows entertainment without a person's being host/hostess. We become alert to things from inside other things, just as we can learn to see a dream in the awareness of someone in the dream quite other than "I." There is no necessary location in awareness, only positions that are taken with degrees of arbitrariness. In meditative thinking we discover that alertness can grow as things are borne in mind without interference in their assembling, legislating, adjudicating presences.

We also come to see that the element of thinking is not necessarily an activity by someone. The allowing quality of alertness that is centered by things engenders intuition and understanding that no one could be said to effect.

This kind of thinking, which is immediate alertness with immediate things, impresses me as an important basis for interpreting. A different kind of interpreting goes on when I apply a set of concepts to data provided by you. That activity is unavoidable, as we formulate a knowledge of something, and we deny it always with the strong risk that we will fall prey to concepts and assumptions that we ignore or overlook. As a basis for interpreting, however, meditative thinging engenders awareness not formed by concepts, but by non-conceptual events. When I am free for the non-subjective immediacies of mind, I am free for interpretations which aim toward exposure with things, rather than conceptual justification. Exposure with things, in their own way of being, is one opposite to that kind of deception in which a person finds him/herself foreign in the world and unable to relate with things and name them as they are.

12. The Fitting and Destiny

People are frequently right when they see conspiracy. They may see a pattern of events that inevitably undermines or overrides what they desire. Often the mistake one makes is looking for "who" is behind such patterns. No one needs to be behind them. A collocation of things can change, often very subtly, the direction that has dominated a society, goverment, or person. The occurrence of therapy itself, for example, can alter an individual's awareness without that person's knowing what is going on. The occurrence of an attentive, deeply affirming therapeutic relation can result in a person's no longer being certain of the pervasive antagonism of his/her world. He/she will experience confusion in relation to things, like people in society in which a fundamental certainty falls into doubt non-voluntarily because of the emergence of very different, highly valent events.

The non-voluntary, directional, fateful quality of those developments can give rise to images of secret agreements. One may be dominated by the fantasy of being singled out by powerful individuals, divine or human, as he/she undergoes a deep alteration of a basic channel of awareness. Or, with good fortune, a person may have fantasies of doing something right that pleases someone or something of great power. But the question remains, how can I keep the run of good luck, the presence of energy, or the prosperity? A deep sense of being wrong and unworthy usually means that a person feels inexplicably responsible for whatever happens that is "bad." That person will also often feel unworthy in relation to whatever good impinges on him/her. In any case, the fateful quality of awarenesses as world-events or individual experience is the center of the issue.

We have seen that mind cannot be appropriately judged regarding its well-being by reference to preferable or non-preferable contents. Within each boundary of awareness are criteria for the desirable and undesirable. We have seen that absolutizing any region, whether consciously or not, appears to create antagonisms in mind that are lived out as deep hostilities and blockages in an individual's life. Perhaps such tensions at times are not only unavoidable, but are desireable, We have found, however, that events need not be denied in order to be opposed. Openness of mind happens as one allows awareness free of personal contol. Things have a free quality of self-presentation, and awareness may collect in many different foci, allowing an individual an intimate alertness to differences as well as alertness in differences. One transcends one's own consciousness. This kind of openness seems to allow differences without antagonism, opposition without rending hostility, refusal without hatred. We have found in the development of this kind of alertness one way in which mind develops as a whole of its parts, while the parts themselves develop their own particularities and differences.

The allowance of destiny may thus be conceived as one way in which an individual transcends his/her own desires. To lose destinies that develop

non-voluntarily often happens in the form of a person's seeking to control
the very creation of the way things are. One tends to lose vast areas of mind
by seeking jurisdiction of the personal over the occurrence of things. That is
quite a different kind of consciousness from that in which a person seeks
what he/she desires in a developed and disciplined alertness in the different,
non-personal awareness of other events. One then may enjoy what he/she
experiences as fortune without needing to feel merit, and one may suffer
misfortune without a need for hatred, bitterness, or paranoia.

How are we to conceive of what is fitting for mind, given its indifferent
openness and its fatefulness for personal preference? The Greeks used the
word *sōphrosunē*,which can be rendered "soundness of mind" or "soundness
of heart," as well as "temperance." It comes from *sós*, meaning "safe and
sound," "well and alive," "whole," or "sure." *Phrán*, which means the muscle
that parts the lungs and heart (diaphragm), was used by Homer to name the
parts about the heart. It could mean the breast that swells with pride or that
one beats in sorrow. It can also mean the heart, the mind, will and purpose.
Sound, wholeness, fullness of life, and well-being are the overtones. When
the emphasis falls on discretion, as it often did in Classical Greece, *sóphron*
had the sense of temperence and self-control. In that light, *sophrōsune*
meant an established, appropriate balance among things, right accomplishment of character, a good control in oneself. The meaning of that accomplishment is the presence of passions that tend to disorder and madness. But
the experience of temperance in relation to intemperate possibilities under-
plays the significance of the destiny of events. The Fifth Century dramatists
were particularly alert to this dimension: the relation of measure to the immeasureableness of destiny. That immeasureableness found part of its
expression in the madness and non-rationality of the events that go on in the
tragedies.

Actors in Classical Greece were in the service of Dionysius—the god
also closely related to madness. The close relation of madness and fantasy
has long been experienced and expressed. But that is also a relation closely
allied with truth. Something utterly true was to be said in drama. Bennett
Simon thinks that the line between madness and sound mind (right measure)
is to be understood in Classical Greek drama as a balance among illusion
and reality, reason and non-reason, tradition and change.[19] That is doubtlessly right. But the kinship between madness and truth, their common
conspiracy, if you will, in right measure, is faded slightly if Simon's
formulation is left in terms of lines to be crossed. The difference between
the chaos of madness and the fitting order of sanity is not a line. It is not like
a border. It is more like shades of light or mixtures of sound. Movements
blend and fall apart. Sounds move in and out of harmony and cacophony.

---

[19] Bennett Simon, *Mind and Madness In Ancient Greece* (Ithaca, N.Y.: Cornell Press, 1977),
pp. 146ff.

And the difference that makes *sōphrosunē* has to do with what is to be balanced at a given time. As Dionysius inspires, people are given an intensity of awareness, a loss of personal restraint, the masks of other awarenesses; one becomes freer for Eros, the One who gives relation. One falls into the divine realm—en-thusiasm—and sees and hears what he/she can no more control than create. Like breathing, this inspiration, in which order and chaos fade one into the other, each appearing as the other's shadow and condition, fluctuates. The balance is always fragile because it is in constant motion. The soundness of the heart is a rhythm, and, like a festival for the gods, it can break lose from its regularity by virtue of what excites it. Yet without excitement and stimulation it grows weak and irregular.

The god Dionysius is very much like the drama that comes and goes so fleetingly and yet can capture one thoroughly. A drama reflects the utter reality of the world in illusion. It is a Dionysian world of truth as it happens with madness and measurement in a moving balance.

Simon has shown how the classical tragedies, particularly those by Euripides, incorporate madness and sanity. In the very drama, he says, illusion and reality, rationality and its opposite, tradition and deep alteration of custom go on. The dramas are illusory and real. Madness and sanity happen in them. Tradition is preserved and changed in their structure. The plays, not one or more "sound" characters in them, are the *sōphrosunē* of these factors. They are a kind of well-being and modulation of these many factors. The tragedy is a whole, a sanity, a fit of differences that make up part of the situation in which people lose their minds. These fifth century dramas present wholeness of mind even as they present insanity, destructive fortune, and loss and death without recompense.

In a wild and frenzied religious dance, with people slashing themselves and blood covering their faces, out of which their dilated eyes stare almost without focus, sanity also is present. The ritual, of which the dance is a part, is like a Greek god. It, silent and distant, gives place to frenzy, like a romp room in a Victorian house. People return from the frenzy to their dark houses. They pick olives and till the rocky fields. The ritual has set apart this ecstatic awareness, with its bloody and probably cannibalistic, prehistoric roots. It has also allowed the awareness, given it lucidity, time, and expression. Madness is present in classical drama, and sanity is present in frentic blood rites.

Sōphrosunē names how madness happens, not its absence. Right measure, appropriate fit, soundness of heart and mind—however we render the word—means that chaos and disorder do not prevail. A whole occurs. The word contains the insight that we live always in orders of disorder, that the sound heart and mind is a region in which madness goes on without conquering the whole. And the whole happens without conquering the madness, loss, foolishness that happen with the other parts. My guess is that also contained in the word's experience is the soul's deep preference for that wholeness that intensifies light and the absence of light to a pitch that ignites all stability and turns mundane regularity into a self-aware measure of change and death.

In the dramatists' presentation of *sōphrosunē*, the measure of sound mind is never an abstract ideal or principle. Nor is it the dramatists' point of view. It is a dynamic event in which a particular course of things is accounted. A kind of story. A finite narrative or a limited poem that is personified before people. The well-being or soundness occurs as the alertness of the play as a whole. It allows its many parts—antagonisms, alliances, vices, and virtues—to unfold in an envisionment of the parts and the whole at once. The envisionment, not what the playwright claims particularly about what goes on, is like the fit of mind, its appropriateness regarding itself. The absence of envisionment appears to promise a chaos of visions that in their insistence on their own priority, have lost that self-alert envisionment which reflects wholeness. Such envisionment gives the rightness of fit, never a directive on what might be fitting at the moment. Yet, when an actor plays out the whole in his/her part, the character will have a fitting power, a genius that is given, said some of the Greeks, by Dionysius.

The whole of the play is not the same as an order. It is more like a presentative place. Plato's dialogues, for example, provide an order defined by a rational inquiry and insight. He thought of that inquiry as an opposite of mythological meaning or non-rational destiny. But the dialogue itself, as a work of art, provides place and time not only for Socrates, but also for all manner of fools, innocents, and open inquirers. Plato, although no friend of the playwrights, allows the dialogue itself to pervade the parts of the discussions and actions in such a way that a comprehension of the whole is quite different from an understanding of how the dialogue is ordered. An event has occurred in which one can participate, not simply as a reader of an essay, but as a part of a conversation filled with emotion and place as well as rational work. Like a Euripidean play, one of Plato's dialogues is closer to a dwelling place, when taken as a whole, than to a position paper. The whole "place" gives moment to the parts and is their meaning.

I stress the difference between "whole" and "order" so that we can see the analogy with mental well-being more clearly: well-being is a whole event that pervades the parts, is not dominated or overcome by the parts, and provides an awareness that transcends any particular perspective. It is not an order. It is a pervasive, non-determinate awareness that has reached immediate awareness of itself. That is the meaning of "measure" when proper balance and soundness are at issue. The measure is found as the parts resound and reflect their whole, very much like genius in playwrighting and in acting.

One of the ideas that has most influenced our traditional understanding of the whole is that of formal unity. Usually the formal unity of mental health is thought of as autonomous identity. Fully developed identity can be experienced, for example, as loneliness without personal collapse, or as a sense of ownness in one's choices, whether they turn out well or ill. Inadequately developed identity is experienced as a sense of distance and absence in relation to what one does. "I was there," one woman said, "being hurt and screwed. I know I was there. I had asked for it. But all I felt was distance. I looked on. But I felt absent." The idea behind the concept of identity is that of an eminent form, a self-aware structure. Therapists may attempt to help build a person's "ego strength," individuality, capacity for responsibility, and so forth. One then learns to cope with the regions of not-I. One seeks a pervasive, formal identity, the I, like the authority of the church throughout its domain, or the jurisdiction of law in a state, or an office that defines the role of the person who "holds" it.

Closely allied with this understanding of identity is an emphasis on moral principles in interpreting life itself. Structures—be they called natural laws, the will of God, universal moral principles, or necessary cultural standards—may be taken to define the happening of all life. Or at least of all human life. Outrage tends to grow in relation to what occurs outside of these forms. One is also then inclined to suppress radical differences in the name of life. Compassion is hard to stretch to the regions that fall outside of the jurisdiction of definitive form.

When the whole is conceived as a form, it becomes a defined or definable kind of being—another part. When it is conceived as an event, however, form itself is relativized to the happenings of particular things, and the whole is found in its own awareness, in which all parts have an immediate part. Continuity by awareness, not by form. We have discussed this kind of awareness by such words as sympathy, compassion, and love. We now see that this awareness of love is not necessarily characterized by sameness of identity or of form, but by openness in individual consciousness for what happens, a "disposition" with living things. When this kind of openness is pervasive of one's way of being with things, of his/her judgments, desire, and preferences, an immediate, non-formal sameness exists vis-à-vis personal identity and the wholeness of world and awareness. This indeterminate sameness, accompanying whatever determinate things go on, is the *sōphrosunē*, the right measure, the fit of mind with things. It is ever elusive, always escaping focus and definition, frustrating our need for specific guidance and for some pattern to help us through times when ignorance, uncertainty, and likely tragedy are close together. It is our being well in all circumstances, being guaranteed nothing in particular, having nothing finally to hold on to, being never totally the same as who we are. It is destiny without a goal or an end, being at once ours and beyond us, like a smiling Buddha, a sketch by William Blake, or the air we breath.

13. The Personal and the Non-Voluntary

Does well-being mean that a person is to be no one self? I have used *self*, *person*, and *identity* as synonyms with consciousness as the name for personal awareness. This convenience allows us to see more quickly that awareness is not like self or subjectivity are. A person may be more or less open to the awarenesses that pervade him/her, with the consequence of one's holding more or less onto the personal way things are ordered. The basic issue is how personal consciousness relates with its vast element of awareness. We have seen that non-personal happenings may be filled with destructive force, with tensions that make personal survival difficult.

Non-voluntary madness can go on as things occur at severe odds with one another. A person may be able to recognize what is happening, if there is a basis for consciousness outside the madness. In that case, with good fortune, a person may be able to avoid becoming prey to the madness. It would be like a person's being able to love in the midst of hatred or a person's being able to see destructive forces in the light of regeneration or hope.

Regeneration can also happen non-voluntarily. One metaphor for such an occurrence is the free land in the United States that engendered a remarkable level of energy, hope, and effort for groups of people who had experienced previously oppression and resignation. A person can also be more or less blocked to new energy. Nietzsche showed with particular genius how a person may resent new life and creation in a consciousness of oppression and restriction.

Whatever is happening with things, however, personal consciousness is founded in it and pervaded by it. Finding the will and evergy to see and hear how things are, capacities for affirmation and refusal, sensitivity to meanings fundamental for one's consciousness, and the inestimable power of that self-awareness which senses itself as worthwhile because it is: those are some of the issues for personal well-being. The immediate presence of awareness is a key to interpreting states of personal growth and decline, and the immediacies that permeate all personal mediations indicate the living nature of what we have to deal with as we find our way in our places and times.

14. Awareness is Historical

B. said that a group of friends had come to her house for dinner. A highly abstract discussion developed around "people's need for love." One woman in particular expounded long on the subject, before a man exploded in anger, yelling over and over that love was real. He accused the woman of hiding behind her talk of love, of being incapable of love. The painful exchange ended with each person at the dinner feeling bad. But, said B., no one pursued the encounter. One man took sides with the woman. Another woman said that she was sorry about "what happened." B. observed that each person there, including herself, felt lonely and separated from people.

They had tried for over a year to develop a supportive friendship and community among themselves. "But when there should have been communication, there was nothing. Just nothing."

In the course of her therapy hour, B. found that she identified with the woman who could talk about love, but could not love. She dreamt of this woman and felt, in her identification with her, great distance from her. "Almost no contact." She could hardly visualize her dreams of the woman, and she felt primarily a sense of absence. "But I felt close to this absence. It felt real. As real as anything I know."

B. contrasted that closeness with the absence of love and close communication with her "comfortable" feeling of recognition and understanding that she enjoyed with another group of casual acquaintances with whom she shared similar values and experiences. "We are at ease with each other. It's very nice. Things flow easily. But it's not nearly as intense, as real to me, as my closeness with the despair of the other people and with this feeling of absence. I miss the intensity when things are comfortable."

B. usually found intensity when she experienced strong desire in the absence of the desired. She is with those people, like A. Alvarez, Sartre, Foucault, and Laing, who experience absence as entrée into how things are fundamentally.[20] We might speak of the absence of fantasy, of being closed off from contact with things, of darkness without light, nothingness, abyss, chaos, and so forth. Usually that type of awareness involves both a sense of threat to life and a heightened awareness of creation. Thomas Mann's *Death in Venice* is a particularly fine literary presentation of the experience. Stravinsky's music also articulates the same sense.

This experience is centered in an absence of *what* is simply real and is accompanied by a strong sense of presence, sometimes passion, often a feeling of both despair and understanding and closeness vis-à-vis oneself and others in the absence that pervades and dissolves things. Alverez finds this absence to be like a vacuum that eliminates presence and draws one toward suicide. Sartre often describes the experience of evacuation and nonpresence that accompanies all presences. B. found herself juxtaposed to all her satisfactions in the experience, and she described her painful feelng of being most alive in her paradoxical sense of closeness with absence.

One meaning of this region of awareness is to be found in the historical character of awareness itself. I do not now have in mind the historical character of the thing that we know or feel or encounter in whatever way. I have in mind the non-necessity and absence of developed character in awareness as such. The experience of absence, pure and simple, is one

---

[20] A. Alvarez, *The Savage God* (N.Y.: Bantam Books, 1972); J. P. Sartre, *Being and Nothingness* (N.Y.: Philosophical Library, 1965); J. P. Sartre, *Essays in Aesthetics* (N.Y.: Washington Square Press, 1966); R. D. Laing, *The Politics of Experience* (N.Y.: Ballantine Books, 1967); R. D. Laing, *Knots* (N.Y.: Vintage, 1970).

dimension of immediate self-awareness. It is a way in which mind is in touch with an aspect of its own being.

Some of the opposites of perfection of being in the dominant, Western tradition of metaphysics have been change, contradiction, and inner difference. Perfection has usually been thought of as unchangeableness. The lives of individuals are obviously filled with contradiction, development, and decline, and one intuitively expects individuals to be imperfect. But one also may expect that the region of imperfections be itself immune to change, contradiction, and inner difference. The Same or the One or Nature have often been named eternal, that is, changeless. Soul has also been seen as a region that is itself deathless and/or changeless. The soul may be corrupted by changing contents. But if it is able to fix itself on changeless things, it will find profound resonance in its own being. It will have come home to its own nature. The expectation of the changelessness of the Greatest Region or the Same has been so deeply a part of our tradition that the question of history has usually been one that had to do with individuals—laws, mores, principles, rules, cultures, and other structures and regions of life—and seldom with reality as such. We tend to conceive of things on the basis of axioms, doubtless principles, and laws that seem to be immutable in at least a limited region. Like souls, axioms may seem to point beyond themselves to a Greatness untouched by growth and decay, a Place without history.

Awareness appears to be like that kind of Place. There have been times when an educated person could not seriously doubt that Reason was essentially an a-historical capacity for apprehending non-historical realities. Our own era was born in that conviction, found equally in the Renaissance Platonists, and in Leibnitz, Spinoza, Descartes, and Kant. If not reason, then the Word of God was thought to be changeless, whether found in tradition, scripture, or nature. By obedience, faith, grace, or their combination, one's soul could find its home in non-historical verity. We have called that return home "salvation," and we have found it in many forms—beatific vision, a life of faith, serenity beyond all particular influences, sacramental life, participation in communities of grace, God-given obedience, and so forth. Pervasive of these ecclesiastical, mystical, and secular experiences of salvation has been a bedrock sense that something in human being that is alive and enduring, is not subject to history. It may well suffer and enjoy the destinies of histories in which it finds itself, but it itself is not historical.

That sense of the non-historical is as evident in Freud's notion of libido as it is in materialists' notions of body and matter and some contemporary theories of brain events and consciousness. In these instances dumb inertness or blind chemical processes replace the spiritualists' notion of transcendent, conscious life. But there is essentially no history, nonetheless.

Our observation is that awareness, as worldly event, is intrinsically historical, i.e., it bears capacity, development, and death. As capacity for seeing, hearing, retaining, etc.—as mind—it happens always in the immanence of how it came to be and of its total absence. It is immediately aware of itself in its objectless sense of absence, total difference, non-justifiable presence.

When one experiences the absence of fantasies, for example, the absence itself is an occurrence of immediate awareness. On the one hand, one may experience that absence as simple dullness and depression. Or one may experience it as a lapse, as a loss of expected life, as being cut off. In that experience is the immediate awareness of no reflection, no creation going on, the strange sense of being aware in the immediate presence of no awareness at all: the opposite of the immediate awareness in fantasy.

When one becomes conscious of this awareness and retains reference to it, other related awarenesses become apparent: the awareness in the possible not-yet, the awareness in present, but unalterable has-been, for example. Awareness happens in the not-yet and the has been, and in both occurrences, awareness happens in the immanence of its own absence. In one case its absence occurs as "able to be, but not yet being there." In the other case, having been, awareness is with its own remainder which is resurrected toward the future only by change in awareness and without eradication of the remainder. In such states, mind is immediately aware in its developmental, historical quality, in its immanent historical character, in what traditionally has been called imperfection.

B.'s own personal history of infrequent experiences of supportive intimacy, coupled with her unusual openness for passion for its own sake, gave her an unusual entrée into the incompleteness of mind with its determinations, absences, gaps, and unbounded openness. She was able increasingly to accept her deep sense of absence and her lack of closeness, without feeling tragic or self-pitying. She had a high tolerance for psychological pain and a low tolerance for narrow satisfactions. As she allowed these aspects, she began to dream and fantasize with a sense of freedom that was new for her. She felt less and less determined by a sense that "something is wrong" and found herself to be acceptable to herself in her distances and lack of satisfaction. She appeared to her therapist to have found closeness with people and things through the immediacy of what we have called the emptiness of her awareness.

15. Love

The seeming unboundedness of mind/awareness/world means the absence of a totally circumscribing law. It means what many therapists have long known, that drawing close to whatever is basic for a person's consciousness is therapy. A psychiatrist commented that most of his energy in therapy is spent in not telling a person who he/she is or what the person is exhibiting. The therapy, he said, comes in the persons's own discovery. That discovery is always an experience and is never only a matter of looking on or observing. Otherwise the psychiatrist could have informed the person, convinced him/her, and performed thereby his therapeutic function. But discovery of awareness does not happen sufficiently through the conscious structures of intellection. By intellect we may guide ourselves, inform ourselves, figure things out, and so forth. But intellection is founded in drifts of awareness far beyond our ordinary educated knowledge. Intellect usually is carried by fundamental interests, desires, and states of mind. It is in the region of "the fundamental" that love and therapy occur.

The apparently unboundedness of mind is its qualitative difference from intellection, which is always bounded by its principles of knowledge. Neither the axioms of knowledge nor the structures of identity can encompass mind. But we are blocked to mind's difference only if we think as though these principles and structures were absolute for our being or self-awareness. We usually relate intellectually in terms of definable structures: roles, rules, principles, expectations, and so forth. We study our personalities in terms of structures: rules of development, social roles and relations that come to define us. We become angry or shocked when rules and roles or principles are broken. We absolutize intellection and person for self and mind.

When a person experiences acceptance without the qualifications of role or principle, a different order communication goes on in comparison to role-governed and principle-governed communication. When a dream is allowed without judgment or analysis, it often stays with a person initially with more power and with a greater tendency to remain. A man found a person in his waking dream turning and bowing to him in greeting and appreciation as he allowed that person without his customary interference. When the hated or feared is allowed its address, the hatred or fear is often changed and a different quality of energy develops. One is freed from their hold. What is unthinkable can also approach, like this single thing, this one person, this red, flying bird coming out of the night. What is not who I am comes, the dancing Hermes; the dwarf, slant headed and unshaven, stupid, leering; the old woman, bent double, long nosed, with her cane. Whatever is present, not conceived, but known and allowed, gives its reality in the openness of the allowance and is in the allowance to some extent affirmed and loved.

This unsentimental love appears to be regenerative, seldom comforting, like the clearness of light that sometimes follows a summer's storm. It is not as much like a lap or womb as it is like release to one's life for no reason. It is a state of mind that immediately gives way to beings because they are aware of double kinship: one in the life of the allowed being and one in the openness of giving way. It is an awareness that awakens a wide range of affections, which are the frequent agents for a person's changing his/her ideas and ways of acting.

The therapeutic occurs as one is able to welcome events, if not always what occurs with the events. In such welcoming one is in the awareness of immediate kinship and sameness. In that awareness one also immediately welcomes his/her own being and discovers the non-intellectual and non-personal truth of therapy as an event of love with regard for the limited occurrences of the boundless region of mind in its sufferings and limited sufficiencies.

When a part loves itself with particular intensity, that love may be the part's separation from the whole. Exaggerated affection for itself is the part's denial of its transcendence, of its mind which is its relatedness in the whole of the world. The myth of Narcissus speaks of what happened when the lovely young man fell in love with his reflection. He lost contact with everything else. In one version he drowns. In another he starves to death. In either case, he loses what is essential for his life: air or food and water. This kind of destructive partiality is seen not only when a disrelated part of me attends primarily to itself and refuses any communication that would intrinsically affect it. Damaging self-affirmation is also seen when I insist that my personal reflection be in all other parts of the world. Then I find something like myself dominating in all experiences. The suffocation that follows may be quick, such as when I am unable to love at all and find my own bitterness returning to me from everywhere. Or it may be slow, as when a group of people over a period of time stagnate by insisting on themselves as centers of value and importance.[21]

In such instances, the self-love of a part, instead of simply enjoying its own being in the whole, attempts to suffuse the whole with its own limited way of being. An immediate alienation and dislocation takes place, something like a refusal by the whole and the other parts, and the self-insisting part's relations become increasingly that of contradiction and breaking away. Falling apart over and over again without creation, satisfaction, or success.

Another kind of love happens when the whole occurs in immediate openness to itself in the occurrence of the parts. An analogy for such an event is when a group of people act in a way that reflects their bonding commitments as they live together in their day to day activities. How they sell and buy and build, etc. make evident their commonality. When a person is open in his/her, let us say, conservative character for the wild and unrully aspects, for parts of him/herself that are immediately attracted to deviation and rebellion, for the awesome transcendence of mind, for the shitty, perverse, boring, etc; and when these aspects are open to the others,

[21] I recall a beautiful lake where a biologist and friend of mine fished. It was clear to its bottom. One spring he found it filled with algae, so thick that they made a scum over the top of the whole lake. A few months later he returned to find it again clear. The algae, he said, had overpopulated to such an extent that it starved for lack of oxygen.

the openness itself immediately reflects the whole as the parts live out their own destinies and preferences. The whole of mind finds this stage of love as various parts become free for their openness. I am thinking of the difference between, for example, the aggressive/competitive aspect's struggling to control the passive/easily contented aspect, and the aggressive one's enjoying its own pursuits while being either indifferently open to the passive one or even being available to compete for the sake of the passive one. Mental accord happens as differences resonate each other in hearing openness. This hearing openness is an immediate awareness of the whole in differentiating activity. It is love of the whole, quite the opposite of both war and absorption, in which love is not an attitude of a subject, but an open accord of the parts at once. The whole comes repeatedly to itself through the way the parts happen.

One form of therapeutic love is like the love of the whole, as people find themselves free to be with each other, without primary regard for judgment or particular agreement, in free allowance for the parts—for the mad ones, the childish ones, the terrible ones, and so on. Free for intimacy and affections as well as for difference, disagreement, and opposition. A commonality emerges in which the occurrence of the whole with the parts has intuitive ascendency. There is immediate insight of the whole, a fitting envisagement that transcends any particular perspective and accompanies the perspectives as mind's freedom in its points of view, a quality of awareness that, as love of the whole, transcends any set of values or desires. It is then that Hermes, the messenger of all the gods to all the gods and to all people, smiles ungraspably.